CHILDHOOD LOST

Edited by

Zelda Marbell Fuksman
Judith Evan Goldstein
Frieda Jeffe

**The Child Survivors/Hidden Children of the Holocaust
Palm Beach County, Florida**

CHILDHOOD LOST

Only about eight percent of the Jewish children of Europe emerged out of the world's moral collapse. They lost their childhood, their ability to trust, their families, the ability to enjoy or rejoice for many years. Many lost the images of their parents, siblings and even of their own young years, unless an immigrant family from before WWII had pictures to renew the faces for them.

It is amazing that these children were able to rebuild an order in their lives. They studied, built careers, businesses and, best of all, created a heritage of new families. This was an enormous struggle. Most survivors accomplished all this by their own will and determination to recapture the road that was planned for them by their lost families.

The only thing that some could not accomplish was how to be joyous without some guilt. Also how to celebrate special events without their own parents or extended families.

They became an island family with friends serving as their extended relations. These child survivors and hidden children became their own ancestors, their own township, their extended integrity and somehow carried their forefathers' heartbeat. These children are beyond the heights of emotions.

As we observe our contemporaries, we are convinced that the human spirit has an ability to rejuvenate, learn to smile, and restore despite the evil that was cast upon them.

It amazes the world that the child survivors have not collapsed or became lost souls. On the contrary, their wills are miracles and memorials of the Six Million.

The quote Never Again will not only be a mantra, but a resolve!
This book speaks for us
For those who were silenced
and
To those who will fight for equality.

CHILDHOOD LOST

Edited by

Zelda Marbell Fuksman

Judith Evan Goldstein

Frieda Jaffe

The Child Survivors/Hidden Children of the Holocaust Palm Beach County, Florida has contributed to Holocaust education, which has had an impact on thousands of students.

This book is the result of the emotional and hard-fought efforts of the many contributors who have told their stories, as well as the diligent efforts of the editorial staff and the book committee.

The Child Survivors/Hidden Children of the Holocaust Palm Beach County, Florida has contributed to Holocaust education, which has had an impact on thousands of students.

This book is the result of the emotional and hard-fought efforts of the many contributors who have told their stories, as well as the diligent efforts of the editorial staff and the book committee.

To order copies or for further information about this book, contact:

Child Survivors/Hidden Children of the Holocaust Palm Beach County
21932 Boca Woods Lane South
Boca Raton, FL 33428

cshchpalmbeach@gmail.com

ISBN 978-0-9896-088-0-0 (lib. bdg. : alk. paper)
ISBN 978-0-9896-088-1-7 (pbk. : alk. paper)

Manufactured in the United States of America
1 – SB – 12/31/13

ACKNOWLEDGMENTS

The Child Survivors/Hidden Children of the Holocaust
extend our appreciation
to
Zelda Marbell Fuksman - Chief Editor
Judith Evan Goldstein - Editor - Project Advisor
Frieda Jaffe - Editor

Norman Frajman - President - Child Survivors/Hidden Children

Book Committee
Pierre Chanover
Mary Eckstein
Norman Frajman
Zelda Marbell Fuksman - Committee Chairperson
Judith Evan Goldstein
Rosette Goldstein
Frieda Jaffe
Benno Lindenberg
Max Markovitz

Hershel Fuksman, Photography

Front Cover Art "Reaching Up" by Judith Evan Goldstein

Expressions of Appreciation
John J. Loftus for his introduction.
Mr. Loftus has published many books including
The Secret War Against The Jews

and

Merle R. Saferstein, whose dedication to Holocaust education
spans a generation. We thank her for her assistance
in copy-editing the final manuscript.
Her selfless contribution is beyond thanks.
Ms. Saferstein has currently published her book ***Room 732***

vi

Contents

AN IRISHMAN AMONG THE JEWS

by John J. Loftus
copyright 9/11/2012

So why is a Boston Irishman like me trying to tell Jews about Nazis? When I was recently asked to write an introduction for a volume of memoirs about Jewish children who survived the Holocaust, I thought it might be a good time to come up with a good answer. So, what is my connection to the Jews anyway?

I got that question a lot, especially back when I was the first Irish Catholic President of the Florida Holocaust Museum. Sometimes I just joke about the Jewish-Irish issue and say "maybe we are related." The Encyclopedia Judaica mentions a Jewish legend that the Irish might be one of the lost tribes of Israel. Curiously, there is also an Irish legend to the same effect.

I was predestined, I suppose, to become a lawyer-historian. I enrolled in graduate school at night for a Masters in Public Administration at the same time I was earning my Doctor of Laws, serving as an editor of the Law Review, and Deputy Campaign

John J. Lofus

Manager for Ed Markey's first run for Congress. (He won.)

As a result of that over-achievement, I was one of a handful of law graduates chosen from across the nation as Law Clerks for the US Attorney General's Honors Program. I wrote a brief that won commendation in the Supreme Court (Pearly Wilkins vs. the United States) before I even passed the bar. That was really cool, but after two years, I found brief-writing boring.

In 1979 I immediately volunteered when President Carter re-opened an investigation into whether Nazi war criminals were hiding in America. Because I spoke German and was a former Army officer with an intelligence background, I was instantly hired as the first staff lawyer for the unit.

My new boss, Walter Rockler, had been one of the original prosecutors at the Nazi Bankers Trial at Nuremburg. He told me that the Nuremburg trials had been fixed, and many rich people in America and Germany who should have been prosecuted as Nazis were protected.

I got to go to Suitland, Maryland. It is a nice little town just outside Washington. That's where America's secrets are buried, literally. There are twenty storage vaults underground. Each vault is one acre in size. Did you remember the last scene in the Movie "Raiders of the Lost Ark"? That's what the vaults are like, but not as organized.

Sometimes I wrote the code words in ancient Greek and the censors thought they were doodles. Most of the time, I just memorized them. Eventually, I read the secret files on the Holocaust, most of which will not be declassified until 2015-2035. I want to be there when the last file is opened. I will be 85 then, but maybe I can make the next generation of Holocaust historians make sense of it.

The worst of the worst of the Nazi war criminals from Eastern Europe had been living in America, protected by embarrassed bureaucrats.

I obtained permission from the CIA to tell the story and blew the whistle on *60 Minutes* in 1982. It caused a bit of a scandal. There was a minor media uproar afterwards and I became a two cent celebrity. Congress demanded hearings, Mike Wallace got the Emmy Award, and my family got the death threats. It was a great tradeoff. It was worth it. I was embraced by the survivors of the Holocaust, many of whom became my closest friends.

One day I was speaking when I noticed a very old orthodox rabbi weeping. He spoke no English, but his loving associates told me why he cried. He had proclaimed that I was a "Ger Zadek" one of the thirty six righteous people who live on earth at any one time, for whose sake the whole world is saved. It was a lovely legend and the nicest compliment I have ever received.

Since I did not go to jail, I became the unpaid lawyer for every wannabe whistleblower inside the USA and more than a few allied intelligence agencies. I was poor, but honest. The American Bar Association Barrister Magazine named me as one of "Twenty Young Lawyers Who Make a Difference." I liked the "Young" part.

Still I could not forget those Jewish victims of the Holocaust whose files are still buried in the secret vaults. These Holocaust survivors have had their stories lost to history. Not that there is any comparison between the two. You should never compare the pain. Every ethnic group has suffered a mass murder in their past, all lumped together (incorrectly) under the term "genocide."

But there is only one Holocaust, and it happened only to the Jews.

The Holocaust was different from every other genocide in history because of its intent. Hitler's goal was to extinguish the race of Jews from humanity, to erase its seed from the gene pool for all eternity. To accomplish that goal, he intended to murder every Jewish man, woman and child on the planet. He would even kill all the Jewish babies to end the existence of the Jews forever and ever.

Hitler intended to rub out part of the human race. It was the greatest crime in human history.

In the old days when I felt better, I used to take children's groups through the Florida Holocaust Museum. Eli Wiesel told me it is his favorite but I wonder if he says that to all of us. On the first floor there is an actual boxcar used to transport Jews to the Holocaust. It stands on the actual rail lines to the Treblinka death camp.

When the conservators were preparing the box car to exhibit, they found something horrible inside, maybe something wonderful. It was a little girl's ring wedged inside the floorboards. Historically, we do not know much about the ring. From the silver marks inside we know that it was made in Europe about the time of the Holocaust. From the empty sockets, we know that it once contained five jewels, all of which are gone. From the size of the band, we know that the ring fit a little girl between ten and twelve years old.

That is all that we know with certainty. But we know what probably happened. You know what happened to that little child. She probably bargained the jewels for survival, probably for bread or water. Then one day, there were no more jewels left and the little girl realized that for her, there would be no survival. She knew she was going to die.

For some reason, the little empty ring was still valuable to her and she did not want the Nazis to find it. She probably hammered it in with her heel into a crack in the floorboard so that no one would ever find it. But, by a miracle, a half century later that very boxcar ended up in our Florida Holocaust Museum where we found that little girl's ring.

We have the ring mounted in a little case just beside the boxcar. I tell the children not to be sad that we do not know the little girl's name, nor be upset that all her jewels in the ring are lost.

"You are the jewels" I tell the children. Every one of you, who keeps alive the jewel of memory of that little girl, keeps her alive forever. You children are the jewels of Justice, the gems of History, the flashing diamonds that connect our living memories back to the fire of the Holocaust. You are the last generation of children in the world who will ever have met a Holocaust survivor. You are the witnesses to the witnesses. For the sake of that little girl, and for more than a million other Jewish children like her, you must remember. Memory is their victory. You are their jewels.

YOU MUST REMEMBER.
John Loftus, St. Petersburg, Florida

I STILL TREMBLE WITH FEAR

by Anya Bogusheva Baum

For me, Slutsk, Belarus - (White Russia), situated on the Sluch River, was a place of wonderful memories. It is stated that Jews lived there for over 400 years.

The countryside around Slutsk produced a wealth of grain, which the Slutsk merchants purchased and shipped all over the Russian empire. Slutsk had eighteen synagogues and study houses called *yeshivas*. It was a vital Jewish community. It was a center of economic and cultural life that extended to the small communities around.

A number of renown Yiddish authors like Abramovitsh, Sholem Yankif (Mendele Moykher-Sforim) and important rabbis, came from this city. It also had the distinction of scribes producing Torahs.

Before the Soviet takeover, Slutsk's Jews engaged in commerce and the trades. The town was full of Jewish tailors, cobblers, bricklayers, dyers, carpenters and merchants.

All this came to an end with the October Soviet Revolution in 1917. The Bolshevik government suppressed religion and the spiritual Jewish life. The number of Jews decreased to about 8,500 in 1926. The historic and beautiful synagogues of Slutsk were confiscated and one by one their leaders were forced to flee to avoid deportation to Siberia. The Jewish community of Slutsk lingered on, in the last two decades of its existence, destitute of its former splendor.

Anya after WWII

Still, even by these deprived standards, it was a vibrant town, with a Jewish community who adjusted to the hardships of life under the Soviets. They had not lost their identity, even though religious practice was frowned upon, and were forced into clandestine gatherings for prayers. Of all the synagogues only the *Tailors' Shul,* remained.

Before WWII, there were about 12,000 Jews in Slutsk - Bobruysk Region, including refugees from Poland, who ran from the Germans in 1939. Until WWII, the town was predominantly Jewish, today only about seventy Jews still live there.

Since I was born in Soviet time, my experiences are of a hard life. Looking back now as an adult, my dear father and mother struggled to keep body and soul together. Still, we were a happy family, with grandparents and many relations living in town.

My grandfather, Abraham Bogushov, was one of the elders and most affluent by Soviet standards. He was consulted by many to assist with different life issues. I remember him as a distinguished looking man, always dressed in a suit and tie. He spoke a number of languages and earned respect from all. He had two children with my grandmother, his first wife, my father Motel and an older sister Dora. When my grandmother passed away, he remarried and had four more sons. Zima served as an administrator overseeing all food inventories for the country, David became an engineer designing tanks and airplanes, Grisha was on the staff at the Kremlin in Moscow, and Boris worked in merchandising. When the three brothers, who were living in Moscow encouraged and facilitated Dora to attend university in Moscow, she agreed and became a pharmacist. She too settled there.

Father Motel

My father was a very special caring man. He was tall, or at least that is how I remember him, with piercing gentle blue eyes and a calm demeanor. He was a great Father and husband and all who knew him, loved him. He was not religious, yet every morning he put on his *tefilin*, (phylacteries). We spoke Yiddish in the house regardless of the Communist indoctrination to assimilate all Jews to accept the new dogma.

Mother Raya

Father worked as a typesetter for a local newspaper until one night when he was overtired, he injured his fingers so he was dismissed. He served in the Soviet army for a few months in 1939 during the conflict with Finland, and returned wounded, full of body sores and infested with lice. His struggle to get any employment began, especially since WWII depressed all economic development and opportunities, and life was hard for all. Finally Father managed to get a job for the sanitation department, distributing a chemical for

5

the outside toilets. He also served as a volunteer for the fire department.

Mother Raya (Rochel Pikus), was a beauty, elegant by the standards of those days and a high-spirited woman. She was tough and a disciplinarian, who at times used father's belt on my brother, Sam, three years older. Very often Father intervened. But, regardless of this strict treatment, she was a good mother and would fight tooth and nail to protect us. She was an exceptional baker and, to this day, I still remember the cinnamon buttery rolls. During this time, 1939 - 1941, my mother also worked in the town bathhouse.

Our home was a free-standing little house situated in a compound of Jewish and non-Jewish neighbors' houses with a large dirt courtyard. The house consisted of one big room and a small kitchen. We cooked on a wood-burning *pechke* (a brick oven) and had to bring water from a well a distance away. The outhouse was our primitive toilet.

When I was three years old, my six-year-old brother poked something into my ear and we neglected to tell Mother. Before long, it became infected and full of puss. My parents appealed to my father's brother Grisha (in the Kremlin) to help get us the right medical care, which he did. We traveled to Moscow where I was treated and improved, but I still have problems with that ear.

I attended school and finished four classes. All education was presented in Russian and any semblance of Jewish culture was played down. I had many friends, especially kids from our compound and my days were happy.

Grandfather Eser Pikus

Mother's parents, my grandparents, Eser and Malke Pikus had four children, Lisa, Luba, Rochel (my mother) and a son Fema. Fema, an electrical engineer, was in charge of an electric generating station. During the German occupation of our town, he blew up the station. The Germans took his wife, two children and him into a field and shot them all.

Grandfather was an acclaimed violinist who traveled all over the world performing and teaching. He spoke nine languages. He was killed in 1941. He lived in Pesochnoe, now Belarus, thirty kilometers from Slutsk. When the Germans found out that he was a violinist, they made him perform for them. When he tried to escape, they caught him, cut off his fingers and then killed him. They kicked my grandmother to death.

On June 22, 1941, as Father was playing with me, strutting around, carrying me on his shoulders and listening to the radio, we heard the announcement, "Attention, Attention! Germany has attacked us. All men must report and register for the army." At this time my mother's sisters, Lisa and Luba and children were visiting with us from other towns.

A day later, in the evening of June 23, 1941, a squadron of airplanes flew over our town with noisy engines that were deafening, dropping bombs at will. Father told us that we must run and hide; he could not come, he had to report to register. We grabbed what we could and ran to escape the bombardment by hiding in the trenches outside of town. We ran away from one trench when finding a German parachutist hiding there. The sky was lit up with flares, exposing us to the bombers.

When the first bombardment ended, we met up with my father and found that he was wounded by shrapnel from a bomb. He told us to get out of town. He said he could not leave because he was not able to register and needed to do so or he would be considered a deserter.

On June 24-25, 1941, all the roads were clogged by the homeless who were heading toward Bobruysk and away from the front. My mother, brother, (losing one of his shoes during this flight), aunts and kids and I ran for our lives. On the road we met Russian trucks with soldiers who were retreating. We were able to get a ride on a truck when Aunt Lisa showed them her little red book, which said that she was a colonel's wife. We were dropped off in Bobruysk.

In Bobruysk, we found shelter with many others in a concrete structure in crowded conditions. An announcement came that hundreds of German planes are heading our way. The retreating army provided a cattle car train for the escaping crowd. We had no food or water. We traveled with a few possessions, the clothes on our backs, while my brother brought along Grandfather's fur lined overcoat. We ran day and night with the planes attacking. The train sirens screaming for all to get off the stopped train and hide. We ran in all directions and were separated from Mother. Fortunately the train was not damaged. The siren sounded once again an all clear. Hurrying back to get on the moving train, I saw dead bodies and the injured. All scrambled to get on. I was separated from Mother and Sam. I was trembling with fear and worry that I would never see them but my mother frantically ran from wagon to wagon searching for us, and finally we were reunited.

We stopped in a town Arol, where we transferred to a passenger train and again continued to get away from the bombs. My brother's belly swelled from hunger. Mother was desperate to help him. We got some hot water, *kipitok*, (condensation from the steam back to water) from the steam engine. Some good local people who were meeting the train brought food for the travelers. Mother was able to get a piece of bread and milk for Sam, not for me. I felt neglected even though I knew that Sam needed it most. At ten- and-a-half-years-old I had to observe, endure, suffer and try to understand.

Finally we were dropped off in a village about thirty kilometers from Stalingrad where we found safety and thought that here we could stay. We found that even here, among the Russians, anti-Semitism was evident. Some Russian hooligans tested my brother to determine if he was Jewish by demanding that he say the word *"kukuruza"* (corn), which he could not pronounce with a sharp-rolling R. He only could pronounce the R in the throat, like the French do.

Mother saw that Jews were discriminated against even here, so she decided that we continue to Panfilava. Here Sam got work, driving oxen to till the fields. He had an opportunity to learn a trade so Mother let him go to Stalingrad where he learned to be a welder. This eventually became a valuable trade, but still he suffered from hunger. Mother had to bring him food by train, where it was stolen from her when she fell asleep. She finally brought Sam back to the village, where at least we had some food and we lived together.

A scene that is etched in my memory is when Mother was extremely ill and we thought that we would lose her. In desperation and with fear and trying to escape not wanting to see her suffer, I went outside in the snowy cold, dropped to the ground crying and praying to God to save our Mother. I came back into the room and to my amazement, Mother was sitting up in bed asking, "Where were you?"

The bombings were reaching our village but my mother decided that we would not run anymore, while her sisters and children continued their escape and wound up in Kazakhstan. So here we were, the three of us, trying to survive alone. Living from day to day, worrying about Father and the families back home.

Sam took on the role of provider by welding rakes from iron that he salvaged from bombed buildings. For this the locals gave him some food which sustained the three of us from starvation. We were able to eat watery soup in a cafeteria for refugees once day and a portion of a small piece of bread, which had to last the week. My brother and I screamed that we were hungry and could not wait for the daily morsel of bread. Mother threw up her hands and said, "Eat it all now. We will see what God will provide."

In the meantime I contributed by gathering straw for cooking and gleaning the fields for scattered kernels of wheat, for which I got a meager food allotment. On one occasion, the German planes were dropping bombs, and shrapnel was flying in all directions near me on the field where I was. When I returned, Mother greeted me with embraces and tears with disbelief that I was still alive. In this village, I made a friend of a native resident, a deaf girl who on occasion gave me a little flour, a fruit, a piece of bread to bring to Mother.

On August 23, 1942, Germany attacked Stalingrad with all their might. Our town became a repository for the wounded and my mother was able to get work as a nurse for these men. The soldiers were dying in great numbers. Our own need was drastic. Mother was able to get boots and clothes for us and some additional food which was allocated for the wounded who had died.

At this time I became sick with typhus. I was accepted in the hospital and Mom was sure that I would die. In desperation, once again, my mother sent a letter to father's brother Grisha, in the Kremlin, begging for help. Within a few days, we received firewood, flour and a generous supply of foodstuff and even a parcel with shoes, a warm hat and a piece of material for a dress for me. Not being allowed to see me in the hospital, Mother came to the window outside to show me the things sent by the Uncle.

During this time, I lived with a dream that maybe my father is a wandering displaced beggar. I would look at men, hoping that it was Father. With disappointment and worry I saw that it was not him.

The siege of Stalingrad lasted till June 30, 1943. When we heard that Slutsk was liberated from the Fascist troops on June 30, 1944, we found our way back home, hoping to reunite with Father and our family.

We found our house was gone. The Germans had built army barracks in the compound. We had no place to stay. With the help of a Soviet official, who remembered my grandfather and Father, we were able to secure a room in a house with an old lady.

Most shocking for us was to learn of our personal tragedy; losing Father and our entire family in horrific deadly events that all Jews were murdered. Thousands of Jews, adults, children, and babies were killed and thrown into a pit, a mass grave, in the nearby forest. It was in Belarus where the Nazis' wholesale murder of Jews was first tested.

The whole family was murdered while we escaped. It became a tragic existence for us to remain in Slutsk. We suffered both a loss and guilt of why we were able to survive. All were gone. Only Mother's two sisters and families survived in the depths of Russia.

Like many other survivors, people connected, married, created new families and brought some sort of normalcy to their lives. Mother met and married a very nice man, Berl Gittelman, a Polish Jew, who survived as a partisan in the forest, along with his daughter, Feigele. Because he was a Polish citizen, the Soviets allowed us to leave Russia.

My brother Sam was considered a Soviet citizen, therefore he was drafted into the army in 1945 and we were separated for twenty-two years. He remained in Russia and we left. Mother's sister lived in Leningrad. We were in contact with her after the Iron Curtain was somewhat eased and we were able to correspond. She told us that she is in touch with Sam and told him that Mother, Berl, Feigele and I were now living in the States.

During the time when "Save Soviet Jews" became a force to let Jews emigrate from the Communist world, Sam, his wife Sonia and daughter Ala came to America, and we had a reunion full of happiness and tears.

We settled in Lodz. Life for Jews in Poland and in Lodz was not safe, it was precarious. We were threatened with attacks by the Polish anti-Jewish element.

Not seeing a future to rebuild our lives or citizenship in this place, like all survivors, we continued our journey of escape to Czechoslovakia, then to Germany to a Displaced Person Camp, Poking in 1945. Poking became my place of recapturing and establishing a life. I attended the ORT school and learned to become a seamstress, which came in very handy when I needed to earn a living.

Anya 2013

I registered to go to Palestine/Israel at the end of 1947 on the ship Panur. We were met by Israeli soldiers. Seeing Jewish soldiers gave me a feeling of pride and safety. I was only seventeen years old, but I had the ambition to secure housing for myself. I found an abandoned apartment, a bed, and wrote to my mother that they should come; I had a place for them to live with me. They arrived in 1948.

I got a job working for a photographer in his dark room. He took a picture of me and displayed it in the window of his store. This is how I met my husband Erwin Baum, a volunteer sailor from Belgium, who saw my picture and admired it.

We married in 1949 and returned to Belgium. Life there was difficult for us because Erwin was a Polish Jew and could not get permanent status. Periodically we needed to bribe the police who came often to deport us.

We were able to pull some strings to remain for one year and by then we received our visas to immigrate to Canada. We arrived in Montreal in 1951. The HIAS (Hebrew Immigrant Aid Society) helped us with housing and finding jobs. I got a job as a seamstress and Erwin as a furrier.

We established a comfortable life. We were blessed with our daughter Mona who was born in 1960 and who enriched our lives with love, and eventually presented us with wonderful granddaughters, Rachel and Jessica, and great grandchildren, Dillon and Sienna.

In the meantime, Mom and her husband left Israel and lived in Brazil for a while. When they were able to get visas, they came to the United States. This is when I decided to resettle to the States to be close to her. Again, after some adjustments, we established a good life; glad to be safe in a country where we could expect freedom and equal treatment for all.

I must say that nothing was handed to us. I had many careers and jobs, including as a makeup artist, a dealer/importer of art. I performed on the Yiddish stage, designed special jackets that even Diana Ross and Prince bought from me.

For many years, memories and visions float through my head - many dreams and sleepless nights of fright and flight. In 2009, I decided to go back to Slutsk and try to validate and recapture the memories of the place where I was child. I traveled alone and met a former playmate there who took me around and helped me learn what happened to my fellow Jews.

When some people learned that I came to visit, they came to meet me at the hotel. They introduced me to a man who knew where my father was killed and buried. He took me to the ghetto site and to a mass grave of 8,000, among them my father. These graves were dug by Jews who were made to undress, were shot and dropped into the pits. Another grave is of 3,000 Jews who were burned and another mass grave with over 1,000 buried. I also visited the monument to remember the Jews, my father and the entire extended family who were murdered during the Holocaust.

Memorial to the fallen Jews in Slutsk area

I am asked why did I join the Child Survivors/Hidden Children organization. My answer is that I am one of them. I like to learn, hear and feel with my fellow child survivors. I thought that mine was one of the worst experiences, but I have learned that children suffered, they remember and most did not even have a parent left. I heard many life stories and many truths. The Shoah was an evil time in world history. A shameful time. I want to forget, but I cannot, I must not.

PAINFUL TO REMEMBER

by Henry (Zvi) Bialer

Yes, I am a Holocaust survivor, I am a witness of horror. I also must speak of my life, my family and my city Lodz, the second largest city in Poland, that dates back to 1423. This is where our family lived for generations and where I was born on December 1, 1923.

Henry age twelve at a unveiling of a gravestone

Some records show that in the 1790s the Jewish population numbered less than fifteen people. By 1820, a third of the population of about 800 people was comprised of Jews but had limited power to own properties and were held back by other restrictions. Some of these restrictions were lifted by July 1827, and the Jewish population was able to own and build homes and businesses. One of the industries established by Jews was the weaving of textiles, especially using

12

Henry Age - 15

the newly developed steam powered looms. By 1900, Lodz was referred to as the Manchester of Poland. In 1912, the first Hebrew gymnasium was established along with a Yiddish school in 1918.

Life was vibrant despite the daily expressions and threats of hate. The Jewish people strived to honor God and the Polish and Jewish laws. They built families that were honorable and refined by the standards and values of those days.

By 1930, anti-Jewish laws and policies, enacted by the Polish government, were affecting Jewish life throughout the country and life became troubled. By this time, Lodz's Jewish population numbered over a third of the total population of about 600,000.

My father's family came from a nearby small town. His father, my grandfather Eliyahu, who was married to Bluma Rafalovicz, leased a quarry from the local nobleman and managed to provide a comfortable life for his wife and their nine children.

My father Moishe, second youngest of the nine children, was a charming man. His company was sought out because of his good nature, boundless sense of humor, and was a great story teller whose stories attracted an audience. His many talents and abilities as a businessman and writer served him well. He was the editor of the newspaper *Der Yidisher Tog* (The Jewish Day), he also was a director of a small bank, and an importer of wool yarns, which he lost during the 1930's depression.

When my father was of marriageable age, his older brother spotted just the right match for him, my mother Bela Wajntraub. She was an acclaimed beauty which dazed the senses. Her delicate countenance and gentle ways put one in awe, almost afraid to approach her. Father's brother recognized the suitable connections both in status and as a good match and encouraged Father to meet with Bela. My father managed to endear himself to Bela and her parents, which led to an approved marriage. Their relationship was loving, although not demonstrative. Publicly and in front of their children, they kept a respectful bearing towards each other as was appropriate of that time. They had four children, my twin brothers Aron and Shlamek, sister Dorka and me, Zvi. The twins were nine years older and Dora, six and a half years older then I.

My maternal grandfather, Chaim Meir Wajntraub and grandmother Hilda Biber lived in Lodz. He established a number of construction businesses and was a self-educated architect whose advice was valued. He built and owned a number of large apartment houses. He was a known and respected philanthropist. He supported a small *shtibel,* synagogue, a *cheder* and *yeshiva* (Jewish religious schools). My grandfather was a religious man, yet modern in many ways. When he passed away, his casket was not driven but was honored by having it carried and accompanied by a procession of hundreds to the cemetery over three miles away.

Our household was traditional in all observances and kosher, as was the natural state of all Jewish homes and was run with a calm and generous attitude towards all. My mother was one of six children who received both a modern and religious education. She was gentle, always dressed with elegance. Although I felt spoiled, I knew well that Mother's disapproval would be emotionally too painful to bear. She never resorted with warning of Father handing out any punishments. She was easy-going and I cannot recall her displaying anger. She was good-hearted, generous and every Thursday provided handouts to the poor who came for donations for their *Shabbes*, Sabbath, needs. My job was to answer the doorbell and hand out the coins. At times I thought that my mother was being abused by the growing number of beggars from week to week, but Mother always persuaded me that this was an obligation to serve people and God. She stated that it is "Better to be a giver."

My life was content and I felt loved by my family and especially by my sister. When I was of school age, I attended and graduated the Polish public school where sadly I encountered anti-Semitism. Name-calling was an affront, and especially being called a "lousy Jew" which seemed strange since I knew no Jews that were afflicted with lice. I became an avid reader and soon realized that the Polish government was also displaying their anti-Jewish bias by trying to pass laws against the Jewish religious *kosher* slaughter, which I knew was done in a humane way, not to have the animal suffer. I continued my education in the Jewish gymnasium for two years because the Polish school had quotas for Jews. I excelled in my studies and had aspirations to become a doctor.

I was surrounded by an extended family of over one hundred people. Our family gatherings were special where I felt safe and loved. I was exposed to literature, theatre, movies and above all appreciation of our Jewish history and Zionism, the yearning for the return to Jerusalem and the land of Israel. Because Father was an enthusiastic Zionist, he managed to send my brother Aron to study at the University of Jerusalem in 1936 and the following year Shlamek followed.

Our peaceful life suddenly came to an end when Germany attacked Poland on September 1, 1939. Armored cars, tanks and a well-equipped army marched into Lodz with a great roar, occupying our city on September 8, 1939. As people were escaping the city, they were strafed by overflying Messerschmitt airplanes, killing and maiming the throng on the roads.

By September 18, 1939, all Jewish funds in banks were taken over, and Jews were not allowed to have more than two thousand zlotys. Jewish businesses were taken over by the Germans. Jews were forbidden to use public streetcars, or leave the city without a permit. Cars, bicycles and radios had to

14

be turned in. Services were forbidden and all synagogues were set on fire. A curfew was established to be obeyed under the threat of death. The separation of Jews from the Polish population was put into operation by November 16, 1939 when the Nazis ordered that all Jews wear armbands on their arm and on December 12, 1939 the yellow Star of David was to be worn instead.

The months that followed were chaotic and stressful, filled with daily round-ups of Jews for forced labor and witnessing the indiscriminate beatings and killings on the streets.

Edicts, one after the other, overwhelmed everyone. We were not allowed to gather in groups, schools were closed for us, and newspapers were outlawed. All furs had to be turned in. Big barrels were supplied to be filled with all jewelry and valuables. Funds and shortages of food became a big problem for all.

After the war, we learned about the behind the scenes plots against our people. As of the beginning of 1940, SS Brigadier Friedrich Uebelhoer sent a confidential communication to the police: "Jews must be placed in a closed ghetto and all valuables must be taken from them." He said that he would decide when and how the city of Lodz would be cleansed of Jews.

On October 13, the Nazis appointed a *Judenrat,* Jewish Council of Elders and on November 9, the city was officially annexed to the German Reich.

The Lodz Ghetto was established on February 8, 1940. All Jews had to relocate there, dragging their meager belongings on sleds or whatever means they could manage. It was located in the northern section of Lodz where many Jews were already residing. On March 1, 1940, "Bloody Thursday," 164,000 Jews of Lodz were forced into the ghetto bringing only what they could hurriedly manage to transport. The Germans tortured and killed as they herded people in a bloody march into the sectioned off area. It was not enough to create these cruel living conditions, the Nazis made us pay for our food, security, sewage removal, and all other expenses. They also decided to make one Jew responsible for the entire Jewish population of the Lodz Ghetto. They chose Mordechai Chaim Rumkowski, *a Judenälteste* (Elder of the Jews), or head of the *Judenrat.* In this position he reported directly to the Nazi ghetto administration, headed by Hans Biebow, and had direct responsibility for providing heat, work, food, housing, health and welfare services to the ghetto population. He performed marriages when rabbis had to stop working, his name came to serve the nickname of the ghetto's money, the *Chaimki*, and his face appeared on the ghetto postage-stamps.

In April 1940, a fence went up, surrounding the ghetto. On April 30, the ghetto was ordered closed, and on May 1, 1940, eight months after the German invasion, the Lodz ghetto was sealed with barbed wires and became the first Polish ghetto to be closed off. Once the ghetto was sealed, it appeared that not only did we get locked in, but it stopped non-Jews from entering. We were fenced in with German sentries ready to kill. The main streets that had streetcars running through them were not part of the ghetto; overpass bridge-walks were constructed over these streets to connect the ghetto areas. Some thought that perhaps the sealing off was a good thing, allowing Jews autonomy and protection from the outside world.

Soon after the formation of the ghetto, Hans Biebow used the ghetto manpower to open factories. He established these by robbing the Jews of their properties and earned great profits. Because of these profits that were gained by the Nazis from Jewish forced labor, the Lodz Ghetto was not liquidated as were other ghettos during the implementation of the "Final Solution" and continued to operate until August, 1944.

We were fortunate to rent one room from a resident of that section and shared the kitchen with them. We were able to transport my parents' four-poster bed, which in later times, we tried to cut up for burning wood, but the hardness of this mahogany and not having the right tools, we were not able to cut it up to be used for firewood.

Right from the beginning, over 43,000 persons died from disease, cold, and lack of food. Skeletal bodies on the streets and great suffering became common place. Escape was impossible and help from the outside was non-existent. Even though all these conditions destroyed the moral, secret theatres offered some escapism from the tragic brutal life and conditions. Some children were able to attend make-shift schools and a limited edition of a newspaper was produced.

I was a frightened youngster trying to find some consolation, especially after seeing executed men hanging from the gallows for days. I looked for comfort, but all I could see and experience is that everyone was in a state of disbelief and shock.

Father was lucky to get a job in charge of a bakery, which enabled him to get some food, and we were able to use his rations; this helped Mother, my sister and me at home. I too was able to work. Our ration cards and special printed ghetto money became our means of keeping body and soul together. Soup kitchen were formed, which handed out a watery slop to the desperate. The sick that wound up in the hospital disappeared; they were killed.

In 1941, the people who were not working in factories were selected and were deceived by being packed into sealed large vans. The doors were slammed shut as they were driven to a nearby forest. Exhaust fumes, carbon monoxide, were routed into the interior, suffocating the trapped victims. After reaching their destination, the dead were buried or burned.

Soon the Germans started to bring in Jews from the outlying small communities. They were tricked into believing that they were coming to a better place.

From January 16, 1942 to May 1942, 55,000 Jews and all 5,000 Roma were deported, murdered in gas vans at the Chelmno extermination camp. In

16

September 1942, they ordered all children and elderly to report; 20,000 were sent to extermination camps.

By October 1, 1942, the population of the ghetto was cut by half, to a little over 89,000, due in part to the systematic extermination of children, some accompanied by mothers, the elderly and sick. The conditions for the residents became worse. On June 23, 1944, deportations to the Chelmno death camp resumed.

August 25, 1944 was when my family and I were selected to leave Lodz ghetto to the assurances that we were being sent to a safer place stating "Not a hair will be taken from your heads." We were instructed to take only a small suitcase and were packed into cattle cars one hundred persons in each. I lived with the hope that indeed our lot would improve, surely it could not get any worse. My father, mother, sister and I were able to stay together, which gave me a sense of some security. At least I was with my family.

After one day and night of travel in the sealed cars, we stopped at our unknown destination, which turned out to be Auschwitz. We came to a stop. The doors were opened and suddenly, men in striped costumes, vicious like animals, screamed and shoved us to get off the cars. It was a scene of chaos and confusion. Still clinging to each other, we were torn away when we were directed to line up, men and work-worthy boys were weeded out to one side and women and children to the other. And then from this subdivision, the healthier and younger looking men and women, among them my sister were selected for life, labor force, or experimentation. The elderly, women with little children, and children were selected for the gas chambers, as we learned later. Mother was selected to go to her death, most likely chosen because she wore heavy glasses. Josef Mengele, the "Angel of Death" attended many of the selections of the arriving transports of prisoners.

Our selected group, men and boys, were taken to a barrack where we were told to undress. They shaved off our hair, including the body and were taken to the showers. Standing there, among the mass of men, I felt stripped of all dignity, clinging to my father. After the showers, we were issued flimsy linen striped uniforms but fortunately we were able to retrieve our own shoes.

Exhausted, dehumanized, without any food during this entire travel and transfer, we were glad to be led into a barrack with plank-like shelving, three levels high, to be used for sleeping. Being young, I chose to go up to the highest level, which turned out to be a smart move since we did not have to suffer any dirt coming down on us. There was a large pail that was to be used for a bathroom at night and which was emptied each morning in a hole near the latrine, a shed with a long bench with holes stationed over a pit as toilets.

The camp was surrounded by electrified barbed wire fences. Many who could not cope with this evil life chose to grab the wires and end their lives. Others committed suicide by hanging themselves in the latrines.

When we settled into the barrack, I dared to ask the *kapo*, (a prisoner trusted by the SS to oversee the inmates in the concentration camps), "Where did they take the women, my mother and sister?" He pointed to the tall smoke stacks at a distance, which were spewing out a dark smoke, and he said, "There is your mother." His comments were without emotion, without pity for those burning or for me to learn about such a thing. I still could not believe it and hoped that Mother and my sister would be used for work.

We slept on the hard planks not feeling our bodies, not remembering a dream. At 6:00 in the morning, we were awakened with shouting to line up for the daily morning *appel*, body count. We were kept on the *appel platz*, selection place, for hours in all kinds of weather. The fragile people just fell to the ground dying. They were left to lie there without anyone daring to take them to the hospital or even look at them. The hospital was a death sentence within itself. No one ever came back from there. When I developed a urinary infection, I was not encouraged nor would I consider going to the hospital. Somehow, healing occurred on its own and I recovered.

After three weeks in Auschwitz, my father and I, along with many, were sent to a sub-camp of Gross-Rosen Concentration Camp in Germany. Here we worked in a stone quarry. Using the jack-hammer shook every part of my body. Emaciated and at the end of my strength, I felt like this tool had control of me. Other times I worked with an iron pick breaking off stones from the walls of the quarry. My strength was ebbing, but my anger was without control. When a German guard slapped me, somehow I held back from striking him with my pick. I knew that I and ten other inmates would be hanged as punishment for my violent act.

Other work we had to do was build a railroad line on the mountains. Walking in the deep snows was impossible in my delicate Lodz shoes. I was able to trade some saved bread for shoes that had wooden soles and fabric uppers. This kept my feet warmer but the buildup of snow sticking to the soles was like walking on stilts. And each shoe accumulated different levels of snow so that walking was an off-balance struggle. The only way to resolve it was to bang my foot against a nearby tree to knock off the buildup. But I could do it only one foot at a time. I could not hesitate in the line or I would be beaten or worse.

The bitter cold, malnutrition and grueling work caused many to die. Another struggle was to keep warm in the threadbare clothing. I discovered that the empty cement bags were made of four layers of strong brown paper. Removing the two inner layers, which were clean, I created insulation by sewing them into our jackets, for me and my father, keeping us protected from the bitter winds. Many others followed my example. My father expressed his pride that I came up with such a good idea and which helped many people.

We were sent to three other sub-camps of Gross-Rosen for different work and when they ran out of work for us they made us move rocks from one place to another and on the following day, move them back.

One German guard, a sadist, enjoyed his power and contrived a game to kill prisoners. He would toss his cap like a frisbee to fly away about thirty feet and ordered a prisoner to get it. As he was doing so, he shot him claiming that the man tried to escape.

Beginning in February 1945, the Russian front was getting closer. The Germans made us leave our camps on the infamous "Death March." We walked for six days and were followed by a horse-drawn wagon which picked up anyone who could not walk. At first we could not believe of this compassion, but soon we found out that in the evening, they took them into the woods and shot them.

Every night they brought us into a barn where we fell into a stupor to rest. In the early morning the usual *appel,* counting the prisoners, would be performed and we continued to march.

The food allocation for the day was a ladle of watery soup. Some were lucky to get a piece of potato floating about, and a meager slice of bread. The hunger was beyond description, but I was very disciplined and hid my bread to eat or nibble on later throughout the day. If the non-Jewish prisoners, who were co-mingled with us, would have known that I had that bread hidden in my jacket, they would have killed me for it. People had no feelings, loyalty, lost their humanity and compassion.

Because my father was known from Lodz, some fellow prisoners extended to me an acknowledgement and a sense of camaraderie. Most did not have anyone to feel any friendship or kindness from or for.

On the sixth day of the march, Father could not walk anymore. He said, "You walk as far as you can. Someone has to remain, you must live with hope." I insisted to stay with him and said, "Whatever happens to you, I want it to happen to me. I am staying." As the column was passing, he shoved me towards his friends who got a hold of me and literally had to drag me for fifty feet, taking me further away from Father. At this distance they let me walk, and I knew that I could not backtrack to him. I would be shot.

That evening no prisoners were shot. I lived with hope that Father was alive somewhere. We arrived at a railroad station, loaded onto cattle cars and transported for six days, without water; rolls were thrown in and whoever was lucky to grab one had some food. I hardly survived. Noticing drops of condensation on the rusty hinges of the car doors, I worked my way towards them and licked the droplets of water. This moisture was condensation from the heat of the inmates in the cars and the cold on the outside.

Father was in another car and died in this transport, which was called the Leichen Transport, the transport of the dead. When the cars were opened, bodies just rolled out. One third of the prisoners died. My great pain and regret to this day is that I was not able to be with my father to comfort him in his final hours. When I found out that my father was not alive anymore, I could not cry, could not feel. Tears would not come; I was numb.

We finally arrived to Flossenburg Concentration Camp and were taken to a sub-camp where we worked cleaning the snow from the roads. My strength was ebbing, I could not work anymore. I was sent to Buchenwald to be finished off. I arrived in the evening with nine others. The next morning they took us together with other prisoners and marched us to the crematorium. As we came to about fifty feet from the crematorium gate, a *Feldwebel,* a German sergeant, approached shouting, *"Halt,"* stop. He came in front of us and called out my name and the other nine who arrived with me. We were not on the scheduled list for being killed that morning; the list was signed by the Commandant the evening before our arrival. He marched us back to the barrack while the others were gassed and burnt in the crematorium. We knew that this reprieve was only temporary and we would be killed on the following day. In the meantime, the U.S. Army was getting nearer and this fact suspended the crematorium killings.

Still, each day the orders to line up for the *appel* were shouted. *"Ale Juden eintreten,"* all Jews get out. We knew that this was a threatening order. Some of us who managed to become friends, stuck together. One of the guys who did not look Jewish went out of the barrack and surveyed the situation. He came back telling us that this was a selection. The four of us hid under the barracks and managed to escape that selection. The next day, again all prisoners were taken out for an *appel*. An air raid sound chased us all back into the barracks. The next morning again we had to report to the *appel* grounds. My strength was fading, I could not march. I fell to the ground and made believe that I was dead. Bodies were strewn all over the field. A German soldier passed by and kicked me to see if I was alive. I did not move, so he left me for dead. He did not want to waste a bullet on those he believed were dead. Those that showed any kind of life he shot.

After the selected were marched away, I snuck away and hid under the barrack. The next morning, April 11, 1945, all the German guards ran away. We were liberated by the American 3rd Army. We were an emaciated group. I was told when I was liberated and hospitalized that I weighed fifty-nine pounds. The soldiers caught a couple of pigs and made soup to feed us. Many of the survivors, including me, became very sick from this too rich food. On April 12, 1945, I came down with dysentery. I thought I was at the end of my existence. I looked up to heaven and questioned, "After surviving five years

Henry Landsberg, Germany

of captivity to die now?" I found it a cruel conclusion to my life.

The Americans organized a field hospital for the prisoners. I reported to this hospital. Taking one look at me, they immediately admitted me. After three months in the hospital, with care, regaining my strength, I walked out guardedly to search for myself, for my family, for a renewal which I did not know where to start. I often said that I am a true American because the blood that is in my veins is from the transfusions that were donated by Americans.

While I was in the hospital, my sister, who also survived, found my name on a list in Lodz. I received a letter from her that was sent through the Red Cross. I did return to Lodz but only long enough to attend my sister's wedding. She told me that when she tried to get back to our home, the Polish squatters slammed the door in her face. From our extended family of one hundred people, only a handful survived.

Like many survivors, I found a home at first in the DP Camp Landsberg and after being spooked by the protective fencing around the camp, I decided to get a room outside of camp which I shared with a friend.

Henry 2013

I lived in Germany for two years until my brother-in-law got papers from his brother, who came to the United States in the early 1930s, for all three of us to travel to America. On August 11, 1947, I arrived in New York and started to rebuild my life. I attended evening school and worked at any job that I could get. After a number of jobs and ventures, I started an automobile business which became my lifelong career.

In 1958, I celebrated a wonderful reunion with my two brothers and their families in Israel. We shared tears of sorrow and joy to be united again.

Until January 2010, I never was able to speak of my experiences, suffering and losses. But now, with the help of friends, I felt compelled that I must record my survival story to share with the world and to share with my wonderful children and grandchildren and my wonderful best friend and wife Vera.

To state that I am the Patriach of the Bialer family is both painful and full of honor. I walk on the path of my father and mother. Their lives were not wasted because we continue and carry on with honor, kindness and charity.

I have an obligation to tell the world of the evil that we had to endure and let it be a lesson to bring understanding and appreciation of life.

When I am asked to share a message, I want to say that "Leave a message of good will and help others as best as you can. We pass this way only once."

PROPELLED TO SURVIVE

Vera Bialer

I have struggled for a very long time about whether I should record my family's survival during the Shoah. Although my memories are in bits and pieces, my vague recollections still carry fragments of pain.

With urging from my husband, Henry, and others, I was convinced that every voice, every memory, no matter how brief, fractured and unpleasant, should be recorded.

Grandfather second from left

Grandfather close-up

So let me start first to tell you about my birth city, Budapest, Hungary where Jewish presence goes back to the 3rd century. In the seventeenth century, after the Ottoman rule was driven from the city, Jewish life was established and grew. It was a fragile existence especially under the Hapsburg rule, which imposed anti-Semitic laws and expelled Jews from Buda and forced them to live in the city's Obuda district. Many of the city's 250,000 Jews lived in this area where there were many great synagogues in the Byzantine and Moorish style. This locality in WWII, actually enabled the Nazis to imprison and seal the Jews into the ghetto, surrounded by walls.

My mother's father, my grandfather Marcus, died before I was born. He had two daughters, my mother Rosa Engel and her older sister Margit, who was murdered along with my grandmother in the Holocaust.

The family was somewhat religious but still lived a more modern life. My great-grandfather on my mother's side was very religious. He owned a bauxite mine, a tavern, *kretchme*, and a general store in the town of Gant. He employed a great many people and his family lived comfortably. He and his wife died before the outbreak of WWII. They had five children, including my grandmother, and of those, only two survived the Holocaust.

On my father's side, my family had achieved recognition in the non-Jewish world of Budapest to a degree that my grandfather even served in the Embassy in Austria where he resided.

My father, Laszlo Roszler, was one of nine children. Four died in their young childhood years. The remaining five all survived the Holocaust.

Father was a handsome and charming man who was educated to be a chemist but his love of the arts inspired him to open a theatre where he produced shows for the general public. My mother and father led a life of society connections in Budapest and attended many

Mother Rosa, Vera, Father Laszlo

social events every night. They dressed with elegance and in the height of fashion. I was always in awe to see them dressed and ready to go out and admired my parents, as Mother's perfume permeate the air when I hugged them good night. We led a relatively secular life in Budapest, which was a modern and sophisticated city.

I was born on September 14, 1939, the month the war began. Because of my parents' involvement and social obligations, I was cared for by a nanny but I remember especially with fondness, the love and cuddling that was showered upon me by my Aunt Erzsebet. She was married to a non-Jewish, very prominent, high ranking officer in the Hungarian military who used his connections to save us by establishing hiding places.

Starting in 1938, Hungary, under Miklos Horthy, passed a series of anti-Jewish measures in copying the Nuremberg Laws. The first law, on May 29, 1938, restricted the number of Jews to 20% in each commercial enterprise, in the press, physicians, engineers and lawyers. The second anti-Jewish law, on May 5, 1939, defined Jews racially. People with two, three, or four Jewish-born grandparents were declared Jewish. Their employment in government was forbidden. They could not be editors of newspapers. There were quota limits for Jewish actors in movies and theatres. Private companies were restricted to employ not more than 12% Jews. Two hundred and fifty thousand Hungarian Jews lost their income. Most of them lost their right to vote, only thirty-eight privileged Jews could vote.

When Hungary joined the German axis, they protected us for a time. The government refused to deport Jews. However, they did establish forced labor camps for young Jewish men, which included my father who was taken to a labor camp in the Ukraine mountains. It is estimated that about 30,000 Jews died there. Father did survive, but he came back toothless and emaciated. We lived with many deprivations and uncertainty. Tensions were high and much changed for the Jewish population.

On March 18, 1944, German tanks rolled into Budapest. They set up the fascist Hungarian Red Arrow Party. They shot Jews at random in the streets. Groups of Jews were rounded up and marched to the banks of the Danube River where they had them take off their shoes, and then forced them into the icy waters and shot. Somewhere between 13,000 and 14,000 were killed this way. Today a touching monument of dozens of bronze shoes lie seemingly abandoned at the edge of the Danube.

Robert Csikszenty

During this time, we were hiding with my aunt's non-Jewish husband, Robert Csikszenty, who was of royal lineage. I saw people taken away and marched down the street. I still recall a specific scene of a little boy who was grabbed off the street and taken with the others to the river and drowned there. I was not fully aware what was happening, but the air was charged with fear and everyone's face reflected terror.

In the spring, Adolf Eichmann arrived and implemented the deportation to the killing camps. Jews from the countryside were relocated to the city from which selections were made and sent to concentration camps. Eichmann set up a Budapest Jewish Council. Freedom of going about the city was forbidden and Jews were forced to wear a yellow Jewish star. After the deportation of the majority of Jews, those who were left were herded into two thousand homes. Inside, conditions were shocking for the 100,000 Jews.

The winter of 1944-45 claimed many lives, while plans were made to deport these Jews in July and August. Within three months, about 500,000 Jews were sent on trains to Auschwitz.

The city was bombed sometime during the beginning of summer of 1944.

24

Around that time, we transferred to a building which was designated for Jews. The bombardments by the allies made all run for shelters. I remember that Mother and I and many others were hiding in a shelter in the building where there was a round port window and I did not want to leave it. Being only four years old, I did not want to obey Mother and wanted to stay and watch the outside. Mother could not budge me away from this dangerous spot, but as it turned out, it was the place that saved our lives. When a bomb destroyed the shelter, Mother and I were propelled through the window away from the collapsing debris. All others were killed in the rubble. Mother scooped me up and we ran to a Christian friend who kept us for a while.

Another memory that comes to mind is when we were hiding in between two glass windows in a small space that had been designed for a flower bed, a hothouse. This area had accumulated snow, which on this day was melting. We all stood in this freezing melted water which reached up to my chin. I, along with nine adults, stood motionless for hours while the SS officers were drinking and socializing with my uncle Victor in the apartment. He had returned to the city from Paris with Christian papers, passing as a non-Jew. I was four at that time, but I fully understood that an involuntary sneeze could cost nine lives.

Our search for safety was endless. Mother found a priest who hid me in the attic with a few others. He brought us food and water. I was moved from shelter to shelter deprived of security and endured starvation. I survived under a false identity. I recall being told, "Your name is Kati Kovacs. If anyone offers you food, you are to tell them you just finished your meal and are full." Even though I was weak with hunger, I still had to pretend that I had access to plentiful food so as not to arouse suspicion.

Raoul Wallenberg came to Budapest as secretary of the Swedish Foreign Ministry in July 1944 with instructions to save as many Jews as possible. He issued thousands of Swedish identity documents to Jews to protect them from Nazi deportation and is credited with ultimately saving as many as 100,000 people. He worked with the Swiss Consul Carl Lutz, as well as Portuguese and Spanish legations to create "protected" houses and a "protected" ghetto to house the Jews with international identity papers. Wallenberg was last seen leaving the city on January 17, 1945, right after the Soviet army liberated the city.

Finally in 1945, the Soviets liberated the city and we were free to try to rebuild our lives. We managed to find shelter in a bombed building with extreme damages, which Father repaired. He also established a lab which was taken from him by the Communists who were now in power. The lab developed a method for distilling wine and making cologne. He was told that he would run it. He did defy them and did not want to relinquish his secrets of these processes nor would he join the Communist party, so he was arrested and taken to jail from 1953 to 1954. When he was released, Father found creative ways to support us but which were very dangerous and instigated inspections often.

I attended school, excelled in my studies and finished three years of high school. I lived an assimilated life, not identifying as a Jew. Certainly under Communism, religion was not permitted. But my parents and I connected to our Jewish heritage by even fasting on Yom Kippur.

My social life was among young people from school. We adjusted to the dogma of atheism, Communism and altruism as the Communist dogma was professing. We lived with freedom, yet with a sense of fear, not daring to defy the established government and rules.

This Communist rule became a recognized oppression and a spontaneous nationwide revolt resulted against the government and the influence of the Soviet union. This uprising lasted from October 23 until November 10, 1956.

During this event, we hid in a shelter while our building was strafed by tanks. Russian soldiers succeeded to take over the building and we had to get into the courtyard. Mother smeared my face with dirt to make me unappealing to the marauding soldiers. For close to three days we were interrogated by them with the aid of a translator, determining if we were the rebels.

This terrifying experience and seeing many of my friends leaving made me firm in my decision to also leave. I announced this to my parents. I was only sixteen years old. They understood our situation and went to the Israeli consulate to get a visa to leave. We left most of our belongings behind. The year was 1957.

We first traveled to Genoa, Italy and stayed in a hotel for immigrants and then transferred to Naples and finally after a three months wait, we boarded a ship and arrived in Israel in 1957.

Vera 2013

The situation and conditions in Israel were difficult. We did not know the language, we had no jobs, and the housing made available to us was primitive, without running water. Even though Father was a brilliant chemical engineer, he could not get work. I worked at menial jobs to help us survive. But my focus, and of course, my parents' was to continue my education.

We somehow adapted to be among Jews and even though life was hard, we were free.

After about a year in Israel, I met a nice young man from the United

States and we married in 1958. I immigrated to New York in 1959 but with great difficulties because I was considered a Communist since Hungary after the war became a Communist country and under the Soviet influence.

My drive to continue my education was relentless. I passed a GED exam, entered college and eventually earned a Computer Science Degree. This opened up doors for me, and I enjoyed a rewarding career in the computer science field.

After about eleven years, my marriage failed, although we remained good friends and good parents to our children.

Eventually I remarried in 1978 to my dear best friend and husband Henry Bialer. He has been a wonderful partner and a parent to my children and my five grandchildren. Our melded family has brought us happiness and a feeling that the future of our children and grandchildren is in good hands. For years, I never thought of myself as a survivor of the Holocaust as I had not been deported to a camp. But upon reflection and with the opportunity to hear stories of others, I have come to realize that my loss and suffering was also significant and worthy of sharing. The telling of my story is important for me, for my family and for the future generations.

A GIRL LEFT BEHIND TO SURVIVE

by Judy Laufer Blackman

Judy after war - in USA

Vienna, Austria was a great magnet for oppressed Jews of Europe. This was because Jews were allowed participation in the 1848 Civil War and were permitted to form their own autonomous religious community, which served the Jewish population of Vienna and of Austria as well.

Full citizenship rights were given to the Jews in 1867, leading to a large influx of immigrants from the Eastern part of the Austro-Hungarian Empire, especially from Bukovina, Galicia, the Czech lands and Hungary. A total of 200,000 Jews lived in the new, tiny Austria.

My father, Salomon Laufer, ran away from his *yeshiva* obligatory orthodox studies in Krakow, Poland to Vienna in his teens. He immediately started a small trial balloon enterprise of selling notions, thread, needles and ribbons. When he was seventeen, he joined the Navy and fought for Austria in WWI. He distinguished himself by saving a number of officers during battles and was awarded many medals for his courageous deeds.

He married Blima Springer, also an immigrant from Poland (Podgrodzie). She was a most striking young woman. Their match was one of great attraction, love and devotion. Together they built a business of elegant textiles and ready-to-wear, such as the costume *lederhosen* – leather shorts. Their location and quality of goods attracted the affluent society of Vienna.

In time, Father brought his family from Poland and set up each one in some business so that they could provide for themselves. Our comfortable apartment in the Twentieth District, on the third floor adjoining the store, provided luxury with a refined elegance, a live-in maid, and a young companion who oversaw the children a few days a week. We spent summers away at a resort.

I was born in 1923, joining my two-year-old sister Eleanor. Our home life was very much Viennese; we spoke only Austrian while my parents would occasionally revert to Polish when they wanted to keep us from understanding their exchange. My father's strict expectations of his daughters were that we excel in our studies, maintain good manners, accomplishments and not bring shame to our name.

We attended public school and never felt anti-Semitism. Most of our friends were Jewish; we spent social times together. In the summer we volunteered on farms, learning about farming so that we might become good candidates to go to Palestine.

The "*Anschluss*" – joining of Austria and Germany, began with fanatic attacks on Jews by Austrian rabble. This was March 11, 1938, when Vienna prepared to receive Hitler. The ruffians dragged anyone that appeared Jewish, beating them. They attacked synagogues, looting department stores and raiding the Jewish flats. They made the rabbis scrub toilets with the *talit*s, prayer shawls, and robbed all their valuables. The Jew-hating did not need Hitler to teach them. We learned that they were inherent with hate. Every day we heard screams and shouts of abuse. Little boys with their exposed side-locks were attacked and pulled at viciously. I too tasted the burn of the swishing switch on my legs. The lines for food where always overlooked by a line of SS, peering at the gathered and punishing any infraction that they imagined. This was the daily evil that was perpetrated against Jews.

Kristallnacht, the night of broken glass, November 9 - 10, 1938 was a horror nightmare. None could comprehend what was happening to Jews. The 267 synagogues, throughout Austria, were destroyed. Seven thousand five hundred businesses and homes were devastated, over niney Jews murdered, and 26,000 Jews were rounded up.

I tremble as I recall the vision outside our window when the Austrian populace, including Father's card-playing friends, were marching, carrying swastika banners. The shouts, "*Juden*" felt like a dream!

Mother's pleading "Let's get out," only got a reply from Father, "I can't go anywhere and take away the roof from my children."

Three days later, the arm of evil reached our home as Father and many others were arrested and held at a schoolhouse cellar lock-down, as the police were claiming that the men were kept for their own safety. Father was held for about four days. Mother tried to have him released. Many family members of the imprisoned came to the basement window to just take a glimpse of their loved one. Somehow Father was returned to us. We remained mostly home trying to keep a low profile, but after three weeks, the police appeared again, arrested Father and sent him to Dachau Concentration Camp. This was a training center for SS concentration camp guards. This routine became the model for all Nazi concentration camps.

During WWII, the Austrians constituted only 8% of the Third Reich's population, but comprised 14% of the SS and 40% of Nazi personnel involved in genocide.

Mother again went into action and appealed to the officials showing them Father's medals and honors and telling them that he saved Austrian officers. This apparently helped because they released Father but they demanded that we get out of the country. Mother signed this paper thinking that it was for all four of us. In the meantime, she transferred money, American dollars, to Italy for "*shifs karte*," ship tickets, so that we would be able to get away to America. We were all packed, carrying valises down the stairs but my sister and I were pushed back and were not allowed to join our parents on the truck. The permit to leave was only for my parents.

So here we were, two young girls left alone in our apartment with a neighbor, who was well-paid, to overlook our safety. A spinster aunt came periodically to look in on us. We were in a state of shock. What were we to do? Where should we go to get reunited with our parents? By this time opportunities to get out were scarce. Eleanor was in a stupor and did not venture out of the apartment except only for meals, which were given out twice a day by the HIAS. I became the one to look for ways to survive and look out for both of us. Within a few weeks, we received letters from Mother that they were in Brussels with words of advice for us to care safely for ourselves. This was the strong message in every letter.

Food became scarce because Hitler took everything to Germany. We could shop only between four and five in the afternoon, when all was picked over and the prices were doubled for Jews. Our ID cards we had to carry were a giveaway that we were Jews. The photo showing the left ear meant that you were a Jew. Every Jew had a middle name added, Israel for men and Sara for woman. In addition, the passports had a big red J stamped on them.

We continued to live in our apartment. As I look back at myself in those days, I wonder where I got the guts to defy the Nazi system by sidestepping some of the rules and even attend a movie with my friend Macy Altman. This scene of trying to bring some sort of normalcy to our lives suddenly was interrupted by three Gestapo wearing tall black boots, shouting with sarcasm, "There is a stink in the house! There are *Juden, Jews,* in this house!" Just as I was about to rise to get out, Macy held me back saying "Don't go, it's a trick." And indeed we heard shouts and shots outside. Those that left were arrested or worse.

Soon the letters from Mother stopped. We did not know what to think, after all, we were just sheltered, naive girls. We learned later that Father was nabbed in the streets of Brussels and sent first to Perpignon, a slave labor camp, and then to Auschwitz where he was killed. Mother was hidden in an attic of a Gentile couple for twenty-seven months. They also hid the friend of my mother's sister in the basement.

Somehow, with the help of the HIAS and advice from some elders, we learned that the two of us would be able to leave Austria for Italy. Arrangements to leave on the last ship out the "Rex."

We packed very little, just what we could carry and arrived in Italy. We stayed for a couple of weeks exploring the sights and tourist attractions by attaching ourselves to adults as their children so that we could get on the streetcars free, since our funds were only for a loaf of bread and a little cheese. My daring and resourcefulness came from a place that to this day I am amazed at.

Our ocean crossing was uneventful. We arrived at New York harbor around Christmas 1940. The sight was overwhelming. The skyline of high-rise buildings glistened with a profusion of lights. I felt that I had arrived in a dream world somewhere out of a fairy tale.

We were met by my uncle, my mother's brother. Our destination was Detroit choosing the shortest route, Niagara Falls, the Canadian side. We were detained there because of our Austrian passports with visible stamps of the swastika. We remained for five days with a Jewish family until our family in Detroit was able to clear our journey.

Arriving in Detroit, Eleanor and I were split between two families, an aunt and an uncle. My life was bleak, I thought coming to America I would find safety and comfort from family, but it was difficult to adjust for all. Finally I accepted a job as a baby sitter to live with a family and care for their three months old baby. It proved to be confining. I felt that I could not grow and make a life for myself. I was now seventeen years old.

After bouncing from a few jobs I met Joe, my future husband, although quite a bit older, I found him to be a good match who would emulate the devotion that my parents exhibited to each other. We were married in 1942 and soon my husband was drafted. We spent four years in the armed services of my now wonderful, free country, the United States of America.

All the while we searched, through the Red Cross, for our parents' whereabouts. Finally in 1946 we were informed that Mother was alive. Learning of Father's death in

Judy 2013

Auschwitz carries a pain to this day. We learned that many members and friends had disappeared in the death smoke of the Holocaust.

Finally we were reunited with Mother. It was both a wondrous and startling time because she discovered that her young daughters were now wives and mothers.

My Holocaust life story has left me with many terrible and frightening memories of the evil that befell the Jewish people and my own family. Even though threatened of being a Jew, I am proud to be one! I love being a Jew!

My two daughters, Sheila and Marilyn, their children and grandchildren are my circle of life. They represent and shine brightly as members of the Jewish people, and I look at them and thank God that we survived to have such a family.

MEMORIES HAPPY AND TRAGIC

by Helene Hertz Daniel

I search the corners of my mind about my life, especially after we moved to Aachen, a spa town in North Rhine/Westphalia, Germany. It is the western-

Brother Alfred and Helene - Germany

most city of Germany, located along the borders with Belgium and the Netherlands. My life there was something like a fairy tale.

I still remember the elms and oaks in the woods surrounding the city. There was a fresh smell of the pine needles permeating the air, and in the autumn, before the wind came to sweep their leaves away, the sun glistened on the last beautiful, golden splendor of colors. For a youngster, there were hardly any problems in the world.

The following will give you an overview how we lived, with an insight and understanding of what the evil meant. We were able to escape from the grips of the killers, but not early enough to escape the evil that was all around us and against us. Tragically, we lost a large number of my family.

In Aachen, as in all of Germany, Jews were integrated as German citizens. They served in the army and navy and contributed to every field of science, business and culture.

Conditions and life changed after the appointment of Hitler as Chancellor of Germany on January 30, 1933 supported by his Nazi party.

Because they needed funds, in the fall of 1938 they strengthened their ambition by confiscating Jewish property by force and for a nominal exchange. That same year, a series of anti-Jewish restrictions were enforced, limiting opportunities of education and full citizenship rights. This was followed by the Nuremberg Laws in 1935, which stripped German Jews of their citizenship and restricted all freedoms including that Jews could not marry non-Jewish Germans.

In November 9-10, *Kristallnacht*, crystal night or the night of broken glass, a night of abuse was directed against all Jews, their businesses, synagogues and homes. Many were beaten to death. Over 30,000 Jewish men were arrested and taken to Dachau and other concentration camps, where life was brutal. Most were released on condition that they leave Germany.

Helene in Purim Costume - Germany

Ironically, the Jewish communities were fined one billion *reichsmarks* for this violence and four million *reichsmarks* to repair the windows. Jews were blamed for the violence of *Kristallnacht*.

I was born on August 6, 1925 in Linnich. Our family lived in Germany for many generations without any maltreatment. My father Max Hertz, born in 1892, unfortunately lost his mother, Helene Levy Hertz, soon after his birth. His father, Herman Hertz, had several siblings who helped care for my father and absorbed him into their family. The aunts and uncles, Alex, Wilhelmina, Lisa Mina, Jacob, Norbert, Simon and their spouses were murdered by the Nazis. Father served in WWI.

Father was a serious but kind parent. His focus, as well as my mother's, Rosa Moses, was their business, and so the care of me and my brother Alfred, thirteen months older, was relegated to a governess, who was my companion and dear friend. The governess lived with us until 1937. I attended Jewish school where we also learned Hebrew. I had many friends, Jewish and non-Jews and felt no anti-Semitism.

Our department store in Linnich was the largest in town. Also it had a separate fashionable custom tailoring department. Mother too had her own studio, designing hats, where she employed a number of workers. These businesses provided us a life of luxury and affluence. We were considered assimilated Jews and were very comfortable with our non-Jewish neighbors and friends. Our home was a six-bedroom large house, with every convenience that was available at that time, including a chauffeur, who later helped us sneak in valuables to Holland.

I recall riding my bicycle accompanied by my governess to my uncle Alex's house. They did not have children, so I became their beloved niece who was welcomed with affection and indulgence.

I was introduced to culture and when, at the age of seven, I saw the opera

"Hansel and Gretel," I was frightened when the witch wanted to push the children into the oven. Mother calmed me, saying, "It's all make-believe." Little did we realize then that ten years later millions of children and their loved ones would be shoved into the ovens, and it would no longer be make-believe.

Aachen Synagogue

In 1937, the Gestapo stood in front of our store, photographing the non-Jewish customers entering. Father was forced to sell their businesses since they were no longer permitted to deal with non-Jewish customers. He had to sell both, the businesses and our home for much less than their value.

We moved into a rental, three-bedroom apartment, in Aachen, where it became a welcome stopover for many displaced Jews. Father helped many get into Holland, whose borders were heavily patrolled. Once he was caught by the Dutch police, paid a fine, and was told not to try again.

That year, 1937, was also our family's sorrow when my dear grandmother Dinah passed away.

On November 9, 1938, *Kristallnacht*, on my way to school, I watched as my beloved synagogue was burned to the ground. As I looked at the faces around me, I saw Jews and Gentiles crying and shaking their heads, but nobody lifted a finger to stop the fire or dared to. All was burning, the beautiful Torahs, the precious ornaments. My memories of a once perfect world burned on and all that was left were ashes.

I did not continue to school that day on the advice of a Gentile friend and went home to tell my parents what was happening. I witnessed store windows being broken, looting, and when the owners tried to call the police they were arrested. Jewish men and young boys were arrested and shipped to concentration camps.

We were surrounded by the Gestapo and by Nazis. Afraid of their abuse or being arrested, we decided to hide in the coal cellar of our building. When the Gestapo came to arrest my father, the maid told them that he had left town. They informed her that she was no longer allowed to work for Jews. I parted from her with sorrow and tears pouring.

We soon were joined in our small apartment by many acquaintances and family members from small villages, who were in need of shelter. It became so crowded that I had to live with a Gentile lady, my mother's seamstress, and repaid her with doing household chores. I was thirteen years old at that time.

By this time, October, 1939, my father knew that we could not remain in Germany. Germany had invaded Poland and other countries and seeing and hearing about the abuse that Jews endured, Father found a way to have us escape to Holland. Holland was only one hour away, but the borders were well-guarded. Because my uncle Alex's wife had family in America, they sent us a visa and with sadness and gladness, we sailed on the Staatendam out of Rotterdam for the United States that fall.

Our entry into this haven, the United States of America, was with expectations for a safer life and, of course, adjusting. We finally felt free. From a six bedroom house in Linnich, with domestic help, we now lived in a one bedroom apartment where Mother had to overcome unaccustomed challenges to become a homemaker.

My brother and I went to high school, and we became the virtual parents of our parents since we both spoke English. I did the shopping, paid bills and quickly became an adult.

In the summer, I got away from the stifling heat and city life when I found a job as a mother's helper in hotels in the mountains. The first summer, I earned $30.00 in four weeks including room and board.

What does it mean to be picked up and snatched away from your safe environment into a world that is completely alien and strange to you? In the beginning I learned that the best way to deal with this pain is to keep secrets. The best way to deal with loss is to never talk about it. I spent many years with this hermetic seal over the past. This way I didn't even know that a large part of myself was missing. One cannot explain the emotional process one goes through, letting go of family, letting go of your dreams.

If the bare facts tell of hardship and deprivation, the emotional experience of family members transcends them. There is no trace of martyrdom or self-pity in our story of the past.

The intelligence and quiet dignity and courage of my parents and their strength of character reflect the influence of our proud, close-knit immigrant family and the adversities we encountered that broke everything but our spirit. We made a life for ourselves in the United States.

We escaped the hell of Germany and prayed in vain that so many of our friends and family would not fall victims to Hitler's murderers.

In 1945 the war was over and I was thinking of getting married. I was twenty years old. We learned about the mass-murders that occurred in Europe, the many loved ones that we lost.

I wondered if my friend, Kurt Daniel, survived? I searched through many agencies who were of no help. Then one day we received a call from a friend who read an ad in an international paper, "Kurt Daniel, Belgium, looking for a family, Max Hertz, USA." I answered the ad and we were happy that this was my friend Kurt who managed to escape the Nazis. He was alone. He lost all members of his family and we were the only friends he knew.

At this time, I applied for a job with the Holland America shipping line and was hired because I spoke three languages, I wanted to get to Belgium hoping that those adolescent feelings of a young teenager transcended to adult feelings now. The war can change many things. Many friends converted, married or had other interest.

A friend, Marcel, who was in the diamond business, traveled back and forth to Antwerp, which was the diamond center at that time. I arranged for him to meet Kurt in Brussels. When he returned a month later he said, "I am going to make your wedding bands."

And so, affidavits were mailed and approved. Two years after the war ended and all red tape cut, Kurt sailed on the Marine Tiger and arrived in the States on August 11, 1947. We were married on November 16, 1947. We were blessed with a wonderful family, a daughter, Dianne Sonia, and a son, Marc David, and four grandchildren, Jason, Michelle, Joshua, Alyson.

The Germans tried to dehumanize the Jewish people, but the result is that they themselves have to live with their shame. All the future generations will be told again and again about the 20th century barbarians and murderers.

We have been asked, "Can we forgive?" We, the children, nephews, nieces, grandchildren, aunts and uncles and friends of the people who suffered at the hands of the Germans, are not in a position to forgive the German nation for their crimes.

To forgive a nation which had invented the death factories? The forgivers speak of new beginnings, not to look at the Germans of the 1990s as the Nazis of the thirties and forties. If they want forgiveness, they have to dig up the bones, search and retrieve the scattered ashes, the scattered mass graves. We don't have the right to forgive. Only the victims have that right, and they are dead!

Helene 2012

The future German generations and current young must learn and be made aware of the crimes. They must be told. They have to be told for the sake of all children and for the sake of the world.

It is now eighty years since the Nazis came to power and seventy-four years since the Holocaust began, based on when WWII, 1939 began. What has been learned? The old hatred is still festering and creeping to the surface and the world and United Nations is keeping quiet.

We, the elders, know of the dark faces of Auschwitz and so many other killing factories. Soon there will be no one left to speak of them. If we don't tell the world what happened, it will happen again.

I am proud of being Jewish because I am a member of a people of courage, learning and dignity. We are a people that produced many Nobel Prize winners, a people of giants in the field of science, medicine, music and literature. We are a people that survived through the years of history, withstood victoriously against hundreds of thousands of Arabs and Romans. The Maccabbees withstood the Syrians and Greeks. My people courageously resisted the Babylonians.

I am a witness of the great courage of my people who fought the Nazis and those who died with dignity with **"Hear, O Israel, The Lord Is Our God, The Lord Is One,"** on their lips.

I am a witness.
I WILL NOT FORGET!

BATTLE OF SURVIVAL

by Kurt Daniel

I was the only child of Sophie and Max Daniel, an attractive couple, who expressed their love for each other and made me feel that their world revolved around me. Father was one of ten children and Mother had one sister and one brother. The extended family of aunts, uncles and cousins were part of our lives. Family get-together were always big events.

Kurt is third from the left on the donkey

Father ran a cattle broker business while Mother managed a dry goods store, which was located below our living quarters in Dremmen, Germany. We were the only Jewish family in town. We lived a mostly assimilated and modern lifestyle, but still observed many Jewish traditions.

Life became uncertain as anti-Semitism started to surface openly. This climate reached its peak in 1935 when the villainous "Nuremberg Laws" were clarified and instituted against the Jews. These laws forbade intermarriage and many other oppressive actions became the energy to destroy the Jews in Germany and beyond after 1939. These enforcements were considered a Jewish problem, an internal German issue by the outside world.

Kurt - Germany

When I turned twelve years old in 1934, it was decided that I continue my education in a private Jewish school in Linich where I lived with my aunt and uncle while spending the weekends with my parents. My aunt and uncle's neighbors, Rosa and Max Hertz, their son Al and daughter Helen (Leni) became my friends. They always included me to participate in all after-school activities.

My Bar Mitzvah in 1936 brought together family and friends in a wonderful celebration of that event. That afternoon I found myself blushing as I heard Leni Hertz's pronouncement that she would marry me some day.

In 1937, not being able to continue my schooling since all higher education was closed to Jews, I was sent to Munchen-Gladbach to work in an office of a clothing manufacturer, which soon closed when Germany told the nation not to trade with Jews. My next stage to maturity was to work as an apprentice for an uncle in his shoe business in Dortmund.

On November 9, 1938, a rock thrown through my window barely missed me. *Kristallnacht*, the state-sanctioned violence against Jews, was carried out by rampaging mobs all through Germany, smashing windows of Jewish owned businesses and private homes. They burned down the synagogues, Torahs, books and everything that was sacred to Jews. Then they fined the owners for the debris on sidewalks and around their property. They killed ninety one Jews and helped in the arrest of 30,000. This was the precursor of the Holocaust, Hitler's and Germany's trial balloon to see what they could get away with. What would be the world's reaction or lack of reaction to *Kristallnacht*. The world was silent and the Holocaust descended over Europe. My aunt and uncle's business was destroyed and looted. They advised me to take the next train home to Dremmen. Arriving home the following day, I found my mother alone, crying at the kitchen table. My father had been arrested and was sent to Sachsenhausen Concentration Camp. His crime was that he was Jewish. He remained there a short time, head shaved, beaten and a witness to the brutality the Germans were capable of. His short incarceration was due to his having legal proof that he was ready to leave Germany for Holland, where some of his relatives lived. He paid a heavy fine and was sent home. An old man walked through the door, although he was only forty-nine years old.

Like so many German Jews, my father thought that he too was a good

40

German and had many non-Jewish friends. They believed that Hitler would not remain in power, and since he fought in WWI, had a distinguished record and won medals, that he would be exempt from harm. The urge to leave and fear was appeased by justifying that there was always hope, mixed with despair, but soon the reality of danger was seen with clarity and reality.

As the situation worsened we sold our house, business and real estate property. We were forced to sell everything for anything that was offered. The same Germans who accepted communion dresses as gifts from my mother when they could not afford to buy them, had no scruples nor could wait to grab what they could without any feelings that the only Jewish family was being abused and forced to leave their town where they lived and built a life. When my father had visited the Hertz family after his release from the concentration camp in 1938, Max Hertz advised that we get out of Germany as soon as we could and that he would do the same.

I will never forget my seventeenth birthday. It was February 11, 1939, when my parents called me into the living room and with tear-stained faces, informed me that a decision had been made to send me to Belgium the following day. "It will only be for a short time," they said. "We expect to follow you, and we will leave for America together." The following day I left in a gravel truck with a few personal possessions. I never saw my parents again.

The trip to Belgium was supposed to be safe. It was arranged through a black market driver who transported gravel for the Germans who were building the defense lines. As we approached the border, we saw the Germans were patrolling the entire area. I was instructed to get under the gravel, breathe through a pipe and when the driver reached a certain farm house, I grabbed my belongings, jumped out and ran for my life. I was met by resistance fighters who escorted me to Brussels. Family and friends met me and suggested that I contact the Jewish agency. They had all the information to find shelter for newly-arrived refugees.

I was sent to a place called Merxplace. It was a sort of prison where an open area was designated for Jewish refugees. When food was delivered by a neighboring farmer, I inquired if he could use an assistant which he welcomed. This work helped sustain my life. After a year at Merxplace, we were evacuated to Exade, another youth camp for eighteen year old boys. Some of the boys that shared rooms with me were later arrested and were sent to work camps and eventually were taken to Poland or Germany. They were murdered or died there.

During this internment, I was able to correspond with my family in Aachen. They were still trying to leave Germany, however there were now many obstacles. The papers that were approved for Holland were useless. People tried to cross the border at night. Those that were caught by the Germans were arrested and sent to a concentration camp, and eventual death. If the Dutch caught them, they returned them back to Germany unless one had a lot of money to bribe the border patrol.

My heartache to this day is why didn't they take a chance, leave everything behind and flee to Holland or Belgium? But their answer was always the same, "Hitler can't stay in power much longer."

In May 1940, the Germans invaded Belgium. They unleashed a series of devastating operations against neutral Holland and Belgium. Unable to match the force of the invaders, Holland and Belgium capitulated on May 27.

We had to evacuate Exade and make our way to a youth camp in Ostende, a place famous for beautiful beaches and hotels. When the Germans approached, we fled to Brussels, which was being bombed. The Germans did not waste time in rounding up Jews of the city and sending them off to "work camps." They were actually concentration camps. "Look for a place to hide. Get out of the city." This is all I heard from friends and the Jewish agency. I remember witnessing young boys had to drop their pants in open daylight on the streets. If they were circumcised, they were grabbed by the Germans and thrown onto a truck for deportation. We were on our own now.

The farmer whom I worked for made contact with a pig farmer located further away from civilization, in Zellik. I was able to stay there; no questions asked and learned to eat pork for the first time in my life. I had a roof over my head, food to eat and smelled like a pig. Here I was still able to receive mail from my parents and learned that my father had to clean the streets in Aachen along with other Jews. My father, cleaning streets! I had never seen my father without a suit and tie. Food was rationed. The need to "get out" was the most important quest. I learned that the Hertz family had left on the last boat out of Rotterdam for the United States and once they were settled would provide affidavits and all necessary papers to help my parents get out of Germany.

The obstacles were mounting. A cousin who was married to a cousin of Henry Morgenthau, the finance minister to President Roosevelt, was contacted without success. There were a few more letters like that and then there was no more mail . . . no more contact. They knew I was safe, had to stay alive, had to bear witness, and must not let the Germans find me. Of course, the latter was not always so easy.

When Germans came to the farm to demand pigs for their troops, I was up in the hayloft. They told the farmer that they would be back periodically. I knew that I had to get out of there. With the aid of false papers provided by the underground and a recommendation from my first farmer's job, I found a good place to hide and work for food in Lembeque. With my false papers, I had the *chutzpa*, nerve, to take a wagonload full of vegetables to sell at the open market on a weekly basis. Some of the unsold products were made available for members of the underground.

One time, on my return trip, a young girl stopped me and very excitedly told me, "You can't go back, the place is swarming with Germans looking for resistance fighters and Jews who are hiding in the area." She took the wagon back to the farm, and I made my way to another suburb of Antwerp. I spent some time at a local church where a few very young orphans were being cared for by some nuns. I was able to provide them with much-needed food.

After a while, the members of the underground told me it was safe to return to Lembeque, and I was given a gun for protection. The family made a false wall in their home where I could find shelter in an emergency. There were times when I was hiding in their Dutch oven in the living room when the Germans were hanging out at a neighboring bar. In my new "living quarters" on a nearby farm, I was able to hide weapons for the underground army. When it was discovered that a German collaborator, a neighboring farmer, gave too much information to the Germans, he was eliminated. Most of the Belgians hated the occupation and the curfews that they had to live with. They despised the Germans and did everything in their power to make them feel unwelcome.

The constant fear of being caught and shipped to a concentration camp was part of my life for twenty-four hours a day. At that time most of us didn't even know about the crematoriums and other atrocities. We soon found out.

The Allies began their bombing runs and France was invaded. The end of the war was approaching. The Germans did not retreat gracefully. It was evident that Hitler and his German "super race" had lost the war, but the looting and killing continued. The underground army and the partisans were now vigorously involved sabotaging German vehicles and retrieving some of the livestock, horses, that the Germans had stolen. I was happily involved in this activity and when necessary, I used our weapons.

When armistice was declared, it was hard to go about without looking over your shoulder. There were still Germans around who were willing to continue their killing spree. One of my friends went to a barber for a much-needed haircut and fell victim to these killers. Shortly after the assassin was killed by the underground. Belgium was liberated by the Allies in May 1945. A great deal of this beautiful country was destroyed.

As soon as it became safe to travel, I made my way back to Germany. I had not been back for seven years. I had to find out what happened to my family. Hoping that they too might be alive, hiding with some of their Gentile friends or perhaps left for Holland. The International Red Cross was of no help. After a long search on my own, I was able to put some of the horrible pieces of the past together. The Jewish population of Aachen was rounded up and put into a "Jew" house at a place called "*Gruener Weg*." There many families shared one room and lived in deplorable conditions. Food was rationed. People were trapped to the will of the German rule. My father was made to work as a street cleaner and performed slave labor at "Kali Kemi," a chemical factory in Stollberg and also worked on improving paint for German cars. The chemicals removed the skin from their hands and arms. When they were unable to perform their work, they were shipped to Auschwitz. *(I have requested that my children not purchase German cars for their use. I see my father's blood on the finish).*

I was able to trace my father's final destination to Auschwitz-Birkenau. My mother was not with him; I was unable to locate her final destination. When and where do I say *Kaddish,* the Jewish prayer for the dead, for my parents? Where are my parents' graves? Do I sit *Shiva, (seven days of mourning)?* Where is my home? Where is my synagogue? Where is God? Where are the tombstones of our murdered families? This open wound can never heal.

I was exhausted and emotionally spent. I felt the outline of my pistol in the pocket of my trench coat. The anger and adrenalin was rushing through my body. It was hard not to become a cold-blooded murderer like the Germans. They killed because of hate, bigotry, greed and traitors to their own citizens. I did not want to live with hate. I wanted justice. I looked at their faces in disbelief. How can they go to church on Sunday, go home and drink their coffee out of cups stolen from the Jews, go to sleep at night on down pillows stolen from the Jews? The city official told me that all our furniture was confiscated and auctioned off along with paintings, heirlooms, silverware, linen and other belongings and the rest was looted. No money was available from my parents' bank accounts nor was Father's life insurance in force. Now over seventy years later, I still have not found justice in what was done to our people, what has been taken away and never returned.

I could not wait to leave Germany behind me. I crossed over to Belgium and never looked back. I wanted to go back to the kind couple that gave me shelter and try to repay them in whatever way possible. I longed for a family, but where are they? My family was gone, no one to bind my life to. I remembered the Hertz family who were like my own. Perhaps I could find them somewhere in America. I placed an ad in an international paper called *"Aufbau,"* Reconstruction, stating "Looking for family Max Hertz, USA, maybe New York."

A friend of the Hertz's saw the ad and took the subway from Washington Heights to Queens to show it to the Hertz's since they had no phones. Contact was made within a week. The letters that followed were full of hope and encouragement. "Please try to come to the US. We will get you affidavits and whatever it takes to get you out of Europe," wrote Helen. Useful gifts arrived from Helen along with perfume-scented letters. Even the mailman when he met me in town informed me, "There is mail from Helen. My whole mailbag smells beautifully."

There were many letters from Helen in the years 1945, 1946, 1947. I was seventeen when we were separated. I was now twenty-five and penniless. Marcel Bernstein a friend and neighbor who was in the diamond business and

Kurt - Belgium after war

traveling to Antwerp, advised Helen that he would meet with me, and look me over while bringing greetings from her. When Marcel returned to the States, three weeks later, he told Helen he would be making our wedding bands.

Marcel had many connections. Passage was arranged on the Marine Tiger, a freighter. I sent Helen a telegram from Le Havre advising of my arrival in New York on August 11 1947. Helen was at the pier to meet me. Our emotion of the "first love" was rekindled and we were married by a rabbi on November 16, 1947.

I developed a career in the real estate business, which helped me rebuild and secure a good life for my family. Our daughter, named after my mother Sonni, was born in December 1950, and our son named after my father Marc, was born in January, 1954.

I see how the Holocaust has affected not only me but in the way we raised our children. Interspersed with the tension and anxiety comes tremendous appreciation for the continuity of generations and Jewish heritage.

Fifty years after the Holocaust, the Mayor of Aachen invited us back to this city. Those that survived attended a formal dinner with their companions. The Mayor apologized for the barbaric deeds of the Germans. We were invited to speak of our experiences at various schools. The students looked at us in disbelief with unblinking eyes. The horror of what they heard mirrored in their faces. They had not been taught anything about the Holocaust.

Mine is one more story, one more witness who can contribute to the legacy of remembering and leaving a lasting legacy of our tragic history to the future.

My grandchildren Jason and Michelle Greenberg, Joshua and Alyson Daniel visited Yad Vashem while they spent time in Israel on several occasions and lit candles for their great grandparents.

Kurt 2012

OVER THE ALPS TO A LIFE OF AN ORPHAN

by Ida Dressner

My parents, Esther Igielnik, born on April 26, 1900, and Jacob Koplik, born on March 26, 1898, were natives of Lodz, Poland. Their love attachment was not approved by the respective parents, so the young couple eloped around 1919.

At first they settled in Germany, and after a time, they immigrated and settled in Antwerp, Belgium. They established a good life by opening a restaurant below their living quarters and invested in a small hotel on the coast.

Mother Esther and Ida

Both of my parents were hardworking and devoted partners whose wish was to have a family. Miraculously it happened fifteen years into their marriage when I was born on January 27, 1934.

I was a most loved child, who was indulged in a good life with every opportunity and advantage that my parents' means could provide.

My mother was employed full time cooking and working in running the restaurant. Most of my care was managed by a succession of governesses. The most memorable one was Regina Blind who was multilingual and spoke Polish, Yiddish and German. By the time I entered kindergarten at the private school, *Ecole Bosquet*, I learned French and had established a capacity for many languages.

My development was guided by Regina, who accompanied me to the ballet and to lavish colorful floral parks. We indulged in afternoon tea on fashionable Kayserlei, where proper manners and behavior was instilled and practiced.

The luscious ice cream and fudge creations bring back memories of a carefree, loved and spoiled childhood. Father also added to my many pleasures by taking me shopping on some afternoons and treating me to the latest imported extravagances such as Coca-Cola and potato chips.

I was surrounded by many relatives including cousin Regina and Joel Sigal who ran a thriving fabric business. Their young daughter Marika was my playmate. The circle of caring relatives were my father's sister and husband, Esther and Jacob Gellhorn and their two older daughters, who did not survive the Holocaust. Aunt Helena and Uncle Mordechai Ungerowicz and their children Ida and Solomon lived in Liege, which was a destination of many enjoyable get-a-ways from our city life.

My mother was a contrast to my father's reticent ways. She was lively, talkative and loved to spend time discussing all sorts of topics which were not shielded from me. I was being brought up with an open, unpretentious mind, with cultural and ethnic diversity. From a child's point of view, life was good and carefree.

September 1, 1939, I recall the worries and discussions about the Germans invading Poland. The radio was on all the time, and our ears were tuned to listen and learn anything new. I knew of the concern from the elders' expressions of worried brows. When Poland capitulated on September 29, 1939, there was still no news from the family. Nevertheless, my parents made no plans or even thought about leaving because they never could imagine that their life would be affected differently than the rest of Belgium and so the months passed with our ears glued to the radio.

On May 10, 1940 Germany invaded Belgium as well as Holland and Luxembourg. Within days, we were awakened to the bombardment of Antwerp. That is when my parents made a decision to leave, while the roads were still open.

My family joined their good friends the Bornsteins with their son, also taking along my governess. And so at the end of May 1940, we motored toward the Belgian coast with a plan to continue to Paris and to the south thinking that we would avoid the mass flight of refugees.

Our progress seemed acceptable until we reached Dunkirk around May 28, 1940 and found ourselves in the midst of a throng of civilian and military evacuation. The British soldiers shared their cigarettes and chocolates with people on the road. I recall that these unexpected treats were soon followed by shrieking sirens followed by the ear-deafening bombardment and strafing at the congested road, killing and maiming indiscriminately all people, whether military or civilian.

Mother and I ran for shelter losing the whereabouts of Father in this catastrophic upheaval. The attack seemed to last an eternity but stopped without injury to Mother or me. Returning to the road, we saw bodies, people, children killed, injured, body parts strewn about. Everyone was numb and in shock. Mother and I located our car on the road and found Father and our companions who escaped injury. We proceeded towards Paris at a crawling pace. Progress hindered by the destroyed vehicles blocking sections of the road. We managed to arrive in Paris where we rested a few days and decided to continue the journey before Paris fell on June 13, 1940.

Our quest to escape continued throughout most of that summer, finding shelter in converted schools as refugee centers. Many people fell apart, not being able to live with such stress. My parents maintained strength under all circumstances.

We traveled very light, wearing the same clothes for days. The infestation of vermin and keeping up hygiene was nonexistent. My memories and mindset were like an adult. I did not question nor complain of any situation and never demanded or asked for food. I knew that the hunger and thirst would be satisfied when possible.

Eventually we arrived to Vichy, France, enthralled by the beauty of this town filled with parks and mineral water fountains. Our stay there was cut short, learning that the Vichy government would soon capitulate.

We continued in our purposeful wanderings to Perpignan, hoping to board a ship to Morocco. This plan fell through when the boat left earlier than we were told. New plans were made just to keep moving with the hope to escape to Spain or Portugal and get on a boat to either the United States or South America. Here we parted from our traveling companions and the car because the Bornstein's managed to get a visa while we could not since my parents were stateless, never having worked through the ordeal of becoming citizens of Belgium.

At this point, my parents decided that they would take a chance to cross into Spain illegally. This effort only resulted in being caught and sent back to France reaching Pau. A big announcement greeted all refugees that a bus will take us to a refugee reception center. The center turned out to be the infamous Gurs, a gathering concentration camp, a prisoners of war compound, which was managed by the French and directed by the Germans. The conditions were inhuman. We realized that we were trapped.

The men were separated from their families and housed separately. The slop soup and a piece of bread were served in rusty cans without utensils. One day, suddenly, we were released. I think that most likely my father bought our way out. We got on a bus and wound up in a tiny village where we kept out of sight for about a week. The neighbors noticed that we were foreigners and thought that we could not be trusted. We continued our journey to Marseilles still in 1940. Here we hoped to get passage on a boat to any safe destination. After an effort of six weeks without luck, Mother declared, "That's it! I'm not living like a gypsy anymore. We've got to go back to Belgium. They are occupying the country, what more could they want?"

My mother and I returned to Antwerp, crossing at the quagmire of a border where my childish charm and command of the German language won over a German officer who guided us through to the right train unmolested.

Mother reopened the restaurant and within a couple of weeks, Father rejoined the family.

It was amazing that our long-attempted excursion of escape brought us right back home, where slowly things returned to normal except the streets were full of German soldiers; marching units strutted through the streets of Antwerp as a symbol and warning of their presence and power.

In 1941, the occupiers were well-behaved and did not show their intent. I returned to the private school and enjoyed my free time in the parks or on the street with my friends.

At the end of 1941, many restrictions were issued on businesses, a curfew was enforced, and all had to wear the yellow star. I was seven years old and when walking on the street wearing the yellow star, I was shunned, harassed and spit upon. The children at school did not display such behavior, so I continued my education.

Before too long the evil intent of the Germans and their collaborators were yelling and shouting at Jews. A scene that still is fixed in my mind is seeing German soldiers tossing a newborn Jewish baby between them and letting it drop to its death in the presence of the pained and screaming parents. This scene and act was the beginning of their coming with trucks in the middle of the night and herding the screaming helpless Jews away. The usual daytime ordeals were to spot a Jew, even a child, abuse, and arrest them. They were never seen again.

The tragedy is still incomprehensible that Jews were helping point out other Jews to the Germans in order to save their own lives for a day or a couple of weeks, still shocks. To this day, I wonder how we maintained strength and sanity after continued abuse and selections, to be able to sleep and go on with life.

In 1942, after closing the failing restaurant, my mother decided to go to Liege to find a place to hide the family since that region was less anti-Semitic. On that fateful morning, mass arrests were made at the railroad station, and they seized my mother. That was the last time that we ever saw or heard from her again.

This tragic news completely broke my father's spirit. He was ordered to report to a slave labor camp, so he placed me in the

Ida Age - 5

care of the Sigals, my cousins. Within a week Father had to report at the railroad station. I accompanied him and remember his encouraging kind words, to be a good girl and with assurance that all this horror will be over soon and we would be reunited. As we reached the bottom of the stairs, Father bent to kiss me and just then an SS man held him while another beat him. Father hurriedly told me, "Turn around and walk away and don't look back." This was the last time that I saw my father. After this incident, I lived my young life as if these horrors were happening to someone else. From that time on, I decided always to hold my own counsel learning that I would be completely on my own emotionally. I never discussed or shared my thoughts, I kept them all to myself and had to depend on my own feelings about people. You learn that some things you just don't talk about. It's too painful and anyway, you are powerless to change anything. I was just as happy that nothing was said because sometimes it's better. You just go along and eventually a child's mind gets distracted.

Regina and Joel decided that only escape would save them. With false identification papers, we removed our yellow stars and each carrying a small valise, including Marika and myself, we boarded a train to Lyons. After a stay there we continued to Thonon-le-Bains attempting to cross into Switzerland. Here we were abandoned by our guide, arrested and I was singled out for questioning at only eight and a half years of age and the most vulnerable. The French captain began his interrogation wanting to know my religion. Realizing the danger for Jews, I answered confidently that "I'm Catholic," and proceeded to cross myself and recite the Hail Mary which I had learned listening to the Catholic children at the private school.

Miraculously, my little group along with the people who were taken in together with us, were ordered to get out of town within twenty-four hours. We were without resources, where to go or what to do when nuns from a local convent learned about some arrests, came to rescue the displaced. They treated us well and arranged a bus for us to be taken to the foot of the Haute Savoie to meet a guide who would walk us across the Alps into Switzerland.

It took seven days to cross the Alps, encountering difficulties of both danger of collaborators and the weather, which landed me in the hospital for a week due to my bloodied feet and distressed physical condition.

We succeeded to cross over, receiving asylum, and were taken to a reception center where we were housed in spartan and crowded conditions. But we finally felt safe.

In January 1943, the children were separated from their parents, and I from my guardians, and placed into foster homes. I was placed with a Jewish Swiss family, resumed school and started my Hebrew school education. After the foster mother had a health problem, in the summer of 1943, I was placed with a Protestant family, the Wetters, who had three adult children. They were the most wonderful people who helped me to live a stable secure life until I was thirteen years old. When I did not accomplish a chore well, Mrs. Wetter told me, "He who has no head has feet." I learned the lesson of living with truth, honor and being decent. I emulated and lived by these creeds all my life. Even with the Wetters, I continued my Hebrew school education; they reminded me that the Jewish refugee organization insisted upon attendance at Hebrew school and that I should honor it.

During all these years, I never stopped thinking about my parents and home in Antwerp. Being reunited was a constant desire and hope. While living with the Wetters, they shielded me from the war news. I was not allowed to read the papers or to listen to the radio news broadcasts. They were very protective. Only when the war ended did I start reading the newspapers. I was eleven years old. My expectations of my parents' return were rekindled with hope.

The Jewish agency tried to send me back to Antwerp, but I broke down and refused to go to the care of cousin Regina. I remained for another half year with the Wetters. Finally after my cousin Ida from Liege and the Aunt and Uncle Ungerowitz were found, I realized that my own parents will not return. I relented and parted from my safe and loving home with the Wetters and their family. I left them in 1947 when I was thirteen years old.

Ida Age - 13

My life with my Jewish family was acceptable, but my aunt was suffering from advanced breast cancer and my cousin Ida was moving to England so I decided to accept the sponsorship from my parents' American friends to go to the United States. In 1948 at the age of fourteen, I came to New York.

Life was a struggle of learning a language and creating an identity and a career to be able to support myself. Within three years I graduated with an academic diploma with honors in English and was singled out for my achievements in spite of all obstacles as a refugee. I started to work for the French American Bank and still continued my education at Long Island University.

Eventually I met a fine young man. We were married and raised a family, Jeffrey and Peter. I have a beautiful family with four grandchildren, Jason, Daniel, Michelle and Michael.

The records of my parents' incarceration and murder came to light in a book entitled *Memorial de la deportation des Juifs de Belgique* by Serge Klarsfeld and Maxine Steinberg, which was published in Brussels in 1982.

The book records the names of all the Jews and others who were deported from Belgium during the Nazi occupation. Also recorded are the dates of deportation as well as the numbers of the convoys.

Both my parents are listed as having been deported through a camp in Malines. They were destined for Auschwitz. My father Jacob Koplik was deported on September 12, 1942. I was informed that Father managed to escape from the labor camp and returned to Antwerp. He was recaptured and shipped to Auschwitz. Based on this oral report, he survived the war but shortly after or near the end of the war, he died of malnutrition and TB.

Jerry and Ida

According to the memorial book, my mother was deported on September 12, 1942, the same day as Father but on another convoy and no trace is left of her after she was sent to Auschwitz.

A CHILD BRANDED AN ENEMY

by Marvin, Mendel (Mendele') Fidler

Kurenets, *(Kuranets, Kurzeniec)* now part of Belarus, was under Polish rule after WWI. Based on the inscriptions on the monuments in the old cemetery, there was a Jewish presence dating back to the 18th century. Kurenets was the center for many small communities around it, with a Jewish population numbering close to fifteen hundred people.

Our family, my father *Itzke,* Isaac, was one of six siblings, three sisters and two brothers, Zlate, Ester, Socie, Harry, and Meyer. Father was a tall, nice-looking man. He was kind with a gentle disposition, soft spoken and had a calming air about him. His father Iser, my grandfather, passed away before I was born. I do not remember my grandmother or her name.

Marvin after WWII

My mother, Chana Pyastunowitz, was a strong assertive lady and was the driving force in our lives. She had three sisters, Ida, Rochel and Gusie and a brother Yankev Leib. Her parents, my grandfather Pesach, nicknamed Peishke, and grandmother, Mina, were also gone by the time I was born.

My parents had inherited about seven and a half acres of land from my maternal grandparents on the outskirts of town where our home was situated. The house was built of logs with a wood shingle roof. Our home was comfortable, although primitive by today's standards. No running water. Sanitary facilities were all outdoors. We had a built-in brick oven where Mother did her baking and cooking, which also provided heat in the cold winters.

They were able to grow their own food, had a cow, a horse and a yard-full of fowl which provided eggs and meat for our family needs. Our home was always well-stocked.

53

Our family followed the traditional values of a Jewish life. They ran a kosher kitchen and observed the Sabbath with a sense of celebration and gratitude.

Mother was a great homemaker and the Sabbath was a very special day when she baked the braided *challah,* twisted bread, for the Sabbath meal and baked a *chollent,* in the oven that held the heat overnight. The *chollent* was a crock-pot type of meat and potatoes all in-one-meal, that sent out an aroma throughout the house with an anticipation for the Saturday daytime meal.

Father also subsidized our income by trading in grains with the local peasants. He knew his way in the forests and was able to discern edible mushrooms, berries and flowers for medicinal purposes. In the winter, he traveled to nearby villages, bartering herrings, salted fish, in exchange for linen rags. The natives grew the hemp plants, spun and weaved its fibers into fabrics. After its usefulness was over became a commodity for the rag collectors.

I was born on February 10, 1931. I was one of four siblings, a sister Mina who was murdered during the Holocaust, Sara who was struck and killed by lightening in 1940, and a brother Iser, murdered in the Holocaust. I was the youngest child and felt special with the loving attention that was showered on me by my parents and the extended family.

At an early age, around the age of five, I was sent to a local *yeshiva* where I was introduced to the discipline and expectations of the teacher. My education continued in the Jewish schools until the Soviets took over our area. Then I had to go to a public school, where we had to learn the Russian language, while the Belarus language was the language used for all other studies. But at home we spoke Yiddish.

In 1939 there were 1,500 Jews in Kurenets and surrounding areas. The history of Jews in the area dates back centuries. They were treated with discrimination and anti-Semitism which was expressed by young and old.

Kurenets was our hometown. We lived among many relatives and with a vibrant Jewish community that was committed to a life of many styles and religious expressions. There were four synagogues in the town.

Most of the Kurenets Jews made a living running small businesses and workshops which were located in the central market of the town. The peasant population from nearby settlements availed themselves of these goods and services.

Following the Ribbentrop-Molotov Pact, between the Soviets and Germany in August 1939, the Red Army entered the district and in September of that year established a Soviet government.

The capitalists and the population that were opposed to their control, their possessions were taken away and they were deported to Siberia and other places deep in Russia. Not standing out as *bourgeois*, capatalists, we were able to continue our life on our own property without much interference. The only change was that religion was looked down upon and Jews had to practice in stealth.

We soon met refugees who had escaped from the German occupied part of Poland, telling horror stories that Jews suffered there. But it was unreal and no one would believe them. They thought that they were exaggerating. Then in June 1941, Germany broke the pact with the Soviets and attacked us on June 22, 1941. The Germans occupied the area until July 2, 1944.

As the Red Army was retreating, panic spread among the Jews who tried to get away to Russia. Many managed to filter through the porous borders.

Immediately, the Germans imposed edicts against the Jews and conditions deteriorated. We had to wear the yellow star of David on our clothes and obey curfews and had to endure shortages of all kinds. We could not maintain any business or work. We could walk only in the gutters of the streets, and Jewish children could not attend school. In addition to the German curse, the local anti-Semites and collaborators organized pogroms against the Jews in autumn of 1941.

When rumors about the killings of Jews were heard, many ran into the nearby forests into their makeshift shelters and eventually many of our youths formed fighting partisan groups.

Jewish men, including my father and brother, were taken away to slave labor. They had to clear trees and growths near the railroad tracks in order to remove cover for the partisans in their sabotage attempts against the trains.

I recall the first experience, witnessing the evil, when two Jewish young men were killed by a Polish policeman at the order of the Germans, but for some reason he was arrested and put in prison. When the SS arrived, they let him out and he, with a number of his cohorts, made an example of using a Jewish rabbi by torturing him and leaving him in the marketplace to suffer. This same bandit abused people periodically, and later we learned that he also killed Christian Belarusians and Poles. When the SS learned about his act against the Christians, they killed him. This news created a celebration in the communities.

The killings continued, especially when the SS came to town and rounded up people who were accused of being Communists. The collaborators gladly pointed them out. About forty-two people were murdered. The captured Soviet prisoners-of-war they held behind barbed wires in the market place without any food or water. Amazingly, some compassionate locals were handing them food.

On September 9, 1942, a large force of police, about 400, arrived at three o'clock in the morning. Jews were gathered in the square to be sent for work. More than half of them were old people and children.

Canvas covered trucks drove the gathered to Mjadelskaya Street where the Jews were herded into a barn and set on fire by the local fire-fighting crew of Kurenets. Those who tried to get out and run away were killed. At the same time the firemen were watching so that the fire would not spread on other houses. One thousand and fifty-two people were murdered in this fire.

We were able to stay in our home till early in September 1942. But we heard that Jews in the nearby communities were being killed. One foggy morning the entire area of town was surrounded by the Germans and their collaborators. By this time, Father had setup a hiding place in the attic through a secret entrance over the stove. Father, Mother and I hid there. Within minutes of our getting up to the attic, a number of Polish policemen entered our home and looked around. Not discovering us, they declared with angry voices that we had escaped.

As soon as we could, hidden by the thick fog, we went to a Belarus friend who worked for my grandfather and actually spoke Yiddish. He hid us in a potato pit and brought food and water. We stayed hidden till it was dark. When we got out of the pit, we saw at a distance flames shooting up into the sky. Kurenets was burning along with all the people that they had captured. At the age of eleven, I was mesmerized by the glowing red sky but what was happening was still quite foreign to me, hard to comprehend.

Not feeling safe hidden in the pit, and having to rely on the farmer, we decided to go to the nearby forest, which was about two miles from our house. Father snuck back to our house to try to bring out some things for our existence, but all was stolen, nothing was left.

We continued to go deeper into the woods and on the following day we met with others who also managed to escape. A couple of days later, we met with my fourteen-year old cousin Mendl, who told us that he and my brother Iser were separated during their escape, and he did not know what happened to him.

We managed to survive by begging and picking mushrooms and berries in the forests. After a couple of months, we met up with Jews from another town, Pastov, who told us that my brother had escaped and stayed with my widowed aunt and son, but they were all killed when they attacked the Jews. This news was difficult to believe, but after seeing the evil that befell the Jews of our town, we knew that Iser was murdered. We heard this news with broken hearts and quiet tears, but we had no time to mourn. We had to find a way to escape the killers.

We constructed a shelter made of branches and moss, which protected us from rain but not the cold. We always had a fire burning to keep warm, but we never could really be warm enough.

This was a marshy area and the water table was very low. Just digging a little hole in the earth, water seeped in creating puddles, which we strained through a piece of cloth for drinking. Food was always at a crisis, which forced us to go begging to the nearby villages. We received a little bread and potatoes and some used tattered clothes, which was a great help to keep us warmer. Sometimes we even got some grain.

With winter approaching we really were more at risk. Since Father knew all the villages around because of his peddling travels, he approached a Belarus whom he trusted to help build a bunker in the nearby forest, a couple of miles away. By this time we were six people; our family of three, cousin Mendel, and two young people from our town, Donia and his sister. Father and Donia built platforms out of branches to sleep on and constructed a primitive stove from rocks. Because we had no outlet for the smoke to escape the bunker, it filled the room, and we had to lay flat below the smoke. A few days later, after a heavy rain, when Father, Donia and a cousin went searching for food, our bunker collapsed. We were fortunate that we were not killed. Father and the men reconstructed our shelter bunker, *zemlanka*, and this time made it bigger and they were able to get a piece of tin from which they fashioned a chimney. Our life struggles during that time were how to fight the hunger, and keep warm.

We stayed in the bunker a couple of months. As winter approached and snow began to fall, on one of our excursions for food we were able to see footprints in the snow, about ten to twelve feet apart, apparently German soldiers had surrounded the village.

The local woman who had helped us before now warned that the Germans were here and to get away. She fed us some *blini* (buckwheat flour pancakes) and we hurried away back into the forest, but we were afraid to remain in our renewed bunker and abandoned it to go to another part of the forest. During this time, we met other Jewish people who had also run away from their bunkers.

We were able to be housed with people in their bunker while Donia and his sister went into another bunker. By this time we were wandering about without any means of how to keep ourselves clean. We were infested with lice. I was the first to be stricken with typhus, which spread like wildfire. All had to overcome this difficult illness without medicine, just our own bodies somehow managed to fight. Miraculously, Father never got sick.

As the weather was warming, all the bunkers were flooded so everyone had to camp outside around a small bonfire.

One time we heard shooting and soon bullets were whistling overhead. All ran into a marsh where the attackers would not follow because they were afraid of the quicksand marshes. When the shooting stopped, a day later when it got dark, we tracked back to our bunker and found that it was blown up, destroyed.

We were told by a young boy from the bunker where Donia found shelter that they were ambushed and all were killed. He was able to run away while Donia was captured alive. He was filthy, emaciated, in tattered clothing. The

Germans paraded him to the villagers to show what Jews in the forest look like and killed him. This was spring of 1943.

Our struggle to keep alive took us to another forest where we met a Jewish family that my parents knew. We spent the summer and fall of 1943 in their shelter. With the approach of winter 1943, once again we built a shelter for us and two other families. There were thirteen people in this *zemlanka*. We spent the winter of 1943-1944 there and hardly survived by begging for food.

We were situated near the partisans who were mostly Russian escaped POW and also a Jewish partisan group that supported the fighters. We felt more secure with the partisans around. We also realized that they were also prime targets. Our choices of finding safety were limited, so we stayed nearby. We also discovered that a cousin, Mulleh, became a partisan and was killed during one of their encounters. No one had time to mourn, everyone tried to keep body and soul together. In the summertime, we were able to manage our hunger by collecting berries, *schav*, (sorrel), mushrooms and begging in the villages. The problem for all during that time was lack of salt.

In the spring of 1944, an *oblave*, offensive blockade, was staged against the partisans and the people in the forest. Our group in our bunker had dug a forty yard camouflaged tunnel to a second bunker a distance away. Fortunately we never had to use this escape.

During all this time the only news we could get is what the partisans told us. We never knew about the concentration camps under the Germans. We did learn that the Soviet Red Army was having successes pushing back the Germans.

In the summer of 1944, the Russian army liberated us. At first it was an effort to return home after all these years and fears. We did. We found that our house was divided into two parts by refugees. We did manage to get back part of the house but after a while we moved to the center of town with a cousin who had a big house. We discovered that all our extended family was murdered. One cousin, ten-year old Chayim, survived with a Gentile family.

Father was able to get a job working for the Russians for a salary. I started school, now age thirteen, and was placed in the third grade with Belarus and Russian kids. I was one of the rare Jewish kids.

In 1945 the Russians offered for all Polish citizens to return to the Polish territory, although still under the Soviet occupation. We had nothing to keep us in this Jewish grave of a town, so we left.

We registered and in March 1946, we traveled to Lodz, Poland where again it was a struggle to find food and housing. I along with my cousin Chayim were placed in a *kibbutz*, a children's home.

In a couple of months my parents pulled me out of the home and we relocated to Stettin. Again we found that all Jews were looking for ways to get out of Poland and settle in DP camps in Germany under the British and American protection and try to find a permanent place to reestablish life out of Europe.

We were smuggled out of Stettin to Berlin on a coal barge and were dropped off to hide in a forest near the waterway. We were then able to get on a passenger boat and finally arrived at the DP camp in Berlin.

Eventually we were transferred to a DP camp Herzog near Hesish Lichtenau not far from Kassel. This DP camp was an old German army camp where we were assigned a room for the three of us and another couple. *UNRRA,* United Nations Relief and Rehabilitation Administration, supported our existence. Father worked in the common kitchen, handing out bread.

Here I became aware that I must try to establish hope for a future and must find a way to secure an education or a trade. I signed up to learn the trade of machining, which is creating parts and metal workings. I attended the ORT trade school during the time that we were in the DP camp.

As much as life was safe, it was far from normal. Everyone was sitting on their bundles looking for a way to resettle somewhere to establish normalcy and a future. We first signed up to go to Palestine, illegally, but they did not want to take us because Father was too old to make this stressful journey. Since Mother had three sisters in the United States, we applied for visas. As our luck had it,

Marvin 2013

just then the US stopped the immigration quotas for Polish survivors. We had to wait and finally our visas were approved. We came to the States in 1949.

Of course the adjustment to a life that was permanent and safe was also filled with doubt if this really would be our home and our safe country. I was eighteen years old. I needed to help my family in order to begin life in New York. I immediately was able to get a job as a machinist and attended night school. Through the early years working in different places, I acquired more and more skills and eventually established a successful business of my own.

I socialized with many young people who were also survivors, but eventually I met an American girl, Rochelle Feffer, who became my wife in 1953. In 1954 I was drafted into the Army and served for two years. I was both proud and apprehensive about being a soldier. Now looking back, I am very proud being part of this country, an American.

In 1957, because I was offered a good job in New Jersey, we moved. Our son Ivan, named after my brother Iser, was born in 1958 and a daughter Mina born in 1971, was named after my sister.

Our children filled our home with gladness and for me it was as if my lost family was rejoicing with me through the laughter of my children. And when our granddaughters Ray and Ela joined our family, this joy grew.

Sadly my wife Rochelle passed away in 1986. It filled my life with loss and sorrow again. But life goes on, as I was told by many.

I was blessed to find a wonderful lady, my present wife Barbara, who has been a sensitive partner to share both pleasures from our families and to understand my long, sad, connections to the Holocaust.

I write this abbreviated memoir in order to leave a marker that I came from a beautiful, loving, extended family and community who were murdered for only one reason. They were Jews.

To spite the haters, I state that I am here, my family carries on and so do the Jewish people.

BARGAINING WITH GOD

by Dr. Daniel George Fischer

The village was called Craidorolt in Romanian-Transylvania or Kiralydaroc when it came under Hungarian rule in 1941. It was part of the Satu-Mare/Szatmar County seat and was situated about fifteen kilometers from town. It straddled both sides of the river Kraszna. The nearest railway station was about eleven kilometers away at Gilvacs.

It was a multi-national village. The right side of the river was inhabited mostly by Greek Catholic Romanians, while on the left side there lived mostly Hungarians and Swabians, Catholics and Protestants. Most of the Jewish families lived on the left side, and the synagogue was built there.

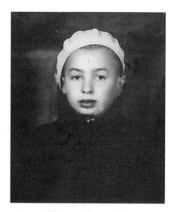

Danny Age - 11

These diverse communities lived most of the time in harmony as good neighbors. Before the deportations, some thirty Jewish families lived in Kiralydaroc. Most eked a meager living, except for two or three wealthier families. The majority were craftsmen and traders, and some were farmers. Today, there are no Jews left there, only the graveyard shows that this community ever existed.

My grandfather, Daniel Fischer, after whom I am named, passed away at the time of WWI. He had established a large general goods store, which served the village and the surrounding populations. By today's standards you might call it a department store, since it carried a variety of goods and merchandise.

Grandfather and Grandmother Jennie Steiner Fischer, raised five children, two boys, my father Julius and brother Alexander who managed to achieve his goal of becoming a doctor. He studied in France and then emigrated to the United States. Father's three sisters, Ethel, Irene, Giselle, and their children were murdered in the Holocaust. Ethel's son, Larry, survived and immigrated to the United States with me.

My father was an easy-going, good and charitable man. He was the major contributor in supporting the synagogue. Even though we lived a modern life, our home was kosher and we followed the laws of keeping the Sabbath. He was a kind, loving, Father, and I don't recall being disciplined harshly by him.

My maternal grandparents, Moshe Hirsch, and Grandmother Zlata Nierenfeld Hirsch, raised a family of seven children. Uncle Willi and sister Rozalia survived. The rest were murdered in Auschwitz.

My mother, Szerena Hirsch Fischer, was an intelligent highly-respected lady. She was an avid reader and in fact, she was reading Margaret Mitchell's *Gone With The Wind* about the time of our own end. I also recall that she began to write her own novel. She helped Father run the store and was the buyer to replenish the stock by traveling to Satu-Mare often.

My brother and I were cared for by Mother and our Grandmother Jennie, who

Mother Szerena and Father Julius

lived with us. My parents employed a maid to help with the household chores.

Our house was situated on the main street. The store faced the street. The L wing of the building was our living area. The backyard patio was surrounded by a luxurious trellised vineyard, a colorful profusion of flowers and a small vegetable garden.

The building had running water and an indoor bathroom, but no electricity. The apartment was furnished with functional good furniture enhanced by crystal light fixtures using kerosene lamps. Mother always searched for the finer things in life and her fine china dishes were her way of expressing it visually.

When I turned six years old, I was sent to the *cheder*, Hebrew school, in the village where I learned the Hebrew alphabet and the prayers. For first grade I was sent to live with my maternal grandparents in Huedin so that I could learn the Yiddish language. Then I continued for three grades in the Romanian school in our village. I understood the difference between the Christian kids and myself and I learned to fit in. I did not feel any personal expression of anti-Semitism, but my after-school playmates were mostly Jewish. After finishing the fourth grade, I was enrolled in a public school gymnasium in Satu-Mare, which lasted for one year.

When Transylvania was turned over to Hungary in 1941, apparently Jews were not allowed to attend public schools. I was transferred to a Jewish gymnasium in another city, Oradea/Nagyvarad, and boarded along with a few boys

62

at a Jewish family's home. The husband of this house was an attorney but was excluded from his profession because he was a Jew. Eventually I was housed in a boarding school for boys until 1944.

I finished the fifth grade and by that time my personal goal of becoming a doctor was quite strong. Actually since the age of eleven I was inspired to follow in the footsteps of my Uncle Alexander, my model.

Danny is in the front row second from the left

In the period between 1940-1944, it was established that only 6% of the Jewish children were allowed to go to public schools, and those who could prove that their parents had fought for the Hungarian army in WWI and were decorated, had priority.

As I look back, our village was not much affected by the upheavals of the Nazi influence, actually not until 1944. In other parts of the country, the troubles began in the early 1940s.

The first anti-Jewish laws in Romania were approved on August 8, 1940, which defined who was considered a Jew. On December 5, 1940, forced labor was declared for Jews and in January 20, 1941, increased military taxes came into being.

Other laws were for Jewish doctors. They were segregated and were permitted to treat only Jewish patients.

Synagogues could be used, only with special approval. Access to beaches was restricted. Theaters and opera companies had to dismiss all Jews. Jews could not own motorcycles or bicycles and had to turn in their radios to the police.

Incidents of attacks on bearded Jews became common, which were inflicted by the indoctrinated hate-filled youths who made fun of them. Eventually, a nightly curfew was imposed in towns across Romania and Hungary.

In late March 1944, after the Germans marched in, edicts of no travel were imposed. I went back to my village and found it still peaceful and normal. This was not to last long. Before Passover, the order to wear the yellow star was issued and enforced.

The young adults were taken away for work service. I thought that I too would be taken away. I got prepared by sewing a backpack from a potato sack and was ready to leave.

At this time Father came to me and handed me a bundle of paper money and told me to hide it somewhere and tell him where. I took two six inch metal pipes, rolled the money and stuffed it into the pipes, and put sealing wax at each end. I then opened up a brick at the foundation of the house, beneath the earth line, cut it lengthwise in half and placed the pipes in this opening and sealed the brick back.

Our store was still run by my parents, but we were ordered to keep it open on the Sabbath. Father obeyed this law. He unlocked the doors, but did not stay to do business. He went to the synagogue to pray. No one of the community came to disturb or take anything at this time.

Soon after, we were ordered to take one suitcase per person and were gathered in a schoolhouse, about one hundred Jews, and held there overnight.

Seeing what was being done to my parents, my old grandmother, and all the Jewish people, a rage fired up in me, which I could not express. The only thing that I could do is write on the wall "They may take Fischer Dani away, but I shall return!" This graffiti was cleaned up by the Gentile kids after we left and when I did return to town, they were surprised that my statement came true.

The next morning we were driven in ox-drawn farm carts to Szatmar, to the ghetto, which was located in the Jewish section of town. It was fenced in and guarded by Hungarian soldiers. We were crammed into one room and were kept there about two or three weeks. Time became elusive by now.

One day, we were told to take our suitcases, one per person, and we were marched through the city, escorted by gendarmes to the railroad siding. Here German soldiers, with rifles ready to shoot, were overseeing this gathering. My grandmother and those who could not walk this distance were taken by truck. We were loaded seventy to eighty people into a boxcar. Grandmother was not with us. There was barely enough room for us. A container was supplied to be used as a toilet. We traveled about three days, not knowing where we were being taken to. As I recall there was no panic in the car. People controlled their emotions.

Through a small barbed wire porthole, I spied the name of a station, "Katowice, Poland." The next stop was our yet unknown destination. The doors were opened to a shouting noise "Raus, raus - mach schnell." Out, out, make it fast. This was yelled by men in striped uniforms. At the same time they were also saying quietly, "Tell them that you are sixteen years old." We had to leave all our belongings on the train.

This was Auschwitz. We arrived on Shavuot, May 30, 1944, and I was at Auschwitz-Birkenau till October 1944.

After the long dehumanizing journey and being greeted by angry yelling, surrounded by SS soldiers with dogs, was a scene that is hard to forget, but the most lingering memory is the smell that was permeating the air. It reminded me of burning feathers.

We were separated from the women and children. Mother and my grand-mother were taken to another side, while Father, Tommy and I joined the men's side where we had to line up five across.

We were marched in front of Mengele, who was standing in his crisp neat uniform. With a slight, tiny gesture of his finger, he pointed Father and Thomas to the right while I was pointed to the left. What I did not know at the time is that they were immediately taken to the gas chambers. My haunting memory of that time is that I did not get a chance to even say goodbye.

My column was marched on a dirt path, between barbed wires, to a large empty warehouse. We were told to undress, to leave our belongings in desig-nated piles and only to keep the shoes. We had to walk through a disinfectant and were issued striped uniforms and caps. Then we were marched to a huge empty barrack where about six to eight hundred of us slept on the bare ground.

The next morning, about 6:00 a.m., we had to form a lineup outside the barrack. We were given a bowl and a spoon and *ersatz* coffee, and were herded back into the barrack. At noon again an *appel* was called and we were ladled a mush, stinky soup. I could not eat it.

At this time, they separated the young boys and walked us to another bar-rack where we were quarantined because some were sick with the childhood diseases of measles, mumps and chicken pox. We were there from the end of May 1944 to July 1944.

Here I asked the overseeing Jewish doctor to help me. This was June 1944. He told me that I needed to get a job and suggested that I take care of the excre-ment barrels from the barracks and take them to the dump for which I got more food.

One incident that still is an unbelievable scene is when a Hungarian boy, who still had not learned about the gas chambers and crematoria, asked a *kapo, kameraden polizei,* "Where are my parents?" The *kapo* shouted with a display of anger pointing at the spewing chimney, "There are your parents!" And with that, he beat him mercilessly with his always present thick walking cane until he dropped dead. The *kapo* walked away without any care, as if he just killed an ant.

After the quarantine, I was relocated back to the original barrack where the *blockaltester*, head man of the barrack, appointed me to be the night watchman. My job was to shut off any lights in case the air-raid siren would be sounded, warning of approaching planes.

Two months later, in July 1944, a selection was called and our barrack was destined for the gas chambers. We were all in lockdown, about four or five hundred men and boys.

There was clandestine bartering going on in Auschwitz-Birkenau. With a population of some 45,000 people in the camp, some found ways to manipulate and buy themselves or a loved one out of a death selection.

The *blockaltesters* and *kapos* were able to enrich themselves by trading a person out of the selection for any valuables that the inmates had or got somehow. What they did is stand in front of our locked-down barrack and grabbed off the yard about seven or eight unsuspecting passerby inmates and took them into the barrack. They were used to replace others who were able to barter their way out or a relative paid for them. This is how they justified the correct numbers. My miracle escape from the gas chambers happened because the *blockaltester* had too many for his *appel* list so he released me. He waved me to go to another barrack.

I was hanging around for about a month and escaped a number of selections. On one occasion, as they were selecting people, I happened to be near a shack where the dead bodies were kept. In the commotion, I snuck into the shack, undressed and laid with the corpses, pretending to be dead. When the selection was over and it quieted down, I dressed and got away to another barrack.

I was only sixteen years old, but somehow I had the wits about me to want to survive. I bargained with God when the end was near in Auschwitz. I said to him, "God, they are killing us all. No one will believe or know what happened here. If I am allowed to live, I will tell the world even though surely they will think me crazy and lock me up. For certainly no one would ever believe what has been going on here."

Until the 1970's, this was my concept of this event, but being a physician and continuing my education, I read a book by Elizabeth Kubler Ross entitled Of Death and Dying where she researched terminal patients who knew that they were dying. She found common psychological processes that were present in all patients. Bargain, anger, and denial were these methods. I realized then that my bargaining with God at that time was this process, my certainty of dying.

On October 7, 1944, women prisoners smuggled gunpowder out of nearby factories to the members of the Jewish *sonderkommando* who blew up Crematorium IV and killed several guards.

In October, I was selected, actually by Mengele, along with many others, to go on a transport out of Auschwitz. We were taken to Kaufering Lager 4, a labor camp, a sub-camp of Dachau, where we were used to rebuild German factories that were bombed in the area.

We were using cement in the reconstruction. I took an empty sack and wrapped myself under the jacket to keep warm. The *kapo* that was supervising our work detail chose to beat me. When he pounded me with his club, a dust cloud of cement powder encased me. This scene made him laugh hysterically and this stopped the beating.

At this time I got sick with typhus and scabies and luckily I survived. I really don't know how.

As the Allies were succeeding in their fight against the Germans, we were taken on flatbed railcars train to the main camp of Dachau. The inmates in the barracks were dying, and I thought that I too will be among them.

After two weeks, we spotted tanks outside of the fences. They attacked the German watchtowers and we were liberated on April 29, 1945. I was to learn later that it was the 42nd - Rainbow Division of the US Army.

I was set free weighing only fifty-six pounds. I had an injured eye from some kind of sliver, which eventually required surgery.

Danny 2013

As many of us were milling about, an American soldier watching over German prisoners handed me his gun and said, "Shoot the bastards." At that moment I understood that if I don't stop hating, it will destroy me and then the killers would have won.

From Dachau I was taken to a hospital in Munich for the eye operation. From there I was assigned to the Feldafing Displaced Person Camp where I found a cousin who also had survived.

After we regained our strength and some weight, we traveled back to my home in the village. Our home and store were totally empty, everything was stolen. I went to look for the money in my hiding place and miraculously it was there, not discovered.

Obviously I was in denial and I restarted the store in the hope that my parents would come back. I operated the store in the year 1946 and part of 1947. Finally I recognized that my hopes of my parents being alive was a dream. The store and village was not for me. I was able to sell the house and left.

In Satu-Mare, now Romania, I hired a tutor to help me take tests and continued my education. I determined that Romania and Communism is not for me. I decided to go to the United States where I had my uncle Alexander.

I crossed borders illegally to Paris in 1948 and eventually arrived in New York in September 1948. I joined my uncle and his family, who lived in New

Haven, Connecticut. Uncle Alex was my model of becoming a doctor. He urged me on to realize my own ambition to become a doctor. I continued my education and after nine years I became a doctor practicing Family Medicine.

I met a wonderful girl, Elaine Shanken, and we were married in 1960. We have built a beautiful family, a daughter Tracy, a son Jonathan and grandchildren, Emma and Oliver and a son-in-law, Cary Geller.

It is my bargain with God that urges me on to this day to make sure that all will know what happens when hatred is left unchecked.

My bargaining with God was my payoff - my great family and living in a country where I feel free, equal and safe.

I am here to witness the evil that was committed against Jewish people. I saw it. I lived it.

I REMEMBER THEM!

Moritz Moshe Hirsch

Zlata Nierenfeld Hirsch

Jennie Steiner Fischer

A YEAR UNDER GROUND

by Nina Frisch

A bright, rose-colored house, with sparkling specks that glittered in the sunshine, was my home in Stanislawow, Poland where I was born on July 25, 1935. It was a comfortable home, with an enclosed porch, and was situated in a neighborhood away from the tumult and center of the city. The house was surrounded by a beautiful garden flush with blooms and trees, which attracted birds, butterflies and bees fluttering about intriguing a child's mind, swooping and flying away with dancing movements.

Stanislawow, now known as Ivanov-Frankovsk, Ukraine, had a population of over 72,000, among them close to 25,000 Jews.

Nina Age - 2

My maternal grandparents, Bayla and Benyomin Albert, lived with us and I loved and hung onto their endearing attention. Both followed orthodox dress and religiosity, while my parents dressed in the fashions of the day and spoke mostly Polish in the house. Even though my parents followed a more modern lifestyle, we kept kosher and observed all holidays.

Nathan, my mother's brother, left home to be educated in Prague and worked in the banking business. He remained there establishing a successful career and even provided a generous dowry for my mother when she married Father. Uncle Nathan succeeded to get to England before being trapped in the Holocaust.

My mother Sala was a devoted daughter to her parents. She was a kind, soft-spoken, and gentle woman who showered me with attention, chasing after me with spoonfuls of food to overcome my poor eating habits. The front gate became my swing as I awaited Father's return from his business with expectation and pleasure. My spills and scrapes falling off the gate also became the source of Mother's scolding and warnings that Father would hear about this.

The Liebermans - Mother Sala, Grandmother Bayla, Uncle Nathan, Grandfather Benyomin

He did but seldom showed displeasure. His temper would flare at times, surprising me that this was possible.

Being an only child, I felt affection around me. I did not worry about the warnings, as I recall, and spent many occasions on the gate, honing my skills in hanging on without injury.

To this day my memories are stirred with the evenings after the Sabbath meal, when my grandmother softly sang melodies to me as she cuddled and rocked me in her lap. Till today that special love and attention still satisfy the child in me. It is where I learned to love.

My parents indulged me with childhood comforts and even fulfilled my wish for a horse by getting a large stuffed animal. I lived a sheltered life. My companions were my immediate family.

Father, Isaac Dannenberg, came from a renowned family, the Liebermans, whose great wealth and possessions qualified them to be known as Jewish "aristocrats." They were respected and honored by all, Jews and Poles.

Father's parents, Grandmother Surche' and Grandfather Yoel, died when he was a teenager. He was one of many siblings, and had to come to grips that he had to shift for himself and learn how to be a man. With some opportunities working in the Lieberman enterprises, he gained knowledge on how to succeed as a breadwinner and businessman and provided a secure life for our family as a merchant, running a textile retail store. His respectful and fair dealings with the Poles established many contacts with people who eventually helped us survive.

When I was four years old, I was puzzled that suddenly the mood in our home became serious and worried faces were apparent. September 1, 1939, turned the world upside down. Germany invaded Poland from the east and the Soviet Union from the west as the Non-Aggression Pact between them was signed, each absorbing a part of Poland.

On September 16, 1939, the Polish government abandoned the city and havoc broke loose. The local riffraff, the Ukrainians from the surrounding villages, and bands of vandals began to plunder anything that they could get a hold of, and pogroms against Jews drove everyone to remain locked in their homes and basements, staying out of harm's way.

On September 18, the Soviets Red Army occupied Stanislawow stopping the gang rule. At the same time, Jewish institutions were closed. Many Jewish leaders were arrested and sent away to Russia. All valuable and useful properties and business were confiscated and taken over by the Soviets. Under Communism, all properties belonged to the government.

When the Germans broke the pact with the Soviets and attacked them, they used their allies, the Hungarian army, to occupy our city. They entered on July 2, 1941, and stopped the pogroms that were being directed against the Jewish population. But during this occupation, they expropriated any Jewish property for use by the army.

Nina Age - 10

On July 26, 1941, German troops occupied our town. Over 40,000 Jews, including refugees from western Poland, the Carpathian exiles, and refugees from neighboring villages sought refuge in Stanislawow because of the abuse by the Ukrainians after the departure of the Soviets. The German soldiers entered the Jewish quarter and arrested Jews, with the help of the Ukrainians. They beat them, cut off their beards, and demoralized them.

By this time, the Germans had perfected their skills of how to steal, oppress and kill Jews and immediately implemented their methods in our town. They ordered that a *Judenrat,* Jewish council, be established and all demands were to be fulfilled. Shortly, a decree was issued for all professional Jews to register. These people, considered intelligentsia, were ordered to assemble at the Gestapo headquarters at the beginning of August. The assembled included lawyers, engineers, doctors, pharmacists, teachers, officials, rabbis and many others. They were held for two days in the courtyard next to the jailhouse where they were beaten and starved. With the assistance of the Ukrainian police, they were taken in trucks to the Pawelcze Forest where they were forced to dig a communal grave, undress and were murdered.

The Gestapo kept a small number of engineers and about ten physicians alive, fearing that they would need them in case of an epidemic in the city.

In the beginning of August 1941, decrees were imposed. Jews had to wear yellow arm bands. Another decree was that all Jews had to hand over all gold and silver, all valuables. The *Judenra*t had to provide maintenance and supplies to the Gestapo headquarters and for the houses of the German generals. Any pretext or excuse to kill Jews was an entertainment for the Germans and their collaborators. People lived with disbelief. The tragic life was not of hope anymore but how to get away from the reach of the murderers.

When we were still living in our house on the outskirts of town, a Ukrainian policeman came storming in and took my dear grandparents away. Father pleaded with them to have pity for these two elderly people, which was answered with a clubbing and a bleeding head. This scene still shakes me to the core as I see my grandmother waiving to me as I stood at the window. I stood at that window for many days hoping to see my grandmother coming back, but this was not to be.

In October 1941, the Ukrainian *"Baudienst"* building service, appeared in the Jewish cemetery supposedly digging large pits to escape air raids, but the reality was a scene of horror not imaginable.

Around October 10, 1941, the news spread that the Gestapo had ordered the *Judenrat* to provide 10,000 Jews to be sent out of the city for work. The Jews realized that a terrible fate awaited them, but only few were able to escape the city. The reality came about at dawn on October 12, 1941, the Jewish holiday *Hashana Rabba*, Day of Judgment. The houses of the Jews, in the center of the city, were surrounded by German police, Ukrainians, and German soldiers armed with machine guns and police clubs. The Jews were ordered to wear their finest clothing and to take all valuables, as they were being taken to work camps. These people were brought to the city market. On the way they were beaten and tortured by the guards, and when they reached their destination, they were required to kneel on their knees in front of the town hall. After, they had to walk not knowing their destination. The weak and the ill were tossed onto trucks. Seeing this march and torture of people, the Jews soon realized that this was a killing walk, everyone tried to find hiding places.

When the selected Jews reached the cemetery, the guards led them near to a wall, and ordered them to turn over all the valuables. In the afternoon the slaughter began. Men, women and children were ordered to strip, were led to the edge of the mass grave and were shot. They fell forward or were ordered to jump inside. The slaughter terminated at sunset. From among the more than 10,000 Jews who were brought to the cemetery, there were still a few thousand who had not been shot. These were sent back home. The mass grave was not covered over that night. Some of those shot who had remained alive managed to crawl out from among the corpses. Some reached their houses, and others died on the way.

After the action of *Hashanah Rabba* which reduced the Jewish population, the Germans decided to gather the remaining Jews and created a ghetto in the most neglected area of the city.

It was now December 1941, and we, along with all Jews, were forced to move to the ghetto, taking very little with us. All windows and doorways on the periphery of the ghetto area were sealed off with bricks and boards. A tall wooden fence was topped with barbed wire which made escape impossible. It was sealed off from the outside around the 20th of December. The entry gates were guarded by policemen of the *Shupo,* German Police, with dogs and

Ukrainian guards and, in addition, were assisted by Jewish guards. It is estimated that close to 30,000 Jews were herded into the ghetto.

We settled in an overcrowded room in one of the designated houses in the ghetto and very quickly, we began to endure dreadful conditions. People were suffering and dying. Mother had us prepare a little stack of emergency clothes, folded and waiting, in case we had to face an *aktzie,* a selection, in the middle of the night.

The Germans employed many Jews outside the ghetto and my parents were lucky to be selected to work details. To this day, I don't know how at the age of about six years old, I was permitted to go with Mother. I do remember that I worked with her sorting and folding clothes of the murdered or the deported people.

On one occasion Mother gave me a Vaseline jar filled with butter to be smuggled into camp. I hid it in my muff. The gate with guards was looming and the vicious German shepherd was glaring at each person walking by. I was frozen in time, walking like a zombie. I was petrified that the dog would sniff out the hidden butter, but luckily I was not detected and as I reached a safe distance, I felt that I would faint from this anxiety.

I was only a child when I witnessed torture and murder but somehow, with the love of my parents, I was able to have faith that my parents were my safe place and they were. Selections, *aktzies,* and murder were commonplace, and were followed with assurances that those left alive were special for their work and so, they blinded and tricked the population to hang on to hope.

On February 22 or 23, 1943, the liquidation of the ghetto was completed. The remaining houses were surrounded, and all the residents were taken out and shot. My father arranged for us to get away into the forests, joining a group of about thirty adults and a few children.

The beautiful pine trees were thick, the air smelled fresh and medicinal. Our hide-away was located in a shallow valley. The adults peeled off wide strips of bark from the trees and constructed lean-tos for shelter and applied mud to the stripped trees to camouflage the missing bark. One day the men left us, a few women and children, in camp to try to scrounge up some food. On that day the Germans looking for *partisans,* guerilla fighters, came across our site. We ran into the depth of the woods, I losing my shoes in this desperate escape and having to continue on the sharp pine needles that blanketed the forest floor, bruising my feet. But we did not dare to stop. We wandered about for three days, surviving only on hazelnuts and sucking the morning dew from the leaves. We soon spotted a peasant's hut. He gave us some soup and water and led us on our way back to the camp. We did not know what awaited us there but, our hope was that Father was there along with the other man. And yes, they were there. Our joy of being reunited again stifled any fears or pain. Mother heated some water to soak, cleanse and heal my bruised feet, when all of a sudden I felt my father's hand grabbing me as I was told to run. We thought that Mother was right behind us as we ran for safety, but when we returned to the campsite area, we discovered that my dear mother was shot in the back. This was August 30, 1943 - a very hot day. We could not bury Mother in a grave because we had no shovels, so she was laid to rest covered with leaves and pine needles. My loss, my heartbreak has never left me. I know that Mother was coming towards me with a fresh bucket of warm water for my feet when she was shot.

Father knew that with the advent of winter, our life in the forest was not possible. He remembered that one of his brothers-in-law was hiding with a Polish man. He sent inquiries with some of the locals that were helping us in the forest to approach Staszek to at least take me into his hiding place. After a couple of days, Father was given an okay to have me brought to hide with Staszek.

A peasant woman came to lead me to Staszek's hiding place. I was dressed like a village girl, carrying a basket of eggs. As we got into town, a German officer approached, which made me almost collapse with fright. Of course he did not associate me as a Jew and just wanted some eggs.

When I arrived at Staszek's, he asked me why I was crying and why was I so sad. I told him that I could not bear to be separated from Father after I just lost my dear Mother. He comforted me and told me not to worry, that things will be okay. And sure enough, right before *Rosh Hashanah*, Father joined me and the group of Jews in the bunker.

This kind young man, about age twenty-five, had a large property with a large enclosed yard where he had a business of upholstering wagon seats and interiors. He, with the help of the Jewish men, dug out a two-room bunker under his house. It was lined with planks and bunks that were folded against the walls, which served as our sleeping beds for thirty Jews. The electricity which was wired into the bunker was wired directly from the power source rather than Staszek's house so that this location could not be found through electric usage. We even had a crystal radio and were aware of what was happening on the outside and the progress of the war.

Staszek, Stanislaw Jackowski, was generous and the best of men. Even though the Jews were at his mercy, he had respect for each and called the men *"pan"* sir. Even when the money ran out, he did not turn anyone away. His plan of hiding a few of his friends became thirty that he saved.

As the hunt for Jews throughout the city and forests intensified, Staszek told our group that the Germans are searching and discovering hiding places in many locations. He thought that we should find other places to hide. But the men decided instead that they would dig a tunnel to the sewer system as an escape rather than through the front gate from Stazsek's property. They worked in an assembly line carrying and dispersing the dirt in pails in the yard of Staszek's property.

74

Another dilemma was looming and that was that one woman was expecting a baby any day. I heard discussions that a sacrifice of the newborn must be made or thirty lives would be at stake. This baby was born the day after we were liberated by the Russians. He was named, *Aqedah* - referring to the bible Isaac's sacrifice "binding." He was saved and wound up in Israel and became our special symbol of our survival.

We were liberated on July 27, 1944. I was now nine years old and could not comprehend what it meant to be free and not afraid. I could not forget the loss of my mother and especially seeing her lying dead in the pine needles. At this age I came to realize that our family was murdered. But still we wanted to hope that somehow, somewhere maybe someone survived.

Looking back, it amazes me how fast our Jewish people tried to create families, pick up the pieces and continue to plan for a future. My father too had to find a center, a balance, for himself and especially for me being a young child. He married in 1945 a kind woman who also had a child, an eight year old daughter, Sylvia, two other of her children were murdered in the selections. We established this melded family and moved to Breslau where we started school.

Nina 2013

Life was precarious and dangerous for Jews after the war so anyone who could, tried to get out and relocate in a safer place. We were able to get out and settled in Germany in a private rental apartment, outside of a DP camp because the camp was overcrowded. My stepmother and Father tried to establish life for me and my little stepsister by giving us whatever opportunities of education that were available to the displaced at that time.

Finally we were able to immigrate to America with the help of my stepmother's two brothers in the United States. We arrived in New York harbor on May 29, 1949.

Of course, establishing and adjusting to a new country, new language was difficult for the parents, but my sister and I were sent to school and discovered the beauty and goodness that this country offered. I wanted to belong to this world. I wanted to be a Yankee and my focus was to establish myself in this country and have roots that I belong here.

I continued my education and graduated with secretarial and accounting skills. My first job was for a small company as their bookkeeper, but after proving myself that I could excel, I accepted a job with Johnson & Johnson where I worked for many years in the Financial Department and actually had a

Staszek top row left and three of the 32 he saved, Father Israel, a cousin and Nina

responsible position with them. I had a career.

I met my husband Martin Frisch in 1953, a sole survivor from the concentration and labor camps, and we were married in 1954. Martin ran a furniture and refinishing business and together we were able to establish ourselves and provide a good life and opportunities for our children.

Our blessing are our two sons, Mark, who is an Obstetrician/Gynecologist and married to Jan, have three children, Joel, Gillian and Julie and our son Sandy, who is an Ophthalmologist and married to Jodie, have three sons, Jon, David and Brian.

Martin and I retired to Florida in 1987, and I became strongly involved in speaking to students. My sad life returned when my dear husband, my companion and best friend, died in 2006.

Today I am trying to find my strength in continuing to live my life with dignity and contributing to remember the Holocaust. I am determined to continue to witness because we must fight the deniers and must applaud those that were the Righteous Among Nations.

Our Staszek, Stanislaw Jackowski, was honored by Yad Vashem in 1968 as a **"Righteous Among Nations."**

LANCUT, POLAND, OUR FAMILY HOME

by Heni Margel Galel

Seventy-four years have passed since the cataclysmic event, the Holocaust, happened against the Jewish people during WWII. Even though I was a young child, my memories are scattered, I must re- member my families who were murdered. I want my testimony to serve as a memorial to my family, our people, and be a lesson for fu- ture generations to learn from our tragedy.

My maternal grandfather, Abah Sauer, re- mained in Poland because he was ill and could not escape the German takeover when we did. We learned after the war that he was taken to Germany and was killed there. Grandmother, Hena, passed away when my mother was fif- teen years old. My mother, Regina, was the youngest of twelve children.

Heni Age - 1

I must mention the names of her brothers and sisters and their immediate families that were murdered in concentration camps.

Her brothers were: Hirsh, Menachem, Naftali, Berl, Itzhak and the sisters were: Golda, Frieda, and Dvora. The surviving siblings were: Sabina, Yehuda (he left for Palestine in 1938), Moshe and Mother Regina. Being just a baby, I never knew them.

Mother's home was traditional-modern. She had opportunities for an edu- cation, which many girls were denied. She took dancing classes and even horseback riding. Mother finished secondary school and attended Hebrew school where she loved to learn about Jewish history and Hebrew.

My paternal grandparents, grandfather Eliezer Nisen Margel, passed away be- fore my birth and grandmother, Channa Saurhauft Margel, was my strong connec- tion and identity to a loving family and ideals for education and a cultured life.

77

My father, Avraham Margel, studied dentistry in Germany where he earned his degree with distinction in 1927. He returned to Lancut and set up a practice. Father played the tuba in the Hazumir Town Orchestra. He also was a talented soccer player.

Father is in the top row fourth from the left

Father's two sisters, Leah and Pnina made *aliya*, immigrated, to Palestine in 1938, a time when the Zionist movement rekindled a vision and desire for Jews to return, resettle and rebuild *Eretz* Israel.

My parents met and married on December 20, 1936. They established a kosher home and followed traditional values but still modern. We lived a privileged lifestyle because of my father's profession. I was born on October 10, 1937 but this good life did not last long.

Eighteenth-century painting of synagogue interior Sometime, after 1786, the Polish artist Zygmunt Vogel, (1764–1826) painted a view of the interior of the synagogue.

A simple exterior in order not to bring any attention to it.

Very simple and modest, clashing with the rich decor and monumental scale of the interior. One of the striking features of the building is the floor, which has been lowered to much below ground level. This device was used in order to bypass the strict limitations once set on the height of synagogues. Lowering the floor made it possible to achieve an impressive height. A monumental architectonic bima, a raised platform from which the Torah was read, whose four columns support the vault, stands in the middle of the main hall. A richly decorated Aron Ha-Kodesh, arc for the Torahs, symbolic stucco and painted elements. Prayers are inscribed on the walls in shallow, semi-circular closed niches.

I want to share with you a little about the area where my family lived. Poland, an Eastern European country, is where Jews established homes and communities dating back centuries. And so did the town of Lancut, where some records show that Jews resided there dating back to 1563. They established a business community and earned a living in many trades. But life was not easy. They were attacked on many occasions in their history.

By 1726, Jews built a synagogue that was the centerpiece of the community in the baroque style. During WWII the Nazis used it as a stable for horses. Since the 1960's it is a museum.

Lancut was known as a city of *maskilim*, intellectuals, and Jewish scholars. Most young people studied in a *cheder*, modern Hebrew school, and *yeshiva*, a religious school. Only a small number attended secular education and some continued their education outside of Poland.

In 1921, there were over 1,900 Jews in Lancut (about 42% of the total population), and 2,700 in 1939. Anti-Semitism grew in the 1930's, creating great hardships and an unsafe place.

On the evening of September 9, 1939, the first German patrols entered Lancut. By September 11, Monday morning, the German troops occupied our town. Immediately they ordered that the Jewish shops be identified with a Jewish yellow star and all the proprietors had to give all their goods to the soldiers, free. And soon they ordered that the Jews hand over furniture and valuables.

The day of the beginning of *Sukkot*, Tabernacle holiday, on September 28, 1939, early in the morning, the Germans gathered the Jews in the yard of the police station and gave an order that by that afternoon all Jews had to leave town.

During the first days, the Germans set fire to the beautiful Lancut synagogue. With the help of the Polish Count Alfred Antoni Potocki, the Jews succeeded in putting out the fire, and only a part was damaged and was promptly repaired. This act of saving their house of prayer was an example of a community that was committed to their heritage and the Torah.

This was followed where Jews, throughout the region, were seized to serve the Nazis in forced labor groups, cleaning streets, their military barracks, clear rubble, clean trucks, tanks and any labor that was thought of for them. While in their presence, they were abused, beaten, humiliated and degraded.

By this time it was known that all young men were taken away for slave labor and a torturous existence of life or death. Because of this, many men ran away to the Soviet side, including my father, even before this edict was announced.

The Gestapo enriched themselves with all valuables and left many murdered in their wake. Many Jews that were driven out of Germany and Western Poland came to Lancut.

A German police force replaced the Gestapo and a *Judenrat*, a Jewish Council, was established to handle the management of the ghetto, which was set up in Lancut on January 15, 1942.

The *Judenrat*'s first selection arrests were at the beginning of July 1942. On August 1, 1942, the Jews of Lancut were deported and were taken to Pelkinia, a town about nine miles from the city to a transit camp. The elderly, the sick and the children were shot in the camp, or in the nearby Nechczioli Forest, about three miles away.

On August 4, 1942, a German SS extermination unit continued with their murder of Jews from Lancut. They were herded near a mass grave and executed by machine guns.

The last transport of the Jews from Lancut left on August 18 and 19, 1942. The remaining Jews, approximately fifty people, were transported to the ghetto in Sieniawa. They were shot to death at a cemetery in May of the following year.

This was the history in brief of what happened to our town and our families. Even though I was not there to witness it, I must include it here as part of my story. This was the place where my family lived for centuries.

The Germans ordered all Jews to leave Lancut. Most ran to the Soviet border, across the San River, which was the dividing border between the Soviets and the Germans as per their non-aggression treaty. The chaos and fear was indescribable. On the other side, we met up with Father and settled for a while with Father's sister, Dvora.

On a couple of occasions, Mother, taking me along, managed to get back to Lancut and discovered that our nice home was occupied by the Gestapo. An unusually daring woman, Mother entered the home and asked to take away a few pictures that were in the house. She also knew that there was some money hidden, which she managed to rescue. On the next crossing, she convinced Father's mother, Grandmother *Chana*, to come with her to the Soviet side.

In 1940 and 1941, the Soviets sent away thousands upon thousands of refugees who had come from Poland to work camps in Central Asia or Siberia. And so was our family. We wound up in the *Novosibirsk Oblast,* province. Unfortunately Grandmother could not endure the hard life, and she died soon after *Rosh Hashana in* 1941.

Father managed to get a place for us, which we had to share with a few families. The work that they were required to do was to cut trees in the thick forests, *Taiga,* of frozen Siberia. The work was brutal and the *natchalnik,* manager-director, pushed the refugees beyond endurance to meet unrealistic quotas. Without proper clothing and limited nutrition, life was difficult to say the least. People died from disease, hunger and hard work and exposure, but no one was holding guns and killing Jews.

By the fall of 1942, when the Polish Anders army was being formed outside of Poland, we were freed from the Siberian forests and were allowed to resettle in *Jambul* about 555 km, about 350 miles, from *AlmaAta* in *Kazakstan,* then a state of the Soviet Union. This was near Aunt Sabina, her husband and my three cousins.

Father was sent to a *kolchoz*, communal farm, nearby where he worked all week and came home on Sundays. This is where my memories became real. We had enough food and even some new clothes, new shoes, which were sent to me by my Aunt Sabina.

I recall an incident when I was playing outside, a woman approached me and asked for directions. She wanted me to go along to help her and she promised me candy. She led me away from our dwelling and out of sight, where she stripped me of my new shoes. I came home in a state of distress and not understanding why this happened to me. I was just four years old.

I know that our life was not easy, because Mother became very ill and had to stay in a hospital for many months. During this time Father cared for me.

Because Father was a dentist, he was able to make gold caps for the Russians, who loved that fashion and was able to subsidize us with flour and other kinds of food. Not having Mother was difficult to understand at this very young age.

Mother Regina, Father Avraham, Leah and Heni - Berlin DP camp

Being without Father most of the time and not knowing what the next day will bring, no one questioned. It was normal just to survive and not ask or expect. One just accepted that is how it was. Day by day existence, without a plan for the future, was lived by all and no one looked for any miracles. Distress was put aside and one made do as best as they could.

A great event that was both joyous for me and also a bit guarded, was when on September 1, 1945, my little sister Chana was born in *Stantcia Yili*. This event gave our family a feeling of rebirth. I was the big sister and learned to enjoy helping with her care.

During our stay in Russia, no information was available as to what was happening in Poland. Insofar as we knew, our families that we left behind found a way to survive with the Germans.

Finally, when the war ended, we were allowed to return to Poland, together with Aunt Sabina's family. We were provided cattle cars for our return journey, and after many weeks of travel, we were taken to a gathering city for survivors, from all means, to the city of Stettin. Here we found out that the only relatives that remained alive were the ones in Palestine and the ones who found shelter in the Soviet Union.

In Stettin we were overjoyed to find Mother's brother Moshe and his wife Pesia and their five children, who also survived in the Soviet Union. Stettin was a place where we learned what happened to our families and a place where all looked for a miracle by searching posted lists, in the hope of reuniting with someone.

Jews who returned to their villages and towns, were welcomed with a glaring surprise that they are still alive and mostly with expressions of hostility. In many cases they were killed or just disappeared.

When Father went to Lancut, he was greeted with hate and had no hope of reestablishing our lives there. He returned to Stettin with a resolve that we cannot remain in Poland.

Our family and Aunt Sabina shared a tiny basement apartment. All of us were poor and had few belongings. By today's standards, they were rags. One day, when we were away, our apartment was robbed of everything. We spotted some of our things on the market square for sale. But one could not do anything to retrieve or punish the thieves.

There was no future for Jews in Poland. All looked for a way to get away. The continual killings by their very own neighbors took place even after the war was over. The fact that we were citizens for centuries in Poland mattered little to this anti-Semitic culture.

Father was able to get us onto a truck to smuggle our way out of Poland across the border to Berlin. Unfortunately, we were met with shooting at the border and were taken into custody and dropped into a prison in Stettin with rats scampering about. Luckily, the second attempt, we succeeded to sneak across and settled in a DP camp in Berlin.

Because Father had a valued profession, we were able to have a better life and not live just on the handouts from the JOINT, American Jewish Joint Distribution Committee, UNNRA, United Nations Relief and Rehabilitation Administration and HIAS, Hebrew Immigrant Aid Society. I attended a Hebrew school in the camp and also was indulged with private piano lessons.

We were fortunate to find our American relatives who sent us a visa and we were qualified to go to America. But because my parents had sisters and brothers in Palestine, the decision was made to be with our families. In 1949, we made *aliyah*, immigration from the Diaspora, and sailed on the ship Negba to now Israel.

At first we settled in an absorption center where we learned how to survive in a Jewish independent country with all its difficulties and shortages. After, Uncle Yehuda took us in and helped us rent a place in Petach Tikva.

The adjustment for us was difficult and yet, coming out of the hell of Poland and DP camps, there was a feeling of being and breathing free and being part of a place where we were helping to establish a Jewish land. Father worked for the government. Mother stayed home with my baby sister and I had my job, school.

My life as a student was one of great curiosity and wanting to excel. I finished high school and continued in the university where I was accredited as a teacher for primary grades.

I met my husband Henri Galel who was serving in the Israeli Army. He was from Belgium but was able to serve his military obligation in Israel rather than Belgium. We married and found much in common. We both survived the Holocaust and both from strong loving families. Our two wonderful sons Ronny and Yoram were born in Israel.

Henri's family in Belgium was a draw to return there and that is where our boys were educated. We found a great opportunity to come to Chicago where we established a good life and after many years, we resettled in Boca Raton, Florida.

Our boys married great girls and now our family has grown with the addition of five grandchildren. Two boys and three girls. A blessing! Our adorable grandchildren are our past and our future. We rebuilt our families and our Jewish people.

Heni 2013

Henri and I have found a home at our synagogue where we are active by volunteering for many important causes. I am also active in the sisterhood.

The FIDF, Friends of the Israel Defense Forces, need our help and we dedicate ourselves to the Israeli soldiers who protect Israel, which really benefits all Jews in the world.

We are pleased to be members and support the organization, the Child Survivors/Hidden Children of the Holocaust, who have been in the forefront of Holocaust education for future generations.

I am sharing my history of my family and their background. Even though I was too young to establish clear memories of the town of Lancut and the tragic end, I am proud to be able to be the voice for my Lancut family and the Jewish community.

At least 10% of those serving in the Polish Army fighting Nazi Germany were Jewish. Over 100,000 Jews were soldiers and officers during the German invasion, and about 20,000 Jews served in the Polish Free Army, formed in England and the Soviet Union. The Polish Free Army fought in Italy, Normandy and the Eastern Front.

FINDING MY VOICE BUT NOT MY COURAGE

by Henri Glowiczower Galel

My grandfather, Joseph Glowiczower, ran from the Polish Army to escape anti-Semitism, persecution and hardships. The train heading out of Poland made its last stop in Brussels, Belgium, and this is where he got off and made this destination home.

Alone, without a language or any friends to direct him, he headed for the synagogue where he was received with kindness, guidance and even was helped financially to establish a livelihood. This was in the early 1930's. After making some success in a leather manufacturing enterprise, he sent for his family to join him. They arrived a couple of years later, Grandmother Pesia, their son my father Itzhak, and his sister Genia.

They established a home where they felt secure to build a future. In the mid 1930's, my father met his mate Clara Poler, my mother, who also came from Poland. They developed an attachment which led to their marriage. I was born in 1937, a dark-haired, curly-top child who was adored and pampered with a good life.

My father was a well-liked and accomplished young man who attracted a following by his leadership of thought and political knack. He was elected Secretary of the Mizrachi organization. It took up his time completely and forced Mother to demand that he diminish his extra-curricular political activities. And so he curtailed his involvement, although in 1941 the British made available one hundred passports to him to pass on to Jews who were

Mother Clara and Henri - Belgium

looking to get out of the country to Palestine. He was instrumental in saving many, including some members of his own family. By the time he and our family wanted to leave, it was too late.

Our one attempt to get away from harm's way was when Father secured a truck, which took forty members of our family and others to the French-Spanish border. The border was still open and was accepting Jewish refugees. The French police caught us and detained the group in a prison in Paris. Within a couple of weeks or less, we were sent back to Belgium.

No one could believe that the Belgian army would capitulate so fast. May 10, 1940 is the day Germany invaded Belgium. Life for Jews under the German occupation became a struggle. Approximately 45% of Belgian Jews were deported to concentration camps during the war.

All Jews had to wear yellow stars of David. On April 1, 1942, Jews were forbidden to exercise any commercial or economic activity on their own account. All businesses had to be turned over to non-Jewish management. Father turned over all our valuables, money, equipment to his Belgian Gentile friend for safekeeping; the same person who also was instrumental in guiding us in finding hiding places for the family. He connected us with Abbe Joseph André from Namur, who cooperated with Jewish underground groups in finding safe places for hundreds of children and returning them to the Jewish fold after the war. He saved over 3,000 families and has been acknowledged as a Righteous of Nations by Yad Vashem for his selfless kind deeds.

My father realized that his dark haired, curly top little boy, age four, would be recognized as a Jewish child. He linked up with Abbe Andre who figured out that I would be safe among eighty Italian orphans, also dark- haired, who were victims of Mussolini's war policies. The orphanage was located about ten kilometers south of Gembloux, in the village of Courroy Chateau. This was a convent orphanage run by nuns who cared for the children with an iron fist, without comfort or kindness. I, along with two other Jewish boys, brothers, were placed into a separate sleeping dorm because we were circumcised. It would be a dead giveaway and would endanger our presence while being bathed and undressed among the other Italian boys.

I can't remember my emotional state-of-mind as a result of having been left there. It is vague and, yet, I can recall the constant repetition and indoctrination by Father of my new name, Jean Pierre, as I was sternly warned to never greet him as Father. I was to call him and Mother, if she should come to visit, as uncle and aunt. I did not see my mother for over two and half years, while Father did manage to visit on a few occasions. Now, even at this adult age, I cannot fathom how I managed to accept this lesson, but the stern warnings of danger and harm fixed the lesson deep in my head and heart. I never made a mistake during the times that my father came to visit me.

My life in the orphanage was very sad. I was scared and terrorized by the nuns and was punished on many occasions but cannot recall what my offenses were. All I recall is the terror I experienced when I was placed in a dark basement cove under the stairs, without shoes, where huge rats were whizzing about over my bare feet.

Here I was safe from the German reach and did not suffer hunger, although the food was austere and without taste. The black bread tasted like mud. I learned later that my mother sent me numerous packages with my favorite foods, but these never reached me or any of the children.

My two-and-a half-year stay in the orphanage with the nuns was not a total loss. I gained a good regimented, intense Catholic education, learned French and discovered that I had an excellent singing voice and a sense of presence in front of the gathered. I was assigned to sing solo prayer hymns in the choir and served as an altar boy. I was awakened at six in the morning every day to march into the sanctuary carrying a lit candle on a long stick to light the candles in the church.

When I was approaching my seventh birthday, the priest told my father that I need to prepare for my first communion. Father asked him to postpone this event till after the war when the entire family could come and enjoy such an occasion. Of course this ceremony never happened.

On occasions when the German's unmanned V1 and V2 rockets or buzz bombs as they were called, carrying explosive warheads were flying overhead, we ran to the deep basement for shelter where huge tanks with boiling water where located. The horrible ear-deafening sound of the drones' engines made all the children scream with desperate fear. The nuns chided us and threatened that our screams would make the tanks burst, and we would be boiled in the hot water. Somehow we muffled our screams and held onto our fears with trembling souls, not knowing which would be worse the bombs or the boiling water. This experience left a profound effect on me.

During my years at the convent, my parents were hiding with false papers as sister and brother with a widow farmer where they earned their shelter and protection by the varied labors and chores on the farm. To keep the facade, with difficulty and feeling a sense of betrayal to his orthodox Jewish beliefs, every Sunday Father attended church, placing alms into the collection box.

My paternal grandfather Joseph, was hidden in a sanatorium/rehabilitation facility because he had only one lung, while my grandmother was in a hospital at another location under false identity. My aunt passed as Belgian, acting as a volunteer for the patients. My maternal grandparents, David and Raizel Poler, also managed to survive in hiding in a tiny remote village, with only about twenty-five homesteads in the area.

My years at the convent continued with sadness. I don't recall being happy or laughing. I tried to fit in and somehow always was the focus of the nuns' wrath. One day I was sent across the road of the convent to get a haircut at the local barber shop. The man there greeted me but almost immediately forced me into a secluded closet warning me to be completely quiet no matter what. With fear I obeyed. After some time passed, he retrieved me from the closet and placed me in a baker's flour barrel closing the lid over my head. The few drilled holes in the lid let in air for me to breathe. I was transported to another location, which turned out to be a funeral home. Getting out of the barrel and seeing the caskets on display shocked me to the core, as I froze in desperation, not knowing what to do. The family that lived in this location had their little boy take me by the hand and play with me, which quieted my despair. Soon after my arrival, Father Andre appeared and with a kind voice and friendly patting said, "Don't worry, little Henri, your father will come and pick you up tomorrow." This was my first encounter with the priest. His pronouncement of the word "Father" again shook my being. How was I to acknowledge his reassurance? I was supposed to have an uncle, who was to be my father? Somehow, I found comfort from this man's presence and awaited my father with a sense of hope.

At a later time, I learned that the barber was active with the resistance. When he saw the Nazi truck standing at the convent, he would not let me return there. My two Jewish companions were taken away and were never heard from again.

The next day, indeed, my father appeared. It took me a few moments to acknowledge him. He was my uncle for so long that it was difficult to start calling him Father. But with his assuring demeanor and lavishing of love and hugs, I let go of my indoctrinated identity and once again became my father's only son. This was 1944. Although the war was not over yet, Father reclaimed me and brought me to join him and Mother at the farm. I still needed to keep my charade of being Jean Pierre. I enjoyed my five months on the farm, being in this wonderful large park, where everything bloomed and showed a promise of life and hope.

To my unhappy surprise, I found that I was displaced by a new son, a baby brother, Willy. It took me some time to accept a brother into my life. After all, I was just reunited with my pampering parents, I was threatened, but soon my mother took me aside and lavished me with love and consolation that I was her first born and first love of her life. At the age of seven, although a child jealous of being displaced, I was older than my years after my experience in the convent where I had to learn to overcome and endure.

When the war ended, our family reunited from their hiding places and identities. We could not return to our old apartment. We were not able to reclaim it. We settled in a new place and Father restarted his business with the help of his friend who kept all the machinery, leather and money in safekeeping for Father's return.

My grandfather Joseph was my idol, my guide and inspiration. His countenance expressed a complete enveloping of my soul and made me feel safe and blessed. He brightened my life forever with love, wisdom, spirituality and a pride in my Jewish heritage and gave me a special printed prayer, "Tehillim" which I cherish and carry wherever I go.

Grandfather Joseph

He shared with me his own miracle of survival. When he was arrested by the Nazis and sent to a labor camp, Brandock, the men were driven with hard menial senseless work of transporting blocks of stones in wheelbarrows from one place to another and then back again. A young German soldier, guarding the men, observed that my grandfather was carting the stones at a pace twice as fast as the other men. He stopped Grandfather and asked him, "Why are you hurrying in this hard work, at a faster pace than the others?" Grandfather replied: "I thought that if I rush this work faster that you would send me home faster." The German glared at him with bewilderment and said nothing further. The next morning he approached Grandfather and handed him a paper and told him to get out through the gate and "Don't come back!" Of course, he followed orders and found a way to hide in the Sanitarium.

Our home returned to an ultra-orthodox life without compromises. Father's stance was not negotiable and even though I learned to be very independent being away from the family, I fell into step with his expectations.

The first year after the war, I attended the Belgian public school but as soon as the Jewish Committee opened a Jewish school for orphans, an orthodox Jewish day school, I was placed there, and I returned to my Jewish identity with complete immersion. In addition, I attended the *yeshiva* on Wednesday afternoons and Sundays.

Our life and family expanded. My parents had two more children, my sisters Yvette and Suzy. Somehow my mother recognized in me a sense of loss of my own childhood and place in the family. Every night, without fail, Mother tucked me in for the night showering me with kisses and words of love that I was very special in her life. This comforting and reassurance brought me peace and finally an appreciation of my siblings.

My parents worried about my physical return to health since I was skeletal. A doctor told Mother that I should be fed eggs and bacon. When she announced this to my father, he was aghast. We were a very religious family and observed the kosher diet to the letter. Bacon was definitely not allowed. Mother insisted that the doctor ordered such food, so the two of them marched off to see the rabbi who listened and appreciated my parents' concerns and without much hesitation made a compensation that they could feed me bacon. And so, immediately they bought separate dishes and pans for the preparation of my curative diet, and sure enough I did gain weight and strength.

In the meantime, I continued my education, joined the Mizrachi – Bnai Akiva youth organization, which brought into focus the striving for a Jewish state.

When Israel declared its independence in 1948, the celebrations were exuberant and emotional. My young heart was overwhelmed with joy that our losses in the Holocaust, after all, made our people strong.

My life continued within the family and community. My experience in the convent of singing in the choir and singing solo opened up my desire to serve in the synagogue as a cantor when called upon. My father and Grandfather were proud of their Catholic-indoctrinated child who gained his voice and independence there.

When I was twenty years old, I registered to serve in the Israeli army for two years. This experience served me well because I learned another language, established a sense of self-respect, and respect for my fellow Jews who displayed strength and courage to protect their people and country. Here I met my wife Heni Margel. After a proper courtship, we got married and were soon blessed with our first son Ron and two years later with our son Yoram. I continued my education in Israel and became an international guide and travel agent. In 1962 we returned to Belgium where I opened my own business.

After all my successes and gains, I thought that my childhood suffering and experiences were behind me. At the age of twenty-three, terrible nightmares encroached my nights and troubled my peace of mind. I consulted our doctor for help. He advised me to return to the convent and revisit the scary places which attached themselves to my subconscious and caused me a troubled life.

My parents joined me in this hopefully healing quest and followed my footsteps through the convent, revisiting the dark places, the staircase rat- infested cove, the basement with now small modern boilers, which were not threatening at all, nor were the nooks and crannies of the building. As we walked about, chills overcame me and served as a release from the trapped hurts of my child's soul. Mother Superior, who was a nun during my stay at the convent, could not understand my need or fathom what a little toddler had to face and endure. She appeased me and let me wander about.

The barber shop was a grocery store now. I could not explore my hiding place in the closet or in the barrels or reminisce with my savior about the scary events there. I was done with these places and promised never to come back. But still the little child in me made me agree to revisit the convent in the year 2,000 with friends. By this time, it was remodeled into an apartment building and the barber shop into an architect's office. These places were dismantled physically into another time and so were the affects of my traumatic memories.

I did go into the church where I found satisfaction remembering the hidden/visible child who found his voice and courage to sing solo in public and be the bearer of candles to light up the edifice of a God's structure even if Catholic.

Seeing the anti-Semitism growing in Belgium, the depressed economy and no future for our children, I decided to change careers and moved us to Chicago in 1981, establishing a promotion business for the diamond industry in Belgium. We found safety, opportunity, freedom for our children, great friends and associates who enhanced our lives.

In 1995, the warm kind weather of Florida beckoned. Here we are surrounded by our sons and families.

I must state that my long-suffering convent life brought about good things in my life as a Jew. I use this recognized voice, serving in Jewish synagogue choirs and cantoral participation, in which I find comfort and almost a sense of approval by God that he has forgiven me for praying and singing in a church.

On occasion, I am asked to address students about my Holocaust experiences. A student once commented, "Mr. Galel, you don't speak with your voice, you speak

Henri 2013

with your heart." And indeed, the words that come flowing out are painful and heartfelt, remembering my own child's experience. I speak because we must not forget, nor can we forgive the evil that was committed against the innocent Jewish people.

A PROMISE TO MY BROTHER

by Daniel Gurevitz Gevitz

I can't complain. I had a good life, except for my early childhood experiences. So where does one begin now to bring forth what I want to forget? I can't, because that would be erasing the memory of my own dear family and people who were murdered with depraved cruelty. I am compelled to remember and tell. We must take notice that it can repeat if the world will allow the evil voices to lure the masses again into evil acts.

I was born in 1929 in Vary, Czechoslovakia, now part of Ukraine. The forty Jewish families of Vary thrived by hard work in farming and in some trade. They lived apart from the Czech modern society by choice and kept out of the way of the anti-Semitic atmosphere against the Jewish population.

Daniel after war

We enjoyed life among our extended family whose homes were always open to me. Our family, although not wealthy, never lacked for anything. My parents followed orthodoxy, prayed daily and each Friday evening we recited the *Kiddush*, blessing over the wine, and kept the *Shabbat*, Sabbath holy.

I was the youngest son, the fifth child of the family. My three brothers, Nandi, Josef, and Miklos and sister Sari were my protectors. After six years of being the baby of the family, my little sister Rifka took center stage. This beautiful child became my own beloved sibling who followed me around with inquisitive eyes and somehow managed to win me over. My parents, at times overwhelmed with six children, blessed us and considered us as God's gifts to them and the Jewish people.

On November 2, 1938, the First Vienna Award transferred parts of Southern Slovakia and Carpathian Ruthenia to Hungary and on March 23, 1939, Hungary occupied the Czechoslovakian - Carpathian region where we lived and immediately started to enforce their anti-Jewish laws. From that time on, our lives were in a constant state of struggle and turmoil, not trusting the country, countrymen or our future.

My father, a shoemaker, was stripped of his license, a requirement to do business, and had to resort to working illegally in order to support the family. He was caught and often jailed for a week or two. The townsfolk made life miserable for the Jewish community, breaking windows of businesses, killing farmers' livestock and doling out constant harassment. I recall often being chased by older boys and when caught, I was beaten and dumped into trenches or dragged through mud. This was their entertainment. Sometimes I was forced to go to church. I will never forget the time when a gang of these boys held me and shoved a strip of bacon down my throat while shouting, "Now you die, Jew!"

My paternal grandmother Szantos' family presence in Vary can be traced to the 17th century, yet the family had been forcibly removed from their home and taken to a ghetto in March of 1944.

On the last day of Passover, walking in the street, I was accosted by hoodlums who grabbed me by my sidelocks and asked, "Jew, where are you going? Go home." The roundup of Jews took place the following day.

To keep the Jewish community relatively calm and orderly, we were told to pack our valuables and whatever else we wanted to take for a "relocations" program. To complete the ruse, we had to make lists of the possessions that we were bringing along. As we entered the school, which served as a gathering place, we were issued receipts for our belongings, which were then taken from us and not returned. After spending the night at this school in Vary, we were taken to the ghetto in Beregszaz, an abandoned brick factory, where we were kept for a few weeks. After that, we were herded into cattle cars heading for Auschwitz.

Our journey of suffering in these sealed, overcrowded cattle-cars, confined and dehumanized, broke the spirit of many. Arriving at Auschwitz, we disembarked to the shouts and threats of the guards. We were led to the "selection" site. An inmate, whose duty was to assist in the process, whispered to me, "Say you are sixteen years old – don't ask me why." I knew that this man saved my life. I was just a few months past thirteen years old and learned the lesson of survival - to grab at any hope. I was separated from my mother, father, grandmother, sisters and extended family. I never saw them again.

There was no work for us in the couple of weeks that I was confined in this death camp. Food was nearly non-existent. Sometimes I would get a piece of rotten cheese, hold my nose while eating it.

Luckily, I was in the same barrack as my brother Miklos, who had learned about the ovens and insisted that I sleep with him that night, avoiding a selection. And so I lived to see another day.

For some reason, my brother and I were shipped to Buchenwald. Here I lost my name and although it was never burnt into my skin, I was assigned number #55011. One or two weeks later, I was among the slave laborers at Dora, the underground factory where the V-2 rockets that bombarded London were manufactured. Forced to work from pre-dawn to darkness, we did not see sunlight for almost three months. My job on the assembly line was to apply one lone screw. The monotony, hunger and lack of sleep often made me doze off until a guard's whip brought me back to a state of alertness.

Workers were plentiful and easy to replace, so the guards used us for their sadistic entertainment. When an inmate slipped between two railroad cars while unloading rocks, the guards brought the cars together wedging him between the connecting discs, which crushed him like a pancake. At other times, guards blindfolded prisoners, making them run down an embankment and using them for target practice. The SS took great pleasure in shooting the disoriented inmates in the legs or backs.

One hundred inmates, including me, were subsequently assigned to a garden detail. When no one was looking, I would eat a piece of raw potato or a few peas. I was now alone, my brother had been dispatched to Ehrlich, another labor camp. Before we separated, I promised him that I would survive. Ehrlich was on the other side of the mountain where cruel guards constantly threatened the inmates with their ferocious dogs while they were forced to dig water lines. My brother never returned.

In March of 1945, as the Allied armies approached, we were marched from Dora to Bergen-Belsen. Lice-infested, sick with dysentery, soaked with urine and excrement, we were forced to sing while watching those who collapsed on the way were torn apart by vicious dogs. Given mere morsels of bread and scooping up snow for liquid, our bodies could hardly digest anything. I hid a bit of bread inside my shirt which was stolen as I slept. The desperation, starvation and loss of integrity brought out the worst in many.

Bergen-Belsen was a place where survival was not possible. People just died! No facilities, no food, or water and no place to rest one's body. The mounds of corpses were in piles mountain high in the yards. The inmates were so weakened and ill that they could not even dig pits to bury the dead. My will and understanding of what it meant to be human was dead. We just waited for the end to join the mounds of the decaying dead. All hope was gone.

April 15, 1945, at 1:00 p.m. is a time and date forever etched in my mind. A Canadian soldier suddenly appeared before us. "I am a Jew!" he proclaimed in Yiddish to the decrepit assemblage of frightened skeletal beings. I was sick with a raging fever and could hardly comprehend the shouts, "We are free!" A girl, Malka Steinmetz, from my hometown, whose brother was with me all through the camps until he succumbed to tuberculosis, nursed me back from near death.

94

Soon after, British soldiers allowed the liberated to go to the local town and gave us a free hand to do what we wanted. Coming upon a woman pushing a baby carriage, some wanted to kill the baby. Remembering the murder of my little sister, together with others, I stopped the would be avengers. "What are you trying to prove? We are not the barbarians! We will not stoop to their level."

My two brothers, the only other family members to survive, were liberated from Mauthausen. Another brother, always a rebel, we assumed was killed while trying to escape. My grandmother, father, mother and sisters were murdered in Auschwitz.

In spite of all the hopelessness and suffering, there was a spark of will to survive. After all, I promised my brother Miklos.

My life began again after February 11, 1947, the day I came to America. I was able to rebuild my life and somehow put aside my bitter memories.

With a business partner, I operated a sportswear manufacturing company in Allentown, Pennsylvania. I got married and had a family; three children, a son Michael and daughters Susan and Judy and seven grandchildren, whose likenesses give glimmers of the faces of my lost family.

In our retirement, my wife Barbara and I settled in southern Florida where we enjoyed the weather and being active in our synagogue and many charitable events. Sadly I lost her in 2002.

Daniel 2011

Just this September 1, 2012, I celebrated my second Bar Mitzvah surrounded by my dear children, grandchildren and friends. My first Bar Mitzvah was held in Vary in 1942 with experiences of fear.

This time I experienced mixed emotions. I mourned for my lost family, but I also rejoiced with tender feelings and a feeling of victory to see my family around me and recognizing a certain smile, a glint in the eye that reminds me of my dear family who were destroyed.

At times images of my "other life" show themselves, a world so fanatically obsessed with dehumanizing and then slaughtering Jews. To this day I consciously will not buy German products to give them further profit from my hard-earned Jewish money.

I often wonder, how it was possible for survivors not to become criminals, how we were able to make something of ourselves? I guess it's who we are. We are good people, not out to hurt anyone.

MY FAMILY'S SEARCH FOR SAFETY
Hungary - Austria - Belgium
France - Israel - United States

by Madeleine Fogel Goodman

My parents, Shmuel Fogel and Sosia, (Serena) Shechter, were cousins. They were married with blessings from family in Hungary, where they were born and lived.

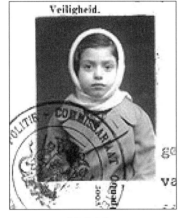

Veiligheid.

Madeleine

My maternal grandparents resided in a small hamlet on a farmstead and eked out a living by keeping hives for honey. They also cared for a small orchard, kept a couple of cows, poultry and a vegetable garden, which provided a meager subsistence. They raised a large family, only my mother, one sister and I survived.

My father earned a living as a fine tailor of men's and ladies' apparel. He especially enjoyed many delightful hours creating attire for his beautiful, high-spirited, accomplished and pleasantly plump young bride, my mother, who was happy to walk about in all her splendor, showing off her outfits on the way to synagogue.

Our way of life was of ultra-orthodoxy. As is the custom of orthodox Jews, Father performed all rituals of his piety, wore a hat/*kippa* and Mother followed the blessing, *mitzvah,* of devoutness and modesty by shaving her head and wearing a wig.

After many years of childlessness, the young couple decided to move to Vienna in 1926 in the hope of securing medical help for their problem. And indeed on September 21, 1932, I, Madeleine, Magda, Fogel, was born followed by my sister Paula in 1934. Our arrival brought great joy to my parents and the families on both sides.

96

Our comfortable apartment on *Schloss Strasse* was in an area where many Jews resided. I am sure this location was chosen by my parents because it was within walking distance to the synagogue and the ritual bath, *mikvah*, just across the street.

Father worked for a large tailoring concern, which did not provide sufficient income, so in his free time and evenings he took in private tailoring for a number of customers. Even with this extra work, the income needed to be subsidized by my mother's earnings. Because she was an excellent cook, she had paying guests for kosher meals and kept a paying border in one of the rooms.

Life was normal. We, the children, felt safe and loved. Although Mother, who was fast to anger and just as fast to forget, made sure that we behaved and were respectful of her will. We enjoyed many happy hours at the Amusement Complex and will never forget sitting on my father's lap, listening to his comforting voice as he read wondrous Bible stories to me.

My first memories of fear began when I saw the apprehension expressed by the adults around me. It was March 12, 1938, when Germany's 8th Army marched in and annexed the First Republic of Austria - the *Anschluss,* Annexation, followed within a half a year, on November 9-10, 1938, by *Kristallnacht,* the night of broken glass.

All over Germany, Austria and other Nazi controlled areas, Jewish businesses had their windows smashed and contents destroyed. Synagogues were a prime targeted for destruction, including defilement of Torah scrolls and prayer books; all was set on fire while the local fire departments just stood by to prevent the fires from spreading into adjoining non-Jewish properties and buildings.

Kristallnacht is the watershed of my carefree life. The daily events of our precarious existence was to be on constant guard of new oppressions and abuse. I recall that on the night before *Kristallnacht*, Mother insisted that my sister and I sleep in my parents' bed away from the window where our beds stood. It was strange that my mother had a premonition to keep her daughters, six and four, away from the glass because that night a brick came crashing through the window shattering the glass all over our beds. Surely this would have injured my sister and me. Evil crept into our daily life.

Soon the Gestapo appeared at our apartment ransacking our possessions and were about to take it all away. Mother, with her strength and audacity, presented our Hungarian passports, which protected Jews, since the Hungarian premier declared that his Jews be protected. Before leaving, the Gestapo replaced all, however just a few days later they returned and cleaned out all our belongings of value.

My parents, with their skills of survival and finding solutions to impending danger, decided to send my sister and me on the *Kindertransport* to England. This was around January or February of 1939. When the train made a stop in Belgium, my aunt and uncle, who were informed of our arrival, removed us from the train and we remained living with them. We were two unhappy children, not finding parental care by the relatives. But soon after, Mother joined us, rented an apartment and rescued us from our sad existence. My enterprising mother again found ways to provide for her family by cooking and feeding people for money. And so we lived in Brussels until Father smuggled himself from Austria into Belgium and joined us.

One day, the Belgian police came to our apartment and arrested my father. Not wanting to be separated, we insisted on going along with Father. We all were imprisoned in the Chateau Thierry, an ancient castle, which housed all captured illegal aliens.

After a time in the prison/castle, we were released and continued our track to seek safety. We walked for three days trying to constantly avoid the German *Messerschmidt* airplanes, which were strafing, mowing down anyone in sight. Scrambling up a steep hill, I slid into a ravine which landed me right near a Belgian soldier pointing a rifle. At first I believed that it was not a German, but soon realized that the soldier lying in position to shoot was dead. I was shaken yet found myself, at eight and a half years old, reaching mature decisions for survival. I scrambled my way up the incline to get away from this scene and being a target for the flying German aircraft.

Rejoining my family, we succeeded to get across into France. Again we were intercepted and confined in a detention camp. The stables and stalls with straw bedding which had been used to house horses became our residence. We were released from this imprisonment when France and Germany signed an armistice.

Once more we continued on our odyssey searching for a corner of safety. Finally in 1940, we reached Nice and were reunited with Father's brother and his wife. We found a dwelling in the old part of the city. Father continued tailoring, while Mother bartered, cooked, sold and traded anything that came to hand.

Nice was included in the "Free" Vichy France zone during the first part of WWII and became a safe haven from war-torn occupied France. This haven offered a semblance of normalcy under the auspices of Italy at that time, Germany's ally. They were lenient overseers and we were able to return to a less threatening life.

I entered public school and I recall that at the time, I used this opportunity and was making progress with my studies. I felt no abuse nor discrimination against us. It seemed that permanence was our life until sometime in the beginning of 1943 when the Germans removed the Italians from their duty over this area. That is when, once again, life became precarious and challenging. Food was rationed and oppressive measures were being enforced. The scramble of keeping out of the eye of the storm became more difficult.

The true meaning of separation, which felt like abandonment, brings me to the traumatic scene as I recall Mother leading my sister and me to a storefront where she quickly hugged and kissed us, saying a trembling goodbye. In April 1943, being only ten and a half years old, although more mature than expected of a child this age, I realized that I had to continue and abide by what was presented. I became aware of the dangers for Jews.

We were accepted at a Catholic parochial boarding school, *La Maison Blanche*, which was run by nuns. Eight Jewish children were melded in among the boarders, although none knew who were Jewish. My sister and I were led into the Mother Superior's office where she gave us new names. Mine was Madeleine Rocher, new place of birth, Dakar, Senegal, new sets of parents, describing my father to be a ship navigator and my mother living with him on board. I practiced endlessly to imprint all this information and coached my little sister as well.

On October 18, 1943, while Mother was out shopping, Father and six others, who were hiding in our apartment, were denounced by the French neighbor, an ambulance driver, who lived in the apartment below us. Father and the others were arrested and sent to Drancy, then to Auschwitz. I believe that he was immediately selected for the gas chambers, since he was an invalid, suffering from arthritis and walked with a cane.

After the war the ambulance driver was arrested, found guilty and imprisoned for collaborating with the Nazis.

During our separation, Mother, carrying papers as a Hungarian Christian, and an aunt and uncle, found shelter in a tiny hamlet. Mother's instinctive talent for surviving brought forth her skills in knitting, cooking, bartering her work for food. They were thus hidden from the Nazi/Vichy net for a year and a half.

Life with the nuns was austere but orderly and we felt safe. We learned to be good Catholic girls, learning all the prayers, catechisms, attended classes and continuing with our education. Our days were busy. We hardly had dared to question or even think about our past life, until one day two women came to the play yard asking for me and my sister by name. Our long hours of both verbal and mental practice of absorbing our new identities paid off - we did not fall for this evident trap. On another occasion when the nuns took us into town, Mother tried to approach and greet us. I was strong of mind to reject and ignored her. This memory still brings me horrible feelings of anguish remembering my mother's face in pain and disappointment.

In the summer of 1944, forty-three girls, who could not return to their homes, were taken to a town in the *Moulinex Valley* where the nuns had a summer residence. Above the valley on either side of the cliffs were mountain forts held by the French résistance on one side and the Germans on the other. The barrage of shootings at each other brought us under their firestorm, and the chalet was set on fire. The resistance came to our rescue leading us and carrying the little ones for over five kilometers to Sospl, into a cathedral. Here we were dispersed with different families in the Moulinex area. My sister was placed with a baker and I with a widow with three sons. The frequent bombardments and shrapnel forced us to stay in the deep stone cellars. This family was kind to me and saved my life. I did return many years later and met with one of the sons who greeted me warmly. I extended my gratitude to him.

In October 1944, we were liberated by the Americans. My first impression was to be cautious of uniformed men, but I soon learned that they were different and among them were Jewish American boys wearing Magen David stars who offered to bring us to America if we were not reunited with our parents.

Mother did find us and took us back to her small apartment in Nice where she struggled to create a stable home for us without Father. My own struggle to abandon my comforting Catholic prayers and customs was difficult. It took time for me to return to trust myself to be Jewish. This awakening and learning the details of what happened to my father, most of our family and the Jewish people, brought out a vicious anger that led me to feel like punishing the world for this neglect and evil.

We knew that there was no possibility of returning to our previous homes in Austria so Mother made a home for us in Nice, and I continued my education.

In 1951, I met Jack Goodman, a handsome, amiable and intelligent American boy. He was my hero, my future and indeed after a very short courtship, we got married and came to New York. My mother and sister came five years later.

I established new roots, blending into the American way of life with appreciation and pride. Our family of four children, two sons and two daughters, and five grandchildren has brought a sense of rebirth of my lost family.

With the passing years, my anger has diminished but my memory of my dear father and our struggle will never leave me. The question why, no matter how reasonable the answer, will never be satisfied.

I can never forget my history, but the results of "Hate" has taught me to be accepting of all people. I do not want to be like the "Evil Murderers." I don't want to assume the worst. I look

Madeleine 2012

for good. I will not come down to the level of wallowing in the evil and have it affect my life and my relationship with all people.

I will not be tainted by these horrible memories!

FROM DENIAL TO TRAGEDY
My Fate As A Hungarian Jew
by Gabriel Groszman

I spent the first ten years of my life, until 1941, in Vamosmikola, the same small rural village of Hungary where my parents, my paternal grandfather, and most probably his father, were born.

Gabriel Age - 8

The synagogue was the center of community life in the village. During the Saturday morning services our rabbi's sermons were in *Yiddish*, a language that the Hungarian Jews did not speak, except for the most religious among us. As a consequence, we the younger congregants understood nothing. When I was nine years old, my brother Imi had his Bar Mitzvah celebration. He made his speech in Yiddish, incomprehensible to me and possibly to him as well. However, the pocket watch, which our rabbi gave him as a gift, with numbers in Hebrew and on the back an embossed image of Moses with the Ten Commandments, is an object that I treasure as one of the few family relics which I still possess.

As was customary back then, I was born in my family home, which was relatively comfortable by the modest standards of the village. It had a bathtub with water heated by a firewood stove with coils. The water was drawn in buckets from a well-located in our garden. When in 1945, the Soviet army established a base in our little border village, our house was designated as official bathing quarters for the troops due to its "sophisticated" facilities.

During WWI, my eighteen-year old Father was enlisted into the army and was sent to the Italian front as an artilleryman to defend the cause of the Austro-Hungarian monarchy. He was wounded and was promoted to the rank of Sergeant Major, being awarded three stars for his "valiant service to the nation."

After WWI, in 1920, Hungary was the first European country in the 20th century to promulgate anti-Semitic laws: the *"Numerus Clausus"* limited the number of Jewish students in universities to 6% of the total student body. When I started going to school, I also began to feel that we were treated differently. Our teacher punished the Jewish kids with a stick especially reserved for us, wound with a rubber cord in order to increase the sting. He referred to his cane affectionately as "the little Jew."

As long as I can remember, we had Kathe, an Austrian nanny living in our home, a common custom among the better-off Jewish families. We loved Kathe very much; she was like a member of the family. When Hitler occupied Austria in March 1938, she was ordered to return home as she was not allowed to work for a Jewish family. We all cried a lot and a short while later Kathe sent us a letter expressing how much she missed us, concluding with an affectionate *Heil Hitler*!

When the Nazis occupied Poland in 1939, the Polish army disbanded and Hungary, nominally still neutral, received thousands of soldiers as refugees. A great number of the Polish soldiers were given lodging in the military base of our village. They were under surveillance but could roam freely in the village. The Jews among them would come to synagogue for the *Shabbat* services and were also invited home for meals. After a year, two of them changed their uniforms for clothes, provided by my parents, and escaped without

A fate we wished to avoid: A memorial to those murdered on the banks of the River Danube

102

telling us their destination. Perhaps because of news that they received from the territories occupied by the Nazis, they had a greater appreciation than the Hungarian Jews of what could happen. We lived on an island of ignorance, as an example, I mention a trivial episode.

For the summer of 1941, an orthodox institution organized a summer camp near my village. Our father was prepared to send us, but the project was abandoned when Hungary entered the war. Matters of fate: at the same time as we and our parents were feeling frustrated by such a small setback, the Nazis were setting fire to the synagogues of Eastern Europe with their Jews locked inside, often with the collaboration of the local population.

Soon afterwards, as the consequence of the so called "Second Jewish Law," my father was forced to give up his small store in the village. My parents decided to move to Budapest, the capital of Hungary. This is how we escaped the fatal destiny of my village's more than one hundred Jews. In 1944, all our relatives and friends were deported to Auschwitz. Now my personal childhood friends remain as a bittersweet memory.

More than forty years later, I visited my village on our "Heritage Tour" with the grandchildren, and I couldn't find a trace of its Jewish life. Even the synagogue building was gone. The neighbors told us that after deporting the Jewish population, the Hungarian army used it as a stable and at the end of the war, the property was occupied, for a time, by a clan of Gypsies.

When Hungary declared war on the Soviet Union, Jews from the mobilized classes were also sent to the Russian front as second class soldiers, without weapons, to perform auxiliary tasks such as digging trenches. Three of my uncles were drafted and only one came back. The other two were not killed by "enemy fire" but by the retreating Hungarians who didn't want them to be liberated by the Russian army.

During the summer months, our parents sent us back to our village to spend our vacation with relatives. In September of 1943, only months away before the demise of the Hungarian Jewry, we returned from my village to Budapest to resume our studies. We were traveling together, all the Jewish children, on the same bus and train. Today it seems unimaginable that this happened at the end of 1943 in Hungary, with its anti-Semitic laws and plunged into the war. While throughout the rest of Europe, Jews were being deported and exterminated, we, some ten Jewish children, not even accompanied by an adult, would travel by bus and train without facing any danger.

As the Russian army was nearing the borders of Hungary, Germany, not trusting anymore its Hungarian ally, occupied the country. The 19th of March, 1944 marked a milestone in the life of every Jew in Hungary. There was a before and an after. Our situation worsened day by day. The next day our Jewish school was closed down. In April we were ordered to wear the Jewish star and in May, the 600,000 Jews from the countryside were deported to Auschwitz.

We, in Budapest, were ordered to move into one of the so-called "Jewish houses."

With the Soviet army closing in on Budapest, assaults against Jews increased. There were frequent raids during which people were dragged out of their homes and sent on the routes toward Austria. For some weeks, our janitor hid us in the cellar of the house, but the conditions there were unsustainable.

During one of the night-raids, we escaped by jumping to the patio of the neighboring house and from there escaping to the street. In October, all the Jews of Budapest were ordered to move again, this time to the walled-in ghetto. We were spared from this fate, as we received safe conducts from the Swedish diplomat Raoul Wallenberg, which entitled us to live in one of the houses protected by the Swedish Embassy. However, as the Russians approached the city, the Hungarian fascists from the dreaded Arrow Cross didn't respect the immunity of the diplomatic building. It became usual that they entered, dragging out people to be taken to the banks of the Danube to be shot, their inert bodies tumbling into the river.

My father decided that to stay in the Swedish House was becoming too dangerous. Some time earlier, as a precaution, he had already purchased false non-Jewish documents on the black market. Now the time had come to make use of them. These showed that we were of the Protestant religion hailing from the Eastern Hungarian city of Debrecen, which was already occupied by the Russians. Through a real estate company he found an elderly couple with a large home who, anticipating turbulent times during the siege of Budapest, wanted to have a family live with them. On the way to our new home, crossing the Danube, we were detained by the Hungarian Nazi thugs suspecting that we were Jews, but my father with great presence of mind, pulled out of his pocket the fake Christian documents. In such situations, the normal procedure was to tell us to pull down our trousers and inspect if we were circumcised. We were lucky they didn't do this; we would have been shot on the spot and thrown into the Danube.

Halfway through the month of December, the Russians had already reached the suburbs. In the first days of 1945, amid increasingly intense bombardments and cannon fire, it became obvious that staying in the apartment was too dangerous. Along with the building's other inhabitants, we moved into our new home, the air raid shelter, where we lived together, with about forty people. Rows of hastily improvised beds were arranged; the three of us took a spot right next to our landlords, the Szabós. The couple had already suspected that we were Jews. One day Mrs. Szabó asked my mother, whispering "You are Jewish, aren't you?" My mother answered affirmatively fearing the worst, but the couple didn't betray us. They were religious Protestants and knew well that turning us in would be the equivalent of sending us to our immediate deaths.

During our stay for six weeks in the shelter, we had to be very careful not to make a mistake and reveal our identity to the other occupants. Moreover, in the last twelve days, when the Russians were already on the opposing side of our street, many of the fighting German troops came to rest for a while in our shelter, not a comforting situation for us.

Finally, on the 12th of February of 1945, two men entered the courtyard, wearing the round fur-lined winter caps typical of the Russian army. We knew that we had survived the Holocaust.

Jorge Semprun, the Spanish anti-fascist philosopher, exiled in France, and later deported by the Nazis, wrote in his book, *Literature or Life*: "Surviving was not a question of merit, it was a question of luck. Living depended on how the dice landed, nothing more…" For us, the dice landed favorably.

A few weeks later my brother Imi also returned from the copper mine in Yugoslavia. Through him we learned about the fate of the 6,000 young Jews who had been taken there as slave laborers. The first group there in the summer of 1943 and my brother's contingent a year later.

In September 1944, the Hungarian commander decided to abandon the area, due to the proximity of the Russian troops and the growing danger of the Yugoslav partisans. He initiated the retreat, taking along the first group of the prisoners, and the "privileged" ones, of partial Jewish descent. Very few of these 3,000 youngsters survived the journey of more than one month's duration. They sometimes walked as much as forty kilometers a day, and those without the strength to go on were murdered and thrown into a ditch. The second contingent of another 3,000 left some days later but they were liberated by Yugoslav partisans who led them across the German lines, through mountain paths to an already-liberated city. Among them was my brother Imi. For him the dice also landed favorably.

Two months after the liberation, in mid April 1945, there was already a certain normalcy that made it possible to attend school once again. My school from the orthodox community was destroyed, so I attended the Zsidó Gimnázium, the liberal Jewish high school.

The educational staff of the school was excellent due to the fact that none of the teachers, not even the most capable, could ascend to the university professorships. They had to settle for teaching in the Zsidó Gimnázium. As one of my ex-classmates, now a writer and academic of international stature said during an interview, "The Zsidó Gimnázium was my university, and its baccalaureate was equivalent to a doctorate at any other institution." Our professors had great influence in our formation.

I decided to follow the footsteps of Mr. Pach, our professor of history and economics. He supported my decision and during my last two years before the baccalaureate, he sneaked me in into his classes at the university. At that point, following the liberation, Jews did have access to the universities but fortunately they continued to teach us.

However, with the communists slowly taking over the government, it became clear to my father that the most he could aspire to in a socialized country was a job in some state-owned enterprise, which definitely wasn't in his plans. He succeeded in making the right connection to obtain passports. Once on board the train to Vienna in April 1949, my connection with Hungary was severed forever.

In Vienna I had to start thinking about my future. The very day we decided to exile, I knew that in a foreign country I would have no future as a professional in the field of history or economic history. With my baccalaureate degree from Hungary, I had no problem enrolling in the university, where I chose to major in chemistry. During my stay, I never heard any anti-Semitic remarks, not even in the university where no one knew my religion. I attribute this to the fact that the atrocities were still fresh in people's minds. Only five years had passed since the collapse of Nazism, and it would take a few more for the Austrians to forget about them.

In early March 1952, we said goodbye to Vienna and immigrated to Argentina. In order to travel, we obtained passports from the IRO, the International Refugee Organization. On our stopover in Zurich, we met Cilka, my father's aunt who gave us the telephone number of a distant relative in Argentina, Elizabeth Heda. We called her as soon as we arrived in Buenos Aires. Cilka's referral proved to have unquestionable consequences since six years later I married Ruth, Elizabeth's daughter.

Ruth was born in Czechoslovakia. When Hitler occupied the country. The parents managed to send her, at the time four years old, to Poland, and they crossed the border through the mountains, sheltered by the darkness of the night. Just before the outbreak of the war, they left with the last vessel for England. Ruth spent the years during the war in London, often sleeping in the stations of the city's underground system, sheltering from the assaults of the German rockets. She even practiced ballet dancing during those years. Thus, her story of survival is much less dramatic. After the war Ruth's father, only thirty-five years old, died of a stroke. The widow and daughter immigrated to Argentina where some years later, Elizabeth married a German Jewish refugee, Semi Uffenheimer.

Ruth

Upon arriving in Argentina, I enrolled in the School of Industrial Engineering at the University of Buenos Aires, where the classes I had taken in Vienna were accepted. While studying, I started a business with Ruth's stepfather. The company prospered and our three children were born. As the business grew, we succeeded in partnering with international companies, and these constantly strengthening ties assured us a favorable position not only in the local market but in several South American countries.

During my half-century living in Argentina, I experienced all the joys that life has to offer. The time dedicated to our three children, Susy, Ana, and Andy, always gave us satisfaction. We had the good fortune to be able to provide them with excellent educations at a Jewish day school, from pre-kindergarten all the way through graduation with a baccalaureate degree.

My son Andy began working in the business while studying and after graduating at the University of Buenos Aires, he became integrally involved in the management of the company, greatly facilitating my gradual retirement. I became involved with the *Asociación Filantrópica Israelita* (Israelite Philanthropic Association). During the ten years until our immigration to the United States, I was the Managing Director of the Association's Elderly Home, which gives shelter and complete medical care to more than 150 Holocaust survivors. Thus I had the satisfaction of giving back to the community part of the generosity that society has shown to me.

Susy, our oldest daughter, went to live in Israel immediately after graduating from high school and is still there with our grandchildren Daniela and Gal. Our second daughter, Ana, followed her to Israel a few years later, where she met her future husband Eldad Coppens. They now live in New York with our granddaughter Talia. Our son Andy, and his wife Karina, decided to relocate to the United States and now live in Florida with our grandchildren Eric, Ken, and Cindy.

Gaby and Ruth 2013

With the departure of our children from Argentina, the time had come for us to determine once again which path to take in our lives. We decided to immigrate to the United States to shorten the distances between us and all of our children and grandchildren.

I finalize with quotes of two outstanding contemporaries of the Holocaust.

Stefan Zweig said in his most important work, "The World of Yesterday:" "All forms of emigration inevitably cause a sort of disturbance in the equilibrium."

Elie Wiesel in his prologue to "The Fire and the Light" by Herman Kahan: "A survivor is, in the deepest sense of the word, a witness. He who has escaped death, cheated or overcame it, is obligated to tell his story, if for no other reason than to justify his existence. This is his duty. History demands it. Although the accounts may be similar, they are never the same . . .

Each survivor is entitled to consider his testimony to be the most important, even if it is not the only one."

We all managed to overcome the upheavals of emigration, adapting to the life and customs of our new country and establishing families. And, with these testimonies, we are fulfilling the obligation to tell our stories.

OUR DESTROYED HOME

by Anszel Gun

Jews settled in Rozyszcze in the late 18th century and with the coming of the railroad they grew to a total of over 3,800 people in 1897. Most Jews fled during the turbulence of WWI, returning afterwards to rebuild their lives with the support of the Joint Distribution Committee. In 1921 the Jewish population was 2,686. The Jews owned most of the town's factories of weaving, brewing and milling, and 270 of its 320 stores.

My hometown Rozyszcze, Wolyn, Poland is where my family had lived for generations. It was a small town, yet it gave a city feeling because of the busy

Brother Jack, Wife Manya and Anszel 1947

railroad station. It opened up the freedom of easy travel and trade. Rozyszcze tried to keep in step with the modern times and even had a three-story building, which was a great novelty and pride for the community, especially since most of the houses were single story unpretentious dwellings.

The town sustained a population close to 10,000 people, Ukrainians, a small population of Poles and Czechs, and about 3,500 Jews, according to the 1939 census. Most of the Jews were employed in the trades of tailoring and as shoemakers.

My father, Shmuel Gun, and his sister were united to a ten step-siblings family when my grandfather, Yankel, became a widower. He married a woman with ten children. Father learned to overcome all obstacles and opened up opportunities for himself by learning and grasping how to manage.

Father married my mother, Sonia Ape1, who was from the town of Torczyn. They were an attractive and compatible couple who shared a vision of helping the downtrodden. Their way of life was contrary to their parents' orthodox traditions. Father attended synagogue, on occasion, to please his Mother and during the High Holidays. His free-thinking often was a contention between my grandfather and Father.

Father and Mother worked together and developed numerous ventures including a tobacco wholesale company as well as a wholesale flax export business and an egg export company. He co-owned these businesses with a number of Polish partners because Jews were not permitted ownership.

Father was highly regarded by the Jewish and Gentile community because of his fairness in all his dealing, devotion for the good of men, and the Jewish citizenry. His visibility and good works had motivated him to become a Councilman Magistrate, a representative on the Jewish Federation Council, *Kehila*, as well as a philanthropist to a variety of causes. On Saturday mornings, it was Father's custom to accompany less fortunate people to the city offices to help them with taxation and license problems.

I was born in 1924 and was followed by a sister Raizel, three years later and a brother Yankel, ten years later in 1934. Our house, on May Avenue Number 3, was modern, spacious and well appointed with fine furniture. A nanny/maid supervised the children and ran the household. Because the building offered more space than we could use, Father donated half of the building space for the use by the Jewish *Folk Shule'*, school, which afforded the children of the Jewish artisans to get an education in Yiddish. It actually opened the minds to more modern views of life. My siblings and I also attended this school. In addition, we attended the Polish public school where the Jewish kids were tolerated but were not included in any interplay by the non-Jewish students. There was a tension that was tangible, but I did not experience any violence personally.

In spite of his civic involvement, Father always managed to spend time with us, his children, and unhesitatingly disciplined us with a few smacks.

110

Mother retained her power over us with a stem warning: "You just wait when Father gets home." But our home was a haven of goodness and love.

When I finished my education in town, I was enrolled in gymnasium, high school, in Luck, which brought me in close contact with many of my aunts, uncles, cousins and especially my loving grandmothers Devorah Gun and Miriam Apel. As I look back, my childhood was a happy one but sadly too short.

Our first taste of German occupation occurred on September 1, 1939 when the railroad station and roads were bombed. This was followed by a swarm of German soldiers arriving on motorcycles with attached side cars, which transported two soldiers in each. They intruded into houses demanding bedding, food, eggs, butter and other goods. Their demeanor was forceful and all citizenry was overwhelmed with this violent invasion; not knowing what to think or how to proceed. We did have forewarnings from German Jewish refugees who had come to our town in 1938, telling us of the violent and cruel treatment and murder of Jews in Germany. We heard but could not fathom such behavior, just pushing it aside, not wanting to believe the truth and thinking that they were exaggerating.

When the Non-Aggression Pact was signed by the Russians and the Germans in 1939, the Germans retreated from our town and the Soviets replaced them, coming in without violence, with slogans and promises of equality and hope. The promise of this equality was thrust upon us by nationalizing our own home, and we were required to pay rent from then on. Because Father was supportive of liberal causes before the Soviet's arrival, we were allowed to remain in our dwelling and town, unlike some people of means who had been expelled to Siberia. Father was given a job as a bookkeeper in the local hospital.

The Soviets' arrival was a welcome change after the Germans and so we dared to hope that this war was to be short-lived and that we could continue our lives in peace. Anti-Semitism which had appeared unchecked during the German occupation was now under wraps. The youths were indoctrinated with communist values and a life of dedication to the common cause.

Life for children especially, was one of fun, music, learning a new language, Russian, and a spirit of optimism and a promise of a life without strife. We attended only the public school, where Hebrew and religion was not part of the curriculum and therefore not permitted.

Things of what seemed as a good life, came to an end on June 21, 1941. The Germans attacked the Soviet Union and returned to Rozyszcze. This time with a vengeance, which was assisted by the Ukrainians, who staged a pogrom on the Jews on June 28, 1941.

Without time to adjust to this takeover, the Germans immediately issued edicts against the Jews. I remember the first order was for all Jews to wear white arm bands with a Jewish star. We were not allowed to walk on the sidewalks, had to maintain a curfew and all other edicts that they had practiced and refined in Poland before taking over our area.

The Germans staged two *aktions,* selections, in July, murdering 430 Jews. Forced labor was established. Father finally started to believe the rumors that these Germans were evil.

The order to relocate all Jews to a ghetto, without delay or exclusion followed. All proceeded to a section of the poorest end of town, which was separated by a canal and bridge. We could bring with only what we could carry.

The Germans enlisted the Ukrainians into a police force, equipped with rifles. They assisted the soldiers in beating and bullying the Jews of Rozyszcze as they struggled with the few possessions, which we were able to carry. The agonizing walk by our demoralized people was met by Ukrainians who robbed this suffering humanity. Finally arriving, we had to find housing, which brought our search to a relative who already resided in this area. Five to six families, twenty-five to thirty people were squeezed in to these humble houses with dirt floors and primitive sanitary facilities.

The conditions were a daily ordeal, hunger, malnutrition and disease reduced the population. Many people starved to death, while others succumbed to illness. My grandmother, Dvora Gun's health and will had weakened and she died here. It was a great heartbreak for us that she had to die in these conditions and seeing her children and grandchildren degraded and suffering. Each day we sank lower and lower.

A *Judenrat,* Jewish Council, and a Jewish police was ordered to be formed. The police also contributed to the brutality by making everyone hand over any valuables, such as gold to be turned over to the Germans as they demanded. The ill treatment by fellow Jews was a great blow to the residents who had lost all hope and protectors.

Daily, we were forced into labor squads. My father and I were among those who worked for a local German, Herr Forst, who supervised the collection of cattle and goods from the local population as taxation to the Germans. Our days were filled with terror and hard labor, yet we hoped for some miracle, which might spare us. Father always hoped for our liberation and the possibility to immigrate to a free country.

Every day brought new experiences, beatings, shootings and captures. Groups of people were taken to the outskirts of town and murdered after digging their own graves.

Because of his pre-war connections and good will with some locals, Father was able to place my sister, whose looks were Aryan, blue eyes and blond, with a Gentile family, but after two weeks she wanted to get back to the family; she was terribly homesick.

Around August 1942, we heard rumors of the liquidation of the ghettos in Luck, Torczyn and other towns in the vicinity. Father knew that we too were headed for this end, so from that time forward I spent the nights outside of the ghetto in the barn of an animal compound where I was joined by my little brother Yankel, even though he was too young to work there.

It was August 22, 1942, when all outside workers were ordered to return to the ghetto.

Father insisted that we stay outside and hide. I will never forget Father's admonishment and words, "Children, you are young, perhaps you can survive, escape and try to save yourselves wherever and however you can. I am going back to the ghetto to be with your mother and sister." This was the day that the Germans and Ukrainians encircled and liquidated the Jewish ghetto of Rozyszcze. Only eighty found shelter with Czech and Polish families. Never again did I see any of my loved ones. I was eighteen years old and my brother only eight when we began our struggle to survive.

We hid in the hay in the barn during the day, waiting for darkness of night to search for safety. We walked for about a mile when we heard noises which frightened my brother. By chance we were near a little house with a barn next to it. Seeing a ladder up to the attic, we climbed up and discovered three Jewish men hiding there. With pounding hearts and distrust of anything and anyone, we laid in the attic listening for any noise. In the scorching heat, our thirst became even more pronounced. This was now the second day that we had nothing to eat. Not feeling safe, we just stayed there waiting for a miracle.

In the early morning, the farmer came in to do his chores and heard some unfamiliar noises. He climbed the ladder and discovered the five of us. "You're Jews, right?" He continued to tell us that all Jews from our town ghetto were taken about ten kilometers away from the city. Ditches were waiting for the impending massacre. These ditches were dug by the locals rather than the captive Jews, not wanting to bring on any panic or disturbance among the Jews. Approximately 4,500 Jews that remained in our ghetto were murdered, including my parents, sister, and other members of my family.

The farmer said to us that he was a religious man and that he would not report us, but his family will be killed if we would be discovered here. He advised us that he would let us stay till night and then we must leave. He brought us a bucket of water and a loaf of bread, which we devoured.

That night we descended the ladder. I was in a quandary as to what to do or where to go next. I remembered my father's friend Jaruszhka, a Czech, with whom Father placed many valuables and bolts of fabric during the Soviet takeover. Father always praised him as an honorable and trustworthy friend, so I decided to go to him for help. I asked for directions how to find the village of Uzowa and let slip Jaruszhka's name to one of the men who knew the area because he was in the livery business. We continued on our own, hiding at the sound of any noise. After a couple of miles, my little brother's stamina ran out so I carried him for a while.

Finally arriving to Uzowa, I found Jaruszhka's house and knocked on his window. He came out crossing himself. He greeted us with reservation, inspecting us as we were some apparition. He thought we came back from the dead. He had already heard what happened to the Jews. I told him about our hardship, the killings of all Jews including our parents and our escape, hoping that he would help us. He asked, "Does anyone know where you were going?" I told him the truth about the other three who knew our quest. He looked thoughtful and said, "You know the Germans are going to kill me and the family if I am discovered hiding Jews, but I will do anything that I can to save you. Your father was my good friend and I promised him that I will do whatever I can to help him or his family." He said that he could not keep us on the property but that we could hide in the tall wheat fields and he would bring us food. At night we should come into his barn, but stealthily. We hid until harvest when he suggested that we go into the thickest of the nearby woods to hide and come to him at night for food.

We followed his suggestion and discovered about forty people hiding there, mostly men and a few women. Besides the danger of the Nazis, we were confronted by Ukrainian bandits who carried clubs and sticks robbing us of our coats or whatever they wanted. We were forced to keep changing our hiding places because of their attacks. This safe haven soon was attacked by the Germans, shooting into the woods and killing most, only fifteen survived.

The winters, in the early 1940's were brutal, reaching twenty below zero or more. We could not remain exposed to the weather and especially leave our tracks in the snow. With the help of Jaruszhka, another man and I, who had a little girl with him, dug a bunker in the field. It took a few nights to complete it. It was a deep hole with a camouflaged cover, which housed the four of us; sitting room only, pitch black. We were infested with lice. In the dark of night, we tried to freeze the lice off our clothes in the sub-zero weather above ground. At night I went to Jaruszhka's for food and water.

One day Jaruszhka told us that we must leave our hiding place because it was discovered by a German officer with whom he was hunting in the area. This German noticed an irregularity in the field. Jaruszhka distracted him that it was nothing and said that he may come back to investigate or someone else may notice. He told us that we cannot stay in his fields any longer and suggested that we return to the woods. I told him it was impossible because the conditions would kill my brother. He thought a minute and then said: "I know a man who works for me. He is a young married man with two little kids. He's very poor." Jaruszhka told me that he lives in a house way out on a field with no other houses nearby. If he would agree, that would be a safe haven for you. There are no neighbors for miles."

Jan Prymas, a Ukrainian, agreed to hide us and was glad to get financial assistance for his family from Jaruszhka. But he would have taken us in regardless. He had a good heart and was kind man. He hid us in his potato cellar

114

which was located inside his house or sometimes in his barn. But at night we were able to come out and sleep in the warm, one room house, along with his wife and two little girls. He kept us until the end of the winter. Around April 1943, we returned to the woods.

The following winter, around October, we returned to Prymas. Again we were treated with kindness and they shared with us their meager food. Somehow a Jewish tailor who was passing for a Ukrainian discovered our whereabouts and got the village elder to come with him to demand some linen and a couple of suits. I had to leave my little brother as a hostage and went to Jaruszhka to get these goods. His demands were satisfied and they let us be after that.

After they left, Prymas declared that he would kill anyone who will come for us. This statement overwhelmed me with gratitude and fear. My Ukrainian protector saved my brother and me. Without his and Jaruszhka's shelter, we too would have perished. Prymas said that he will not accept any payment or rewards from Jaruszhka for keeping us.

A few months after that we were liberated. It happened in February 1944. We left Prymas and went back to our house. We found our home stripped. Everything was gone. We were hoping for a miracle that perhaps someone from our family would have survived, but that was not to be. Yankel and I were alone.

I climbed up to the attic and with a broken heart, and yet with great excitement I found a treasure. Our family pictures where undisturbed and also I found the addresses of our family in the United States.

Soon other survivors came out of the woods and into our house. One day, just a few days after we were liberated, we were shocked to learn that the Germans were returning. The front was still fluid and the perimeters of fighting were still around us. We crossed the bridge over the river. We were able to get on Russian army trucks, which took us with them to a little town of Keverts. There we were able to get on a train, which took us to the city of Rovno.

Rovno was liberated, but a lot of shelling was still going on. The underground shelters became now our safe zone, however, being safe from shelling did not satisfy the hunger and cold. We had to wander about begging from the local peasants for a little food. One day we approached a house where an elderly couple helped us with some dry bread and water and in return, we sawed some fire wood for them.

As soon as we heard that our hometown was secured by the Russians, we returned to Rozyszcze. Our house was still empty.

One day a lovely young woman, Mania Wilenczyk, came to town. I was immediately enamored by her, but nothing happened at that time. She returned to her town and I, in the meantime, became very ill with typhoid fever. I was taken to the army hospital where my little brother came to look after me. When

I got well, the Soviets were drafting people to continue the war against the Germans. Even though I was twenty years old, I told them that I was only seventeen. I thought I was safe from being sent to the front, where many young survivors were killed on the first day of service. After living through the ghettos and all other atrocities, to be killed on the front was not my idea of survival.

A few months after the draft board came with a slip and said, "Anszel Gun, we need you to report to the draft board." Having no choice, I went with the man to their headquarters. "You're a soldier as of now," was what I heard. I appealed to them that my ten year old little brother is all alone. We just came out of the fire of Hitler's killing field. They assured me that he would be cared for by the Russian administration. I begged for a twenty-four hour reprieve. "I must have some time to at least talk with him and make some arrangements." This was around September. I found Yankel and told him about being drafted and that I decided to get away. I would let him know when finding safety.

I got to Vladimir-Volynsk, about one hundred kilometers away and changed my name to Myatik Zimmering, got a job working for the NKVD in the office and, after a few months, I sent for my brother. Here once again I met Mania and from that time I could not part from her.

One day a Ukrainian man recognized me. I realized then that I could not continue such a life, to live with fright and to be declared as a deserter would mean to be shot. The war was still raging.

I tried to smuggle my brother and an acquaintance across to the Polish border without papers. I offered a Russian soldier a couple bottles of vodka for which I told him he had to smuggle two people, Yankle, a lady friend to be reunited with relatives in Poland. Fortunately this soldier either wanted the vodka very badly or understood the plight of divided families. Yankel hid under one bench and the woman under the other and so they were transported to the border where they were discovered. They were taken to the police headquarters where they were interrogated and held for three days. After much questioning, they let them get back to the border nearby. After I learned what happened to them, I did not make my attempt to escape to Poland. I began to look for legal ways to get back to Poland through the Jewish committee. By chance, one of the men on the committee was a man who used to do business with my father. He helped us get the papers after he learned of the danger of my being taken away as a deserter and my little brother to be left all alone.

Alone with no other survivors from our family, my brother and I got out of Poland and settled in a DP camp, Bindermichel, in Lintz, Austria.

Mania and I were married there and all of us immigrated to the United States in 1948.

We settled in Michigan and renewed our lives and family, two daughters and a son. Our family has grown and we were blessed with seven wonderful accomplished grandchildren. My brother Yankel also built a family and we are united in our commitment as loving brothers and survivors.

I have often wondered how it is possible to continue a normal life and have memories and losses that wounded my heart, always carrying the memories of our blessed parents and extended family? My answer is that my heritage comes from good and kind people.

My family's motto is to live a righteous life and pass on this motto to the future.

Anszel 2012

HIDDEN IN PLAIN SIGHT

by Roman Haar

Rzeszow - 1941

Father Salo and Roman

As I look at the picture and at the face of the little boy posing with his father, I am saddened and tears pierce my eyes. These were my last days with him. This innocent child had to learn how to hide his identity at the age of six.

I am still aching from my hurtful memories, the loss of my adoring father, aunts, uncles and most of my family who were murdered in the Holocaust

The city of Rzeszow, about one hundred miles east of Krakow, is where my father Salo, *Meshulem*, Haar, was born. He was the oldest of three siblings, a brother Eliyahu, who survived by escaping to the Soviet Union and a sister Regina, who was murdered in the Holocaust along with her husband and my little cousin Gigi.

Not finding a chance for a better life in Rzeszow, Father left his family in Poland and moved to the then open city, Danzig, to improve his life, sometimes in the early 1930's. Danzig, a major seaport on the Baltic Sea for both Poland and Germany, was a city under international protection and a free port without visa restrictions. It became the destination of thousands of Jewish refugees from Russia and Poland who were continuing their journeys of immigration to many countries.

Roman before WWII

118

Father was a bright and amiable man and shortly established himself in Danzig by working as a salesman at a Jewish firm Moskowitz, which sold dry goods and piece goods for tailoring of clothing.

He met my mother Erna, who had a son Joachim born in 1927, from a previous marriage. Mother was not born Jewish, but converted with all the obligations of our religion and followed all the rabbis' dictates. My parents were married with acceptance as per Mosaic laws. Although Father was a modern man and tried to fit into the current society, he valued his family roots and continued his strong connection to Judaism and attended the Great Synagogue of Danzig.

Danzig - 1939 Father, Roman, Brother Joachim and Mother

Apparently Father made a comfortable living because Mother was able to stay at home and be a housewife. Father was a kind and decent man who appreciated his family and honored his obligation as a stepfather, without difference between my half brother and me.

I was born on July 9, 1935 in Danzig or as it was known in Poland as Gdansk. Our life was uneventful. I spent most of my time with the immediate family, Father, Mother and my brother Joachim, who was at times my playmate and my protector.

Registered letter sent to Mother on November 19, 1942

When anti-Semitism became more threatening, many Jews left the country as did our neighbors and friends who were able to get to Cuba. They encouraged Father to do the same, but he did not believe that this threat would be of a long term.

Eventually, and actually, to raise funds to get Jews out of Danzig, the Jewish community sold ritual objects, which are now in the Jewish Theological Seminary in New York. They even sold the Great Synagogue for a fraction of its

119

value. The last congregation gathered there was on April 15, 1939.

Danzig was occupied on September 1, 1939. Those who were transplants from Poland were ordered to return to their country of origin as it was for us, to Rzeszow. We too, Father, Mother and I left in the Fall of 1939.

At the outbreak of WWII there were about 14,000 Jews living in Rzeszow, a third of the total population.

Fortunately we were not yet in Rzeszow when the first German bombs fell on the city on September 6, 1939. It was occupied four days later on Sept. 10, 1939. The anti-Jewish reign of terror began.

When we came to Rzeszow, we settled as best as we could near Grandfather's sister-in-law, Great Aunt Lotka, and near Great Aunt Rucia Haar, in an apartment with a balcony facing the courtyard, which was located on the main street. Father was still able to open a small grocery store also on the main street but with a Polish partner, a front man.

By this time, schools were off limits to Jews and, of course, I only knew German, which was the language in Danzig. Father hired a tutor to teach me to read and write in Polish. The only friend that I recall playing with was Dr. Heller's daughter living upstairs of us. He let us play with his guinea pigs, which the doctor used for pregnancy tests.

Late in 1940, the Germans designated an area for all Jews, which all had to move to. Father helped the family move with us and we shared a small flat, seven of us. The conditions became difficult and overcrowded. An important German factory complex, for the production of aircraft engines, employed Jewish slave labor from the ghetto.

On December 17, 1941 a decree was issued, establishing a ghetto in Rzeszow, and on January 10, 1942 the ghetto area was closed off, surrounded by about a ten-foot-high wooden fence. There were three gateways guarded by Jewish and Polish police. Only those with a job outside the ghetto were entitled to leave, imprisoning approximately 12,000 Jews, about 3,000 of them refugees and people deported from western Poland. Overcrowding, starvation and lack of hygienic facilities resulted in the inevitable epidemics, in which hundreds died.

During this time, Mother talked herself out of going into the ghetto and stayed in our apartment on Main Street, which eventually the Germans confiscated but they let her live in a small room employing her as a maid cleaning woman in the Nazi headquarters (*Ortskommandantur*). She convinced them that she was not a Jew.

From July 7 to 13, 1942, the first mass deportation took place to the Belzec death camp. At the time of the deportation, about 200 Jews were shot for their passive resistance. Father was among them. Another 1,000 were taken to the nearby Rudna Forest and killed there.

On August 8, 1942, about 1,000 women and children were deported from the ghetto to the Peikinia Concentration Camp, where all of them were exterminated shortly after arrival.

As the selections were happening, Mother managed to have me smuggled out of the ghetto and kept me, mostly isolated, in the apartment. When the Germans questioned her at Gestapo headquarters, brazenly she told them, "Look at him, he is blond and blue eyes and speaks only German." And they took her word and did not pursue any further. I slept in the kitchen and kept out of sight. I had a bed in the large pantry, also used as a coal storage.

On a few occasions, I ventured to play on the street and a soldier befriended me. Mother did warn me to be careful and hide my Jewish identity. I knew to hide myself when I needed to use a bathroom since I was circumcised.

I spent most of the time alone, playing on the balcony and had a crow pet which found me and I fed it breadcrumbs.

We learned about Father and about the children and women that were being taken away. I too was discovered and no appeal helped. The Germans were not convinced that I was a German child, and they demanded that I be returned to the ghetto within ten days or they would take action against Mother.

Mother insisted that I stay completely out of sight, not to be seen anymore. When I try to recall how I spent those years, it is almost a blank.

So we passed our time until 1944 when the Russian front was getting closer. Somehow Mother was able to get us back to Danzig where we lived in the outskirts with my maternal grandfather. On the train from Rzeszow to Danzig, late in 1944, when danger of discovery threatened, I was hidden under luggage and clothing.

The Russians moved closer to Danzig, and the bombardments were nightly for a few hours. The city was in shambles.

On March 26, 1945 we were liberated by the Russians. We moved into our own apartment and stayed there until August of 1945. As Jews were leaving Poland, since even after the war was over, it was dangerous for us to remain. So we too smuggled our way to Berlin where we registered with UNNRA who got us out of the Russian Zone to Hanover. From there we were assigned to a DP Camp, Foerenwald.

I was now eleven years old and started school. Again, I had to learn a new language. Everything was taught in Hebrew. Those years, which freed me from hiding, were the best years of my childhood. We grabbed at life and all opportunities.

Because we had Haar cousins living in the United States, HIAS helped us locate them and even though they were very poor, they sponsored us to come to the States. In the meantime, we discovered that my Uncle Eliyahu survived and was living in the DP Camp Lansburg. He immigrated to Israel. We have a wonderful family there.

After going through all investigations and being approved with our visa, we were allowed to come to America. We sailed on the army hospital ship, General Hersey, and arrived in Boston on August 27, 1949. The cousins met us at the port and took us back with them to their small apartment in Manhattan. We stayed with them for a short time.

When Mother saw that they could not help us, she appealed to the HIAS, and they helped us get a cold water flat for which we paid $20.00 rent per month. Mother got a job working in the garment district as a seamstress and I continued my education entering seventh grade.

Roman 2013

School was my passion. I needed to succeed and so I did. I graduated high school and served in the army for two years between 1955 and 1957. After my service, I worked at a variety of jobs and went to college at night. I graduated with a BBA degree from Baruch College and continued to earn my Masters.

With time, I adjusted to the American ways and eventually got married. I have a son Stefan and grandchildren, Caroline, Juliana and Jeremy and a stepdaughter Wendy who is a physician in Washington, DC.

My career was in the pharmaceutical field for over thirty years. It was gratifying and it was where I earned a good living.

My wife and best friend Norma and I retired in Florida in 1994 and are enjoying our life.

As a member of the Child Survivors/Hidden Children of the Holocaust, I knew that I am one of them. I was not only hidden physically but also hid my identity. I became someone else, not a Jew.

This brief memoir is to add to the tragedy that befell the Jewish people. It must serve as a memorial to my dear father and extended family and be a lesson to remain. It must be taught that such an evil can occur again if we do not recognize and prevent it from happening.

"Never Again" should not only be a slogan, but a commitment!

FROM BERLIN ON A JOURNEY TO HELL

by Herman Haller

Very little is known by most readers about Jews of Berlin. Jews arrived sometimes in the 13th century and for centuries they were abused, discriminated against and killed for many unfounded reasons. Between 1446 and 1571, they were expelled and their properties were confiscated. When they returned to live in the city, they were designated to live in ghetto streets and were engaged in money lending and small activities in trade.

After opportunities and freedoms were eased for Jews, by 1933 the population grew to 160,000.

In the years between 1933 and 1939, as Jews had their social and economic rights eliminated, Jewish communal life increased dramatically. Jewish children were not permitted to attend public schools and had to attend Jewish schools. Jews were not permitted to intermingle with any citizens other than their own kind.

In June 1938, the round-up of Jews began as thousands were arrested without reason. On the evenings of the 9th and 10th of November, now known as Kristallnacht, the night of broken glass, Jewish synagogues and shops were vandalized and burned down throughout Berlin, Germany, and Austria. In the months that followed, more and more Jews were arrested or put to work at forced labor camps. About 12,000 Berlin Jews were sent to the Dachau Concentration Camp that night.

Still, in their own sphere, Jewish life remained vital. In 1941 things deteriorated more severely. Many more areas of the city were declared off limits for Jews, and laws were enacted requiring Jews to wear the yellow Jewish star.

Between 1941 and 1943, all the city's Jews were deported to camps throughout Europe, and on June 16, 1943, Berlin was declared Judenrein "clean of Jews." By 1945, only 8,000 Jews remained in Berlin. Those who survived were either in hiding or blended in because they were married to non-Jews.

This was the background where my family lived, thrived and became the unwanted, abused people.

I was born in Berlin on July 6, 1924. My parents Anna and Victor Haller were unfortunately divorced in 1930, when I was almost seven and my brother Alfred four. Father escaped to Palestine before the war.

Back Row: Grandfather Menachem Mendel, Aunt Greta, Uncle Moritz
Front Row: Mother, Grandmother, Uncle Victor, Aunt Bertha, Uncle Herman

We were raised by our Mother and were surrounded by an attentive caring family of grandparents, aunts, uncles and cousins. Our family was observant and the *Shabbes*, Sabbath, was a time when the family gathered for this revered day.

Our apartment was situated in a large building in the center of the city. The tenants were both Jews and non-Jews. My mother's side of the family were in the furniture business, and all uncles and aunts owned stores in Berlin, including Mother. After the divorce, Mother continued to run our store with the help of her brothers.

I remember vividly my grandparents Menachem Mendel and Gittel Grzyb. This name was changed to Gibbs when their children arrived in the United States. They immigrated to Germany before WWI from Poland in order to improve their life and raise their standard of living. Once in Germany, Grandfather opened a furniture business and expanded to all the children.

My grandparents were very religious and followed orthodox Judaism. The celebration of the Sabbath and all holidays were observed with devotion. Grandfather prayed every morning in the small *shtibel,* little prayer house.

My mother, Anna, was one of six children, three boys and three girls. Five survived the war. Before the war and *Kirstalllnacht* in 1938, Greta, their oldest daughter immigrated to Israel, then Palestine, and Morris, Bertha, and Victor were able to immigrate to the United States. Herman, who married a Polish woman, immigrated to Poland before the war, but he died in the Lodz Ghetto in Poland.

I remember, with a sense of pleasure, my kind and loving Grandmother who baked *challah,* a braided design bread, and cakes for the Sabbath. My job, every Friday afternoon, was to go to her house and pick up the *challah* and cakes, which enticed the senses as I carried them to our home.

One day, in 1934, the Nazis or the police came into the *shtibel,* during the services and took all the men to the police station. They were kept locked in the basement without food and water. They stayed there for three days. When my grandfather came home, he said he would no longer stay in Germany. They returned to the city of Tarnow in Poland where he still owned a home. He left his furniture business to his youngest son Victor.

During the war, all the Jews of Tarnow were put in a ghetto. One day they were rounded up and all were shot.

Although we did get along with our neighbors and non-Jewish acquaintances, we did not socialize with them. Our life was bound to our family.

My days in the public school system were difficult. Even the teachers displayed their anti-Semitic outbursts.

I recall the year 1933 when the Nazis came to power. They staged a boycott against all Jewish shops and were carrying signs, "Don't buy anything from the Jews. The Jews are our misfortune. *Die Juden sind unser ungluck.*"

Under the Nazis, Jewish children were not permitted to attend the public schools, so my brother and I were transferred to a Jewish school. I was in fourth grade and Alfred was in second.

My mother continued to run the store by herself until November 9, 1938, *Kristallnacht,* when our store was destroyed and it became impossible to earn a living in Germany. On that date, Mother was very concerned about her sister Bertha and her two very small children, Harry and Ruthie, because she lived in a building where there was a synagogue.

After the night of *Kristallnacht,* Mother sent me to check up on Aunt Bertha who did not answer the telephone. Riding on my bicycle through the streets, I saw the disaster that was directed against Jewish businesses. All display windows were smashed and the stores were vandalized and looted. Glass was everywhere. I could not ride on the bike. The synagogue that was just a few doors away from our apartment building was vandalized and all the *To-rahs,* scrolls, and prayer books were thrown into the street and set on fire. There were bonfires everywhere; all synagogues were destroyed.

When I finally arrived at Aunt Bertha's house, I saw a big mob in front of the apartment building. Her store windows were broken and glass was everywhere. A large crowd was gathered watching the burning synagogue, which was behind the courtyard of her building. The police were there, but they just watched and did nothing to interfere. The fire department was pouring water on the adjacent building to make sure that the building did not catch fire, while the synagogue burned.

As I mingled among the crowd, I found out that the people living behind the store, Aunt Bertha and children, managed to go to some neighbor's house where they were safe. I was afraid to identify myself, but I was actively listening to the crowd to find out as much information about my aunt Bertha and my cousins without being observed.

I rode back home immediately to report what I had seen and heard. My mother was relieved that her sister and the children were okay but under the circumstances, we realized that it was over for us in Germany. We tried to leave but it was difficult.

Alfred Age - 9 - Herman Age - 12

My mother's younger brother, Victor, managed to obtain a visa to go to the United States and was waiting for a passage ticket on a ship that would depart from Antwerp, Belgium. During the *Kritallnacht,* he was already in Antwerp waiting for the ship. My mother was able to contact him and asked for his help to get us out of Germany.

Mother and Uncle Victor devised a plan for my brother and me to travel to Paris to a distant relative via Brussels, Belgium. When the train would stop in Brussels, our uncle would be waiting for us.

Our journey, leaving the family behind, was stressful and worrisome as to what awaited us. We were still children, I was fourteen and my brother not quite twelve. We were instructed to behave as if this was a normal trip. When the train arrived at the border of Belgium, the German passport control came on the train and asked my brother and I for our visa. We had no visas. We showed them our German identity card, with a large "J" on it, which identified us as Jews. We also showed them our return train ticket from Paris to Berlin. We told them that we were visiting an uncle in Paris. The control officer looked at his partner and said, "Let the French worry about these kids." and let us pass.

We were met at the train station in Brussels by Uncle Victor and Aunt Lilly. That is how we got out of Nazi Germany after *Kristallnacht.* Mother could not use this method to escape Germany but our uncle arranged for her to go to Aachen, which is on the border between Germany and Belgium. There she was to meet a guide who was going to take her over the border into Belgium during the night. Unfortunately, Mother was caught at the border and sent back to Berlin.

Our dilemma was, should we return to Berlin? My uncle determined that since we were out of Germany and his ship was arriving to take him to America, he and cousin Emmanuel in Paris would come to take us across to Paris. And so it was.

Emmanuel, a French citizen, was able to go across the borders without difficulties and took us on a train to Paris. The plan was that he would meet us on the Belgian-French border on the train. When the border patrol would ask for passports, he would show his French passport and tell them that we are his children.

Emmanuel had a home in a suburb outside of Paris where we stayed. But he was afraid to let us go outside. We did not speak the language and he was basically hiding us. He knew that if the French police would see us, they would instantly send us back to Germany. After about eight weeks, he decided that it would be better for us to go back to Belgium since their police were more lenient than the French.

We traveled back to Belgium with Emmanuel where he handed us over to the Jewish Agency. The agency was full of Jewish families who fled Germany seeking help and asylum. The police gave us identity papers, but we had to report every three months since we were *etranger,* strangers. The agency placed us with Jewish families in Antwerp. The family we stayed with, the Sterns, were paid by the JOINT, (American Jewish Joint Distribution Committee), for our keep.

While we were in Belgium, Mother received a letter from the police precinct in Berlin telling her that she must leave Germany within eight weeks or be subject to imprisonment or heavy fines. The letter said that she could appeal this decision but that the appeal would be denied because of the Nuremberg laws. I still have a copy of that letter. At this point, she was desperate to leave Germany. Because her sister Bertha's husband had relatives in England, my mother was able to get into England with their help. There was a shortage of domestic help there and if one was willing to work in a household, a work permit to enter England was issued. And so she was able to leave Germany legally.

We corresponded with Mother. The Jewish Agency tried to make an exchange to have us go to England to join her while other children could come to Belgium to be united with their parents. The British would not allow such an exchange.

On May 10, 1940, Germany invaded Belgium. The JOINT could not continue their funding and the Sterns just left their house and tried to get into France. When they discovered that the Nazis had invaded France too, they returned home and told us to leave, because they were not getting any funding for us from the JOINT. We were virtually out in the street. The Belgian authorities did not believe that two children were living by themselves and would not give us food ration cards. My brother and I had a hard time, to say the least.

A well-to-do Belgian family, who knew my little brother, thirteen years old at that time, took him in and hid him where he survived the war. I was on my own. I found menial jobs to support myself. This was not legal because I had no papers to work. I slept where I could. I found a job in a bakery keeping the oven warm all night. Here I slept on the bench where they made the bread. I just lived from day to day until June 1942.

By this time, the Nazis were rounding up people from the street, saying that they needed workers in Germany because all their men were at war. The Nazis closed up a whole area, and I was caught in one of these roundups. I was sent to France to Boulan - Calay, thirty kilometers from the French coast. One could see the "White Cliffs Of Dover" of the English coast. Here the Germans were building the Atlantic wall of defense because they thought that the Allied invasion would come from that side, being the closest distance across the English Channel.

The conditions were horrible. There was no water, no sanitary facilities. The Germans dropped us off in a spot and told us to build a camp. We were guarded by Organization Todt, a Third Reich civil and military engineering group, which is equivalent to the Army Corp of Engineers.

I was there from June 1942 to October 1942. In September 1942, I became sick with typhoid fever. Since our guards were afraid that they would catch this disease, they took me and five others into a hospital in the city of Boulan, France. The hospital made special accommodations for us in their basement and gave us medication. As sick as I was, I appreciated, for the first time in a long time, a clean bed.

After about three or four weeks, the German guards came back and told us that we had to go back to Belgium because they did not need us anymore. Back in the labor camp Boulan - Caley, we saw that it was in fact being dismantled and all the people were loaded back on a train. We were sent back to Belgium and were told that we would be repatriated.

When the train arrived to Brussels, they did not let us get off. They connected additional cars with more men, women and children who came from

Malines, an army compound in Belgium. When the train arrived in Marlene, Belgium, additional families, who were gathered outside on the platform, were herded into the box cars.

I have a copy of my transport record. That transport record was given to me after the war by the association of people that were in Marlene, 1942-1944. They gave this transport record to the survivors to show where we came from.

The transport left Belgium on October 31, 1942. I was number 559 of the sixth transport that was sent to Auschwitz from Marlene. All in all there were 848 men, 94 women and 41 children; a total transport of 983 souls. Only 54 men survived.

After about five days, the train arrived in Auschwitz. We did not know what to expect. We saw a big sign *"Arbeit Macht Frei,"* Work Makes Free. They immediately separated the men from the women and children. We were told to leave all of our belongings to one side.

We saw men walking about with striped pajama-type uniforms. They were sorting our belongings and stealthily were whispering to us, "Walk, walk, walk." We did not understand what they meant by that. We were told that those who could not walk should step over to one side and trucks would be sent to drive us to the camp. All the men who were able to walk marched into the camp. We learned later that all the people who could not walk were sent directly to the gas chambers and the crematorium.

To describe Auschwitz is beyond any human words or imagination. We were completely ignorant of what was ahead of us. SS guards immediately separated the transport. We were told to walk to the campsite.

Inside the camp, all our hair was shaved and numbers were tattooed on our forearms. My number is 72554. We were referred by number only and no longer had a name. When we arrived inside the camp, we were quarantined.

I was assigned to work on a detail called *Werkhallenbau*, which later became *Krupp* and *Weichsel-Union*. We were put to work to build a factory. It was bitter cold, and we had no warm clothing. Krupp today make coffee pots. During the war, they made cannons. They were looking for mechanics to repair the machinery. Being young, I told them that I was an apprentice in a machine shop, and was admitted to work inside the factory. Everyone wanted to work inside to be protected from the elements.

At first, we had to clear the field, mix cement and carry the bricks to build the factory. After the factory was completed, Krupp brought in the machinery, which was badly damaged by bombardment. The Germans then were looking among the prisoners for mechanics and machinists to restore the machinery. When they found the machinery was beyond repair and had to be scrapped, that is when *Weichsel-Union* took over and I worked in the machine shop. *Union* had brought their own civilian personnel. Our *Meister,* expert master, was *Meister* Fischer, a true Nazi and *Meister* Tuschke, a more humane person.

"*Union*" manufactured detonators (*zuender*). In the machine shop, we repaired all the machinery and made dies and gages, etc.

Herr Graeber and *Herr* Schoepfer were *betriebsleiter,* factory manager and director. Both of them were very good Nazi party members. They never talked to us, only gave orders through the guards.

The machine shop was divided into three sections. One was the main machine shop, lathe milling machines, etc. To the right was a thin smith shop and to the left was a "*haerterei*" where the electric furnace hardened machine parts.

The "*Union*" workers were quartered in the main camp Auschwitz 1, which consisted of brick buildings with two floors. The upper floor housed 600 people and the lower floor housed 400. Since the union worked around the clock, the shifts ran from 7:00 a.m. to 7:00 p.m. and from 7:00 p.m. to 7:00 a.m.

Once, when I worked the night shift, I rose early in the afternoon to find additional food since our rations were completely insufficient for survival. I was housed in the upper level of my block. While descending the stairs, I encountered an SS guard coming into the building, going up the stairs. I could not escape. As required, I removed my cap and shouted *achtung* very loudly. He continued to mount the stairs, and I was under the impression that he was satisfied with my performance. All of a sudden, he turned around and called me back and asked for my name. At that moment, I did not realize his sadistic thoughts so I gave him my name. He then repeated what is your name, and I realized what he meant and I answered *schutzhaftling,* prisoner*, Jude* #72554. Then he said, "Follow me, I have to teach you to remember your name." He went upstairs and sat down on a table with his feet resting on a bench and ordered another prisoner to clean his boots. He said to me, "You make 100 knee bends and count." When I got to 20, he said "I can't hear you count. Start from the beginning." When I counted to 100, he said to do 100 more and count backwards. After that he ordered me to lay on my back and do ten pushups. After that he told me to turn around and do ten more on my stomach. I was completely exhausted and could hardly move. So he took his pistol from his holster and pointed it to my head and ordered me to do ten pushups or he will shoot me immediately. With my last strength, I was able to satisfy this monstrous sadist, and he let me go.

By that time the word had gotten around and my comrades were waiting for me outside because I had to report to work at the *Union.* After my ordeal, I was hardly able to walk, but my friends encouraged me to report to work since reporting sick would cost me my life. With the help of my comrades, they almost carried me between them, I was able to report to the factory. Once inside the building, we went to the *haerterei*, hardening shop, which was in the rear of the machine shop and was not in use during the night. My friends hid me inside a tool cabinet to recuperate.

During the night I heard two German civilians, *Meister* Fischer and an *Overmeister*, head of the craft guild, whose name I do not remember, enter the darkened *haerterei*. I heard them open the window and were laughing and saying, *"Siehst du wie die Juden brennen?"* Do you see how the Jews are burning? From that window one could see the crematorium and the chimney's red flames in the sky. They smoked their cigarettes and left. Luckily I was not discovered. I hid in this cabinet with the help of my comrades for several nights until I recuperated sufficiently to continue working.

There was a *kapo* named Schultz. Thank God he was not my *kapo*. He was especially brutal to the women prisoners. I believe he was Slovac. Outside the factory was a partial underground building, a powder room, where they stored dynamite powder, which was needed for the detonators. I knew of the women working in the powder room but did not know them personally. Through rumors we learned of these courageous girls who smuggled out the dynamite powder with the ultimate aim of blowing up the crematoria. They succeeded in blowing up one gas chamber and crematorium. Unfortunately the four girls were caught and horribly tortured and hanged. We were all forced to watch this horror.

I worked in that factory until January 18, 1945. When the Russian army moved up from the East, we could hear the artillery fire. The Nazis decided to evacuate Auschwitz. The "Death March" became the last event to destroy the rest of the Jews. Many people died on the way from starvation, cold, exhaustion, and those that could not walk were shot and left on the side of the roads. We marched to Breslau where they put us on open cattle cars. We were on this train for seven days without food or water. We ate snow to survive. After many torturous weeks walking from camp to camp and sometimes traveling in open coal-train cars, I arrived in Buchenwald. From the 110 people on my cattle car, when it arrived in Buchenwald, there were only seven of us that were alive.

Buchenwald had many German political prisoners that were there for many years. The prisoners took us to a sick bay. I was brought to *Krankenblock* #61, sick block, because I could no longer walk. We had bags of straw and slept three tiers high. My feet were frozen and I was completely exhausted. The seven of us from my car were frozen with frost bite.

Because prisoners in Block #61 were of no use to the Germans, the commandant from the camp issued an order that our starving portions of bread be reduced in half because he said, "Sick people are not productive." So all we got was one liter of a watery slop of a soup per day. No bread. The inmates from Buchenwald were trying to help us as best as they could.

Finally by a sheer miracle, the morning of April 11, 1945, American soldiers liberated us. I was so sick that if the war would have lasted another day or two, I would not be here to tell this story.

When the first American soldiers arrived, I did not realize that they were Americans. I was wondering what kind of guards they were sending us now. The Americans took the sick people out, put us on stretchers and transferred us to a civilian hospital in Weimar, the town next to Buchenwald, where I received the proper care.

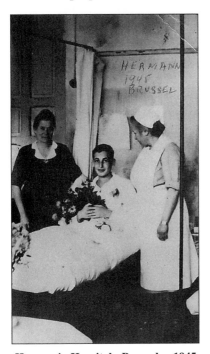
Herman in Hospital - Brussels - 1945

Many of the prisoners died after the liberation because the soldiers felt so sorry for them and gave them all their food rations. Their digestive systems could not handle the quantity and richness of this food. Since we were in a hospital, they knew to give us baby food to slowly get our systems back to normal. I weighed fifty-five pounds.

After the war, there were many displaced persons, survivors. The Allied forces made an agreement that any displaced person could go home or wherever they wanted to go. The government of Belgium had sent a delegation to Buchenwald to find citizens from Belgium, both Jews and non-Jews, to get them repatriated. Since I came from Belgium and I spoke Flemish and some French, I told them that I would like to go back to Antwerp where I used to live and gave them my old address.

The American Army placed me on a transport plane on May 5, 1945, to return back to Brussels, Belgium. The Belgian population gave us a big reception at the airport, and we were immediately sent to a hospital. I was sent to St. Gilles Hospital in Brussels where we were treated by Belgian doctors.

After we regained some strength, we were sent to a recuperating home. I stayed almost one year to get back to normal. While I was in this home, I contacted my uncle in America and found my brother who survived the war. My brother hid in the mountains of Belgium, among Belgian farmers.

With the aid of Jewish agencies, I was able to contact my relatives in the United States. They sent me the necessary papers to immigrate. I came to the United States in September 1947. My brother went to Palestine. My mother remained in England where my brother and I visited her often. She was very ill and refused to come to America to live with me. She died in 1979.

I lived and worked with my uncle on a farm in New Brunswick, New Jersey. Later I went to New York City where I lived with my Uncle Victor and Aunt Lilly and got a job working in a factory. I worked during the day and went to night school to learn English and further my education. I took advantage of all types of on-job training and taught myself much through library books and "how to" books. I self studied electrical work and was able to take a test for the New York City Transit Authority where I worked in the signal department.

I joined the New World Club, a social club for people who were immigrants from Europe. I met my wife Lore there, a transplant from Heidelberg, Germany, who arrived in 1938.

We got married on December 25, 1949. We have two daughters Heidi and Elizabeth, and four grandchildren, Jonathan, Alison, Sean, Amanda.

Herman 2013

We retired to Florida and have found ourselves among Holocaust survivors who also were children during the war. We joined the organization, the Child Survivors/Hidden Children - Palm Beach County, who are active speakers at schools and many other venues. They are contributing to the history of the evil that befell the Jewish people. We were children who were denied every kind of dignity. Our families were destroyed, our childhood was stolen.

I am proud to be part of this hard-working group and to contribute to the tapestry that is the Holocaust.

With gratitude I need to say: "God Bless America" that gave us shelter and opportunities to rebuild our families and our lives.

IN A POTATO SACK TO FREEDOM

by Eta Levin Hecht

Eta with her parents 1939

During the Holocaust, over 96% of Lithuania's Jewish population were murdered by the Nazis, assisted by the local collaborators. As a historian once said, "It was safer to be a Jew in Berlin than in Lithuania."

I often think, how is it possible that I survived the murderous time when the killers took over our world and the rest of the world stood silent?

My life is not one of a hero because I was just a little child during those evil years, but every survivor must record and speak of their own personal experiences and their town's life and destruction. I am compelled to speak in order to add to the total picture of history that was the Holocaust.

The city of Kovno, *Kaunas,* Lithuania is my family town and where I was born. The history of Jewish life spans to the 13th century with the periodic anti-Semitic expulsion and invited return to this country.

Between 1920 and 1939, Kovno, located in central Lithuania, was the country's capital and largest city. It had a Jewish population between 35,000 to 40,000, about one-fourth of the city's total population. The Jewish population of the country was about 220,000. By the end of the war, almost all of the Lithuanian Jews were murdered, higher than anywhere else in Europe. One of the main reasons so many Jews were killed in Lithuania is because of the local Lithuanian collaborators.

Kovno was known for its vibrant Jewish life and culture. It was an important Zionist center. The *yeshiva,* religious school, in Slobodka, a poor suburb of the city, was one of Europe's most esteemed institution of higher Jewish learning.

Kovno Synagogue

I was born on October 7, 1938, an only child. My mother, Rachel Abramovitch Levin, was from a nearby town, Visokedvor. She was the youngest of six children. Her mother, Ette Abramovitch, and father Shaoul Abramovitch, encouraged their children to improve their lives, especially through education, and so she became a teacher in the Jewish school system in Kovno. She sang in the choir at the Great Synagogue in Kovno, which was also the synagogue where my parents were married.

Father, Rafael Levin, was born in Vilna, Lithuania, where at times it was under the Polish control. He was the youngest of six children. He too became a teacher and principal of a Jewish school. He lost his father, Yehuda, when he was nine years old. His mother, Fayge Levin, lived with us before the war. She died in the Kovno Ghetto when I was four years old.

Until the age of two and a half, I had a normal and happy childhood. We shared a small apartment with my grandmother Fayge, who took care of me while both my parents worked.

Because Germany and the Soviets had a Non-Aggression Pact and an agreement to divide territories, they came in September of 1939 from the East and West. They occupied at either end of their borders and divided Poland and other smaller countries to be claimed as their own territories.

The Soviets occupied Lithuania in June 1940, including the capital of Vilna, which the Lithuanians then relocated to Kovno. During their short time in our area they enforced the doctrine of Communism. Many were arrested and their properties taken away. Soviet authorities confiscated properties of many Jews. Hundreds of families, among them factory owners, merchants, public figures, Zionist activists and leaders, were rounded up and exiled to Siberia.

This Non-Aggression Pact did not last long. After the Germans attacked the USSR on June 22, 1941, the June uprising against the retreating Red Army began in Kovno. A short-lived period of independence was proclaimed in Kovno on June 23, 1941.

On June 24, 1941, the Soviets retreated. Before and after the German occupation of the city, on June 25, bands of Lithuanians went on a rampage against the Jews, especially those living in the Slobodka suburb. The Jewish people became targets of hatred and murder.

They murdered more than 3,800 Jews and took hundreds more to the Lietukis garage in the city center and killed them there. This was done not just by the Germans but also by the Lithuanian collaborators.

The murder of Jews continued when the Germans took charge of the killings. And so the nightmare began. Jews were expelled from universities, they lost their jobs, properties were confiscated, possessions were stolen. Jews had to wear a yellow Star of David on the front and back of their garments. They were not allowed to use public transportation or walk in parks and were not allowed to walk on sidewalks, only in the gutter. Jews had to walk on the right edge of a pavement one behind the other.

Then in July 1941, the Germans announced that the Jews of Kovno were to move into a ghetto, which was to be located in the suburb Slobodka. By August, the ghetto was sealed off and was encircled by barbed wires. It was heavily guarded with posts manned by Lithuanian guards. The gates were also watched by German police. Anyone trying to escape was shot.

The housing in the ghetto was primitive. Everyone was crowded together. Our family, my parents, grandmother and I had one tiny room. My two cousins slept in a very small space in the small kitchen, and another family was in another room.

Food was rationed. Most of the time it was a piece of bread and a bowl of soup that consisted of water and potato peels. Men and women were forced into slave labor, working eighty to one hundred hours per week. In fact, the Kovno Ghetto became a concentration camp in 1943. Life in the ghetto was a continuous struggle for survival from hunger, disease and the constant threat of death.

In the autumn of 1943, the SS assumed full control of the ghetto and converted it into the Kovno Concentration Camp. When the ghetto was sealed off in August 1941, it contained over 29,700 Jews. In the following two and a half months, 3,000 Jews were killed. On October 28, the Great Action, *"Grosse Akzie"* happened during which 10,000 persons were murdered, half of them children.

In the beginning, one could not believe what was happening and everyone thought things would get better. After all, Germany was the most civilized nation in the world. Who would think that it would give us Auschwitz?

To keep resistance to a minimum, the Nazis lied and used elaborate deceptions. For example, shortly after the ghetto was established and sealed off, the Nazis announced that they needed 500 volunteers, doctors, lawyers and leaders of the Jewish community for work in the municipal archives. The 500 Jews were taken away and never returned. They were all murdered. Nonetheless, there was an underground movement in the ghetto and there were attempts to help save lives by sneaking young people out so that they could join the partisans and fight the Nazis.

There were individual acts of heroism. My mother risked her life when she smuggled an egg or a small piece of bread into the ghetto for me. The guards searched everyone returning to the ghetto from work. My mother could have been shot if found out.

There were also individual acts of sabotage such as placing defective parts in equipment which the Germans required. The hope was that it would undermine German's efforts in the war. This was done by Jews working in the factories.

The ghetto provided forced labor for the German military. Jews were also employed as forced laborers outside the ghetto, especially in the construction of a military airbase in Aleksotas. The Jewish Council, Council of Elders, also created workshops inside the ghetto for those women, children, and the elderly who could not participate in the labor brigades. Eventually, these workshops employed almost 6,500 people. The Council's intent was that the Germans would not kill Jews who were producing for the army.

Although the Jews were unable to carry out a unified, large scale resistance, they chose spiritual resistance. The slogan was *"Bleiben A Mentch,"* to remain human.

Not to submit to the Nazi dehumanization, the underground provided schooling for children seven to twelve years of age. Children over twelve had to go to work. People wrote poetry, kept diaries that were buried in crates in the ground so that the world would know one day what happened. However, how do you fight when you are starving, are infected with disease, lack the necessary arms as well as fear for the safety of your family? Mere survival was an act of heroism.

One morning, on October 28, 1941 at 6:00 a.m., three months after we arrived in the ghetto, trucks came rolling into the ghetto streets with loudspeakers, announcing that everyone was to leave their home and assemble on "Democratic Square," which became an ironic name for roll call. Anyone found in their home would be shot.

We were instructed to lineup in rows of eight and were forced to stand all day in the cold, without food or water, while a Nazi, Helmut Rauca, sat on a chair pointing left or right as people marched by him.

Our row consisted of my parents, my grandmother, myself and several other elderly people. As we approached the Nazi, he pointed us to the left. My father had noticed that the old, the disabled and children were sent to the left. As we were pointed to the left, Father quickly pulled us to the right. He later recalled that his heart told him, "Don't go to the left." We found out that those who were sent to the left were sent to their death. Ten thousand Jews, 4,000 of whom were children, were selected to be killed that day. This day became known as the *"Grosse Aktzie"* - The Great Action.

After that day, my parents realized that they had to keep me inside. Most of the time I sat under a small table that was covered with a long overhanging cloth. I felt more secure under there as the Nazis were always searching for children and one never knew when they would show up.

One day we learned that the Nazis were coming, so my parents rolled me up in the bedding and placed me on the bed against the wall, like the back of a sofa. I was told not to move. I felt that I was going to suffocate, but I did not move. I was aware of the danger as young as I was.

Years later my parents would discuss events that happened in the ghetto and my mother would say to me, "You wouldn't re-member that, you were too young." But of course I remembered.

Another vivid memory is when I was five and a half years old. Two *Kinder Aktzies* - children actions, of March 27 and 28, 1944, is when the Nazis carried out a massive organized search for children.

A cousin came running to our house warning us that the Nazis were search-ing all the houses for children. We quickly hid under the stairs that led to the second floor. Our cousin leaned an old mattress against the opening of our hiding place to camouflage the opening. We sat there for two days and two nights. It was cold, we had no food and I had a cough which I tried to suppress so that the Nazis wouldn't hear me. We could hear the sound of the Nazis' boots climbing the stairs above our heads. Also we could hear the screams outside of mothers and children. We could see their shadows through the cracks between the wooden boards of our hiding place. The Germans were snatching children away from their mothers and threw them on trucks and took them away. Their destination was evident.

When the *Kinder Aktzie* was over, my parents realized something needed to be done to save my life because our luck would run out. They had to get me out of the ghetto. But how? They had heard that the Jewish underground had con-tacted a priest who in turn had contacts, Christian families, who were willing to save Jewish children. But the priest said he couldn't do anything until after Christmas. This was the end of March. We couldn't wait that long.

My parents were getting frantic. Finally, contact was made with a Christian colleague of my father, a principal of a Christian school, whom my father knew before the war. Father asked him if he would take me in order to save my life and he agreed.

My parents then proceeded to instruct me about my escape. They told me that I was not to admit that I was Jewish, to say that I was Christian. They gave me a new name, *"Elenyte."* I was instructed to say, if asked about my parents, that I was abandoned as a baby. My parents then practiced with me to sit mo-tionless in a potato sack which my mother would carry out of the ghetto on the day of my escape.

The long awaited day of my escape arrived in April of 1944, three weeks after the children action. I was placed in the potato sack. Mother joined the other women lining up to march out of the ghetto to their place of work, carrying the bag like a bag of tools, again risking her life for me. Outside the ghetto gate Mother quickly slipped away while the other women distracted the guard. Mother removed her Jewish star and ran to meet a woman who was to take me to my new family, the Lazauskas family.

I had spent almost three years in the ghetto. I was a child at that time but I never had a childhood. I did not have toys as children do, I could not play outdoors. I did not have companions my age to play with. The only companions I knew were hunger and fear. When my mother carried me out of the ghetto, I did not know whether or not I would ever see her or my father again.

I would like to relate to you an incident that happened while I stayed with the family. One night, planes were flying overhead and Mr. Lazaukas thought we were going to get bombed, so the whole family went to hide in a bomb shelter leaving me alone in the house. They left me because they were afraid to arouse suspicion from their neighbors.

Four months after I was smuggled out of the ghetto, on July 8, 1944, the Kovno Ghetto was liquidated. The remaining Jews were transported by trains to concentration camps in Germany, and the ghetto was burned down. They traveled for days, overcrowded, without food or drink. Many died en route. All felt this was the end.

While they were still on Lithuanian territory, my parents decided that my father should jump off the train, hoping that at least one parent would survive so as not to leave me all alone.

Father jumped from a small window of the moving train and fell unconscious. A railroad employee found him and proceeded to take him to the Gestapo. My father managed to free himself from him and ran away. In August 1944, the Russians occupied the territory where my father was hiding, and he became a free man. Three weeks before the Soviet army arrived in Kovno, the Germans razed the ghetto to the ground with grenades and dynamite. As many as 2,000 people burned to death or were shot while trying to escape.

After my father jumped from the train, the train went to Dachau and Stutthof Concentration Camps - camps of suffering, brutality, deprivation and horror. The fact that there are survivors of these camps is a miracle. Stutthof, my mother's concentration camp, was liberated by the Russians in June of 1945. After I was reunited with my father, we still did not know if my mother had survived.

When my father came to look for me, I had not seen him for almost a half a year. I remember my father asking me if I recognized him. I didn't answer. I was still afraid.

A year later we finally learned that Mother was alive, and Father made plans for our reunion. He sent Mother a letter telling her to remain where she was. Father decided that we should not remain in Lithuania. We escaped from Lithuania to Lodz where we were reunited with my mother.

I remember worrying if I would recognize my mother after not having seen her for a year and a half. I did. We were now finally together again. It was truly a miracle.

We survived the horrors of the Holocaust, while about forty of our extended family were murdered by an evil people who destroyed the Jewish life in Europe.

There was no safety or future for us in Poland so we followed the illegal immigration to a DP Camp in St. Ottilien, Germany and then transferred to a DP Camp in Munich. From 1946 to 1948, we waited for a visa to go the United States.

The DP Camps became the place of renewal and establishing hope of a future. Here is where my little brother Ari, Harry, was born in 1946. I attended the Jewish school in Munich, studying Hebrew for about one year.

We were told to go to France from Germany, that it would be easier to receive visas there. So we went to Paris, France but actually it took longer. We waited for four years. Here, at the age of ten, I continued my education and completed elementary school in four years.

Finally in October of 1952, we came to the United States where my father had a sister, Mary Levin Tolkoff, in Morristown, New Jersey, who had come to the United States before WWII. She and the family sponsored us and we settled near them.

My father got a job in a screen factory and Mother became a bookkeeper in a department store.

I was fourteen years old, and the public school I attended in France somewhat prepared me to be able to enter high school, but

Eta 2013

I did not speak any English. My will to fit in and take advantage of the education was most important to my family and me. From the time I was fifteen, I also worked in the same department store as Mother until I graduated college. I continued my education at Rutgers University, Newark, New Jersey, commuting by train for four years. I graduated in 1960, majoring in economics and languages. After graduating Rutgers, I worked for Johnson and Johnson in

140

their International Legal Department. I also worked at the hospital of the University of Rochester, New York in the office of the Psychiatry Department.

I met my husband Warren in 1959, and we were married in 1960. Our family grew and my own personal joy was to rebuild our family. We have a daughter Rena and two sons, Steven and Daniel and eight grandchildren. Can you hear the laughter and joyfulness that is my family?

My life story on these pages I want to also use as a monument to my murdered family. Their names are not inscribed anywhere. Their graves are ashes and unknown common graves of Kovno Jews murdered.

We, Lithuanian Jews, all over the world, have an annual memorial service on October 28th. We say *Kaddish,* Jewish prayer for the dead, for the Jews who were murdered.

The world cannot forget the lesson of the Holocaust. The revisionists and the Holocaust deniers will not succeed in their task.

> *One of the famous Righteous of Nations, Chiune (Sempo) Sugihara, was stationed as a Japanese Consul General in Kovno. He had issued visas to over two thousand Jews and facilitated these Jews to escape out of Lithuania.*

A JOURNEY OF MANY PORTS SEEKING SAFETY

by Joe Henner

Berlin, Germany was a place where many Polish Jews found opportunities to a better life than in their homeland. Here they established new roots and families, without the daily discrimination and lack of prospects. That is what brought my father and mother to escape their burdened lives in Warsaw and mother from Krakow.

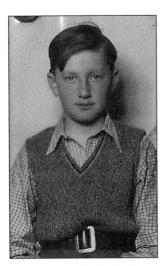

Joe Age - 14 Holland

Father Benjamin found a niche for himself in the poultry and egg distribution business. He met Mother, Fanny, who was a seamstress and added to the income and quality of life for our family. Together they succeeded in establishing a comfortable life for our family, my four older sisters and me.

I was born on March 29, 1925 and was cared for by my loving parents and a maiden aunt who helped my parents with the care of our home and the five of us. Even though we lived a more modern life than my parents had in Poland, we did not abandon our Jewish customs, celebrations of holidays and even ran a kosher home.

We lived in a comfortable third-floor apartment and by the time I was nine, my family had a summer cottage with a couple of acres of land in the countryside. We had over seventy mature fruit trees, which supplied bushels of fruit to many of our friends and relatives who came to visit at the cottage. We also had a vegetable garden. My parents let me spend my summers actually staying in the cottage alone. There was no danger for a boy of ten to remain there. But I do remember that my nights brought forth scary images especially when the branches of the trees banged against the cottage on windy

142

nights. We had a man caring for the grounds, and my time was spent in playing with the local German children. On the weekends, the family came down to the cottage to get away from the hustle and bustle of their work and the fast life in Berlin.

My father was an easy going, quiet man who was slow to anger. I remember his displeasure only once when I took a plum from a store without paying for it. The punishment of a good spanking was painful, but mostly I was greatly hurt that I disappointed my father. Father was a devoted parent who valued his children. Mother too was a reserved quiet lady, although she was more likely to deal with any discretions that she found inappropriate from her children and had a *kanchik*, a leather strap, handy.

I attended regular public school and also a Hebrew school where I was being prepared for my Bar Mitzvah.

In 1937, a great change happened. All Jewish children born to Jewish German citizens were not allowed to attend school. I, on the other hand, because my parents still had a Polish passport, was considered a Pole, not a Jew, and was allowed to continue. But the teachers kept on interrogating me to have me identify myself as a Jew. I don't know why I had the foresight to evade the answer they were looking for.

As a boy of thirteen, I was shocked to experience the reality of what it meant to be a Jew during the terror of *Kristallnacht* on November 9, 1938. That morning I was excluded from the school and life became a continuous struggle for all Jews. I was taunted "Dirty Jew" and was at risk of being beaten by the indoctrinated youths.

Kristallnacht was also when my father was deported to Poland because he was considered a Polish Jew.

It is tragic that my parents did not take the advantage of the two opportunities to leave Germany before the borders closed and the arrests began. In 1933, Father applied to resettle in Argentina to develop a ranch. The only condition was that he had to come without the family and work for five years to prove himself and then the family could come. Of course, this was not acceptable to my father. Another opportunity which became closed to us, was when mother's sister sent us papers to immigrate to America. She came to the United States in 1913, but the American Embassy declined our visa because the quota for Polish Jews was not due for a few years. So here we were stuck.

Soon after Father was deported, a friend of his, a German detective, came to our apartment to warn Mother to send me away from Germany because arrests of Jewish boys would be happening any day. The family decided to heed this warning and sent me and my cousin Joseph Waldman, the same age as me, out of Germany.

Our destination was Holland. Two thirteen year old boys were put on a train on a journey without any papers, and actually not knowing where or what to do. We got on a train at the Holland border. When the conductors and all staff were changed from Germans to Dutch, we got off the train and hung around the station. As the train was pulling away, we jumped on and continued our journey. We were discovered by the Dutch and were arrested but fortunately not sent back to Germany. They turned us over to a Jewish organization who took us in to a children's camp.

This camp, actually situated in a building in Gouda, took care of about ninety boys and girls. We had chores and attended classes. We played sports and a kind Dutch boat owner took us on excursions to enjoy the outdoors and nature.

I was assigned to kitchen duty from early morning to get all the stoves and ovens fired up and boil water. This was my assignment three times a day for our meals. In reality, I liked this responsibility because I felt like one of the grown boys.

We were separated from family over nine months. During this time, my sisters were able to escape to Shanghai, China. At the beginning of 1939, Father got permission to return to Germany, with a visa for three days, to pick up Mother and get out of Germany. They too managed to book and pay for tickets on a ship to travel to Shanghai. This was our only hope to get away. When they reached Naples and waited for the ship, they contacted our camp and advised them to have me join them. My cousin refused to come with me and remained in Holland. He was arrested during the Nazi takeover and sent to Auschwitz where he was murdered.

I got on a boat to England where I was met by a Jewish man who took me around London and treated me to a "hot dog," which I accepted, being afraid to insult him by refusing. I really thought that it was food made from a dog, and of course, learned that it was a delicious sausage on a bun.

My journey continued by getting on a Japanese cargo ship, which also took on passengers. Until uniting with my parents, the ship made stops from South Hampton, England, at Gibraltar, Marseilles, and finally we arrived to Naples where my parents were waiting for me. Here about 400 Jewish people were taken on this long journey of five weeks. We continued through the Suez Canal, Port Said, Singapore, Colombo (now Malaysia), Hong Kong and finally Shanghai.

Arriving in Shanghai, we were met by my sisters who helped us to adapt to this most unfamiliar culture and lifestyle. We were fortunate to have come with some funds and since everything was very cheap, we were able to buy a house, which had modern facilities, where we all lived together. My parents immediately sought a way to make a living for us by opening a European style cafe, where Japanese officers who were educated in the United States, foreign residents and visitors were happy to find something familiar to eat and drink.

Many had to find means of providing for themselves since there was very little support especially after UNNRA and other support organization had to pull out after the Japanese attacked Pearl Harbor. Our situation was by far not dire, and my dear parents tried to help the ghetto community as much as they could. Life was full of hardships. To see the suffering of our people broke our hearts, but we were all in the same boat.

When the ghetto was established in February 1943, we were forced to exchange our home with a Japanese family, which happened to be the house where our cafe was located within the ghetto perimeter. While the ghetto had no barbed wire or walls, a curfew was enforced and the area was patrolled. Food was rationed, and everyone needed passes to enter or leave the ghetto.

I attended school to learn English and also attended the ORT school, where I learned mechanical skills and also to become a locksmith. Eventually I got a job on the outside of the ghetto working in a metal works place where we produced lighters, cigarette cases and even lipstick cases.

The ghetto was under the temperamental egotistic Japanese overseer, Goya. We were at his mercy not to offend him in any way in order to get a pass out of the ghetto to work outside and look how to get some food or means to keep going.

Even though we were sequestered by the Japanese, we avoided coming face to face with a Japanese soldier for fear of being abused. In hindsight, I see that we were in a haven escaping the murderers of Europe.

I remained in Shanghai for nine years. When I applied for a visa to settle in the United States in 1947, it was approved because I was born in Germany. My parents, who were considered Polish citizens, finally were approved in 1950 and joined me in New York.

I sailed to San Francisco and then continued to New York where I got a room in a rooming house. Immediately I searched for a job and got one using many of my learned skills at ORT, working for a car company which was eventually taken over by General Motors. I worked for them for thirty years.

Adjusting to the American ways did not take long. My immersion through the military service and the availability of opportunity, made it easy for me, considering all the struggles of survival that I had gone through. I felt

Joe - U.S. Army

truly an American when I was drafted. I served for two years in a tank company during the Korean war, but I was sent to Germany.

I met Florette Bleeker in December of 1955 and we were married in October 1956. Our son Edward and daughter Randy enriched our lives.

When I look back at the personal history of my life, it has been difficult, but it cannot compare to what happened on the soil of Europe. The killing of innocent people blemished my life with a sadness and mourning. When I think of my lost childhood, my opportunities of a normal safe life, and people who were murdered in the Holocaust, it breaks my heart. They were my aunts, uncles, cousins who lived in Poland. About sixty members of my family in Poland and Germany were murdered and became the gains for the Nazi killing machine. I want to disconnect from this memory, but I cannot.

Joe 2013

For many years I never thought of myself as a survivor. I was not in danger of being killed outright. My immediate family, my parents and sisters survived in Shanghai. But after meeting many survivors, especially after we retired to Florida in 1997, we were drawn to others who had similar histories.

I began to attend meetings of the Child Survivors/Hidden Children and found a commonality and comfort, where my story adds to the varied facets of what was the Holocaust.

On occasion, I speak to students leaving them with an understanding that the Holocaust was not only concentration camps tragedy. It took many forms and ways that the Jewish people were singled out for the Final Solution.

I share my story to add to the history of the exodus of Jews from the European continent, some by ship to places like Shanghai and just a few other places.

The Six Million Jews, their souls were sent through the chimney stacks by the brutality of the beastly people who sought to destroy all Jews.

MEMORIES OF A CHILD

by Adele Bogner Judas

How absurd and painful it is now at the age of maturity, to think back and remember that my earliest recollections are only of hardship, hunger, danger and fear of dying. It is unreasonable that a child of three should have to grasp the concept of pretending and lying in order to protect herself and her family's survival.

I was born in 1936, Adele Bogner, in Belgium. My father, Simcha, and mother Gitel Rifke, immigrated to Belgium around 1930, along with their first child, my sister Henny. My brother Max and I were born in Antwerp. My father, a carpenter by trade, provided a secure life for us.

Our house, a traditional Jewish home, must have been a loving place. I personally have no memories of the good life. My first memories start in May of 1940, when the Germans invaded Belgium. The terrifying explosions of bombs frightened me and reflected fear in the adults around me. The loud bursts were deafening and only the

Adele Age - 10 1946

embrace of my cuddling siblings and parents helped me feel some sense of security.

As the occupying armies entered Antwerp, we escaped the onslaught of the Germans by getting onto a train headed to Switzerland where Mother had a brother who was a Swiss citizen. To our dismay, we found ourselves being transported to the South of France instead and were interned in a concentration camp. We were shuffled about to a variety of concentration camps, Gurs, Rivesaltes and Brens. One of my vivid memories is the barbed wire fencing that surrounded the camps and the straw mattresses, which were our beds in the dreary, overcrowded barracks.

147

When we arrived to France I was three, my brother was nine and my sister was eleven. One particular camp, Rivesaltes, stands out in my memory where the, *"appels,"* selections, were held at 5:00 a.m. every morning in all kinds of weather. We had to stand outside the barracks until the roll call was completed.

On one particular morning, my mother and I were boarding a train, being part of the selection to be taken to Auschwitz. I could sense high anxiety in the crowd and felt it in my mother's hand as she held on to me with a grasping hold that almost felt abusive. Just before the train was to depart, a guard came to check our names and could not find us on his list. With an authoritative voice, he demanded that we get off. To this day I cannot come up with an answer as to this happening. The only name I can assign to this occurrence is a miracle.

Because the Germans valued carpentry skills, my father was considered a valued inmate and was made a manager and supervisor of forty other carpenters. His status extended to my mother who was assigned to work in the camp kitchen, which helped our survival with the additional accessibility to food.

To keep the inmates in a constant state of anxiety, the Germans at times had selections of only men to be sent off to Auschwitz. Another day, to keep the populace off balance in a state of fear, they selected both men and women.

On one occasion, when they were after men only, my father cut a hole in the ceiling of the barrack, just big enough for a human body to squeeze through. He hid there among the attic beams for two weeks. At this particular time the family was together in the barrack and Mother was able to pass food through the hole and remove the waste. When the Germans appeared again and asked me where my father was, somehow I knew that I could not give away his hiding place. As a child of only four, I knew instinctively what to say. It was a fearful time and a struggle for survival.

During the next three years, I recall being taken to a number of children's homes and one in particular, Beaulieux. Although my daily life was more comfortable, I felt forlorn without the presence of my parents.

In June 1943, the O.S.E. *"Oevres au Secours des Enfants,"* an organization that helped children escape, helped us, my sister, brother and me on a journey to safety to Switzerland. My recollections of that journey are vivid to this day even though I was only six.

We were put on a train, traveling for two days, and found ourselves at the border of France in Annemasse where fifteen other children joined us accompanied by one adult. Our stopover at Annemasse, for two nights, was spent in being briefed and coached on what to do, when and how to cross the border and what to say in case we were caught. After this intense indoctrination, on the third evening, my siblings and I and an adult lady took a trolley to the outskirts of Annemasse. Eventually we were led to the nearby forests to meet a guide who would help us cross to Switzerland. We waited that night, hidden

148

under a tree, lying flat on our bellies until the other fifteen children were able to join us. It was a very dark night.

I was scared and tried to find comfort by holding on to my sister. After a time we heard the sound of footsteps, which turned out to be our crossing guide. We had to overcome many obstacles on this stealthy journey into Switzerland. We crossed many rows of sharp rolled barbed wire fencing in order to get to an open field. The older children helped the little ones over the barbed wires and suffered many cuts and injuries to their hands and arms. We were carried by the older children to keep us warm and protected while crossing a small shallow river. We finally arrived at the clearing where a huge barbed wire fence, six feet tall, stretched in either direction without an end, out of view.

My sister, being the oldest, ordered that my brother and I stay close to her and not be separated. Max was a very agile youngster and soon climbed to the top of the fence. Suddenly he heard a voice saying in French, *"Halte la, a combien vous etes la?* Halt, how many are you there?"* Frightened by this sudden voice, he jumped off the fence back to the French side and joined us running to seek a hiding place. We hid in bushes, holding our breaths, until the guards left with those who had crossed, and they were seized. Our guide then explained to us that they were on the Swiss side and that the children were safe.

After we climbed over that fence, we began to speak in loud voices so that we would be heard by the guards of the Swiss side. These guards were accustomed to these tactics since many had escaped to freedom from the Nazis and the Holocaust.

Finally safe on the Swiss side, all the children were taken to an interrogation office where each one had to wait to be questioned. Even though I was only six years old, they did not spare me from the interrogations and questions, such as "Who helped you over the border?" At last they took us to a place where we were locked up for the night, leaving us on straw mattresses without food or water. The next morning we could see a schoolhouse across the street. A woman, who lived in that building. apparently knew why we were there, asked how many are we. She returned soon with nineteen rolls in a basket. The boys collected and connected their belts and dropped the belt/rope out of the window to raise the basket with rolls to us.

Since my memories begin with concentration camp life and hunger, these white delicious rolls where a revelation that such food existed. We were kept for another day of interrogations by the Swiss, then transported and quarantined for three months in detention camps. During this time, the Swiss government was making sure that we were not bringing in diseases. Also that our relations, in my case my uncle and aunt in Zurich, would take care of us. But sadly when they found out that we would become their responsibility, they declined to take us in. At that time I looked at it without any hurt, but as I reached my adult years, knowing the refusal of so many to take in Jews, my own relations' act became even more unforgivable.

We were sent off to a children's home in Heiden where we remained until June 1946. At that time, with the help of the Red Cross, we were reunited with our parents who were lucky to have survived the many concentration camps.

Fifteen hundred children, who had taken refuge in Switzerland, were returned to Brussels. Many found only horror stories.

My siblings and I were greeted by our mother and father. By this time I was nine and half years old. I did not recognize these strangers and held back from hugging them. When I saw the embraces of my sister and brother, I was reassured that I too should hug them. Still, I asked in a careful voice, "Are you my mother?"

My parents had been liberated from the camps and returned to Antwerp where they found complete devastation. Nothing was left of their apartment or their possessions. Those apartments that were intact were cleaned out from all their contents. My father's trade at this time was most useful. He was hired to rebuild all the synagogues in Antwerp.

Adele 2012

Now as a parent and grandparent myself, I look back at my childhood and realize how difficult it was to be separated from my parents at the age of six. It was far from a normal upbringing to be a prisoner at the age of three, not knowing what the next day would bring. Will I be alive tomorrow? It should never be a question that a three-year-old needed to worry about.

Although I, like many of us who went through the Holocaust, cannot remember all the details of the experiences. What I do remember has left an imprint of the past in my heart. Memories that should have been of parks, zoos and birthday parties were replaced by barracks, beds of straw, hunger and the fear of dying. The young innocent years of childhood, with all the special attention, encouragement and love of parents were taken away.

I arrived in the United States in 1958. I was determined to revive and rebuild my life and family. My husband Kurt and I have a lovely family, children and grandchildren, who follow Judaism in the orthodox tradition.

Our yearning for a life in Israel finally came to fruition in the Spring of 2007. We have resettled in Jerusalem, close to our daughter and family.

CHILD'S TEARS STILL SPILLING

by Kurt Judas

Ihringen, a small town near the French border in the south of Germany, was the ancestral home for the Judas family for generations. Jews were already present in the mid-13th century. All were murdered in the Black Death persecutions of 1348-49 and the Jewish settlement was only renewed in the mid-19th century, with the Jews maintaining a population of 150 to about 180 people - 4% of the total population until the Nazi era.

Kurt 1946

Jews played a leading role in the town's economic life as retailers and wholesalers. Seventeen of the twenty four Jews serving in WWI received the Iron Cross. The Jewish population in 1933 was around 163 souls. Under the Nazis, around three-quarters emigrated. Of the thirty six expelled to the East, three survived the war.

My father, Leopold, one of thirteen siblings, earned a living in the family business, a trader in horses. He married Cary Ramsfelder in 1931, and soon their life was enhanced and complete when I was born in 1932. We lived in comfortable circumstances and felt secure among our neighbors. The family practiced Judaism by keeping a kosher home, observed the Sabbath, and supported the beautiful synagogue of the town, which the community and other nearby Jews attended.

As an only child, I felt happy and protected. When I reached school age in 1938, I was sent to my aunt's in Freiburg to attend school. By this time, the forty-eight Jewish children were separated from the German student body by having two schoolrooms assigned for us. On the weekend, I rejoined my parents and family.

Life for Jews, by 1938, became a puzzle of how to live, how to adjust, and how to keep safe. The nightmare of WWII years began the morning of November 10, 1938 after the "broken glass," *Kristallnacht.* Some fifty Jews including myself, at the tender age of six, were paraded in front of the burning synagogue to see it being consumed by flames. All the Jewish men of the town where arrested and sent to Dachau. The families were placed off-balance, bewildered as to what all this meant. After a few weeks, Father was released from the camp, returning a broken man.

All our possessions, our businesses were confiscated. We were forced out of town. I recall the tragic picture of my parents and elderly widowed grandmother trudging with difficulty, pushing the meager belongings in a pushcart for twenty miles to Freiburg. Our search for housing and safety made us move numerous times. Life was a constant struggle. Business and employment for Jews became nil.

On October 22, 1940, most Jews of that region were deported to the concentration camps in France, close to the Spanish border, Camp Gurs and Camp Rivesaltes. We were sent to Gurs, which was an internment camp in the foothills of the Pyrenees Mountains of southern France. It was originally constructed to hold Spanish Republican soldiers fleeing the Franco regime in the wake of the Spanish Civil War.

Around 4,000 German Jewish refugees were added to the French left-wing political leaders. Twenty-two thousand prisoners passed through Gurs, around 18,000 of whom were Jewish; 1,100 internees died in the camp among them my grandmother, Bertha Judas, who died of typhoid and dysentery after six weeks in camp.

Many Jews were sent on to Drancy or Auschwitz, but there were also a number who escaped, were released, or were able to emigrate. Transit camps functioned as collection centers for prisoners, most often Jews bound to extermination or labor camps of Eastern Europe.

Leopold Judas   **Carry Judas**

We endured inhuman conditions. Barracks and straw mattresses were the norm. Young children were kept together with their mothers. Fathers were put in separate compounds. Food became very scarce.

152

After about six months, we were taken to another concentration camp, Camp Rivesaltes. There the howling winds, the inclement weather, abominable hygiene facilities and starvation existence made havoc of our lives. These camps were under the administration of the Vichy collaborators. It held 8,000 internees, 3,000 Jews, with a population of 3,000 children. At this location, somehow my cousin was able to rent a farm at Caussades and rescued our family out of camp. Under the darkness of night, two families, aunts and uncles, squeezed under the wires and were taken to a waiting car and driven to the farm.

We had visions of a safe haven, but no such luck. We were apprehended and returned to the camp. At this time, deportations had started.

Camp Gurs

In the middle of 1942, the Final Solution was implemented, ordered by Eichmann. As many as a thousand people per convoy, including children, were shipped in cattle cars for their final journey to Auschwitz. My father was taken on Convoy #31 sometime in 1942 to Auschwitz. I never discovered if he was sent to the gas chambers upon arrival or was killed during his internment. Convoy #62, November 20, 1943, sent off 1,200 deportees, among them my mother. One hundred and sixty four children were under eighteen years old and eighty five under twelve. Only 241 men and forty five women were selected for labor. The rest were marched directly into the gas chambers.

Mother, who had the foresight or just wanting to improve my life, permitted me, age ten and my seven year old cousin, to be among the approximately

153

6,000 children who were periodically smuggled out of camps to orphanages. At the first home I learned French and attended classes. The memories of this place bring bitter silent tears whenever I think of the place. For the first time, I was among strangers whom I wanted to trust but who abused and betrayed me and have left scars into my senior years. After a few months my cousin and I were transferred around to a succession of homes. The next was a French castle, where the resident children spoke Spanish. To my surprise, and I don't know when or how, I found myself speaking the language and do so to this day.

We eventually found ourselves placed in a Jewish home at *Montintin* near *Limoge*. All through the war food was scarce. Eating grass or finding berries and nuts on excursions was a lucky Godsend.

OSE - its full name is the Union Mondiale Pour La Protection De La Santé des Populations Juives et Oeuvres De Secours Aux Enfants -- operated eight homes throughout France in an effort to rescue children from the Nazis.

It became apparent by the end of 1943 that keeping many children in these homes was very risky. The OSE was worried for the safety of the children as the Nazis were overrunning France. On April 6, 1944, in the town of *Izieu*, the Germans succeeded, by the order of Klaus Barbie, to apprehend forty four Jewish children and their five adult caretakers who were transported to Auschwitz where they were immediately gassed.

One day, riding on a bus together with my younger cousin, the lady accompanying us suddenly leaned over toward me as she whispered in my ear, "These are your falsified ID papers," as she slipped them into my hands. My new name became, Charles Julien and my cousin became Maurice Julien. In an instant, I changed from being Jewish to Gentile. A slip of the tongue could mean life or death. We were dropped off at a farm at Neyron near Lyon, with an elderly couple by the name of Bourats, who risked their lives to keep us. I attended school in the village where, at times, I was beaten by my teacher for no reason. At any hint of Germans in the vicinity, we ran into the forest to hide.

The war years and the confinements were slowly coming to an end. Bombardments by the Allies could be seen for miles. The smoke and flames rose skywards. In 1945 the OSE representative retrieved us and placed us in an orthodox home in Hirondelle. The war was over.

Those lost childhood years only bring back memories of the struggle for survival. Like in a dream, I no longer had to play the part of a Gentile youth. No more going to mass on Sundays. No more kneeling before graven images. When I crossed my heart I sometimes wondered why me? But I was alive.

Off came the coat of many colorful facets of Christianity but to my greatest disappointment, I tried to put on the coat of Judaism; alas, it did not fit. I was a young boy lost. It was like the whole world was on one side and I was on the other side. I was alone. Suddenly my sense of family and belonging surfaced. I remembered my mother, my father. What could have happened to them? Why did my mother abandon me? The searches for my family on the lists were fruitless. During my adolescent years, my thoughts found consolation and comfort that someday, sometime, someplace my parents will come strolling down the Avenue of the Righteous. We will fall into each other›s arms and once more we will be reunited.

As I was being prepared for my Bar Mitzvah, I steeled my heart and soul to place all my energies to life and a future.

Kurt 2012

In 1946 my cousin and I were allowed to enter the United States to join our aunts and uncles who received us as their own. I was fourteen and a half years old.

My American immigrant family arrived before the war, and their life was one of struggle to make ends meet, but they took on the responsibility of their nephews and guided us to adulthood. I continued my education and at my family's urging, I decided to become a baker, which served me well all my life.

At the age of twenty, I was drafted into the army and was sent as an MP to Japan. I am proud to state that my service to my country, America, is an honor and privilege.

Adele and I married in 1959, raised two wonderful children and now we are grandparents of ten. We retired to Florida in 2001 and have found ways to serve and be part of a community. We are members of the Child Survivors/ Hidden Children of the Holocaust group. I serve as a volunteer for the Sheriff's Department as a COP (Citizens Observer Patrol) and volunteer at a Boca Raton Hospital.

And as my wife Adele writes, our yearning for a life in Israel finally came to fruition in the Spring of 2007. We have resettled in Jerusalem, close to our daughter and family.

MY ROMANIA, MY DESTROYED HOME

by Hedviga Gruenstein Jungstein

It is important to learn where my own suffering began and the evil that befell the Jewish people in Romania. The Jewish community of Greater Romania was diverse and numerous, with roots in the histories and civilizations of the Regat, of Habsburg Austria, of prewar Hungary, and of the Czarist Empire.

Hedviga Age - 16

Out of the prewar Jewish population of 800,000 in the three provinces, of Wallachia, Moldova and Transylvania, at the end of the WWII only 400,000 Jews remained in Romania.

In Transnistria around 200 different labor and concentration camps were set up for Jews throughout the 118 counties in the area. About a third of the people at these camps died of malnutrition, and the remaining were killed without warning, in the most brutal ways.

On October 16, 1942, 150 young women were told that they would travel to work in German hospitals. They were brought to the forest, where they were raped and killed. Such evil and brutal killings were the norm.

The Antonescu regime, together with German troops, tortured Jews until August of 1944. Many others died when they were moved to regions further west, such as Bassarabia, Bukovina, and Tirgu Jiu.

Methods used to destroy large numbers of Jews did not include gas camps or other methods used in Nazi Germany but more primitive practices such as suffocation, starvation, and hanging.

Gypsies were also victims of the Holocaust; 26,000 were deported, around 7,000 were massacred, and 3,000 starved to death. They were not considered enemies but inferior beings that had to be killed in order to keep the Romanian race pure.

For many years I had the feeling that all who heard a little about my survival thought that I appeared from the ashes of the Holocaust. They could not visualize that I, we, came from loving homes, good lives, education opportunities, friendships and hope for a good future.

I was born on May 10, 1924, in Baia Sprie in Northern Romania, a beautiful resort town graced with beautiful scenery of mountains, a mining town, which provided jobs for many. It was located fifty kilometers from the city of Satu, where the Chasidic Satmar Jews originated. Baia Sprie had a small Jewish population of about seventy families.

My mother Esther was a beautiful and spirited lady. Her looks and fashionable clothing exemplified a picture of modern elegance. Father Josef, a talented goldsmith and designer, ran his own business selling jewelry made from precious metals. Mother was also involved in the store. Her sincere dealings, charming ways and charisma drew customers to the store. The business thrived.

Father was reserved, and treated me and my brother Rommy, two years younger, with caring attention. I was very much attached to Father, appreciating his musical abilities, playing just about any instrument, and also his acumen in his knowledge of nature. Often he took me along to explore the nearby forests to teach me about the various medicinal plants. With his example and encouragement, I learned violin. Father was my teacher.

My mother's father, my grandfather Michael Liebowitz, was taken to serve in WWI and never returned. Grandmother Miriam, the beautiful Miriam, as she was called, raised their eleven children on her own. She did not want to remarry, because she did not want a stepfather for her children. She raised her children, running a catering business for Jewish weddings. Ten of the children were killed in the Holocaust.

We lived a comfortable life in a home that was situated near a brook. The rippling sounds of the flowing waters still bring feelings of a time of peace and affection. Because Mother also worked in our store, we were able to afford help to keep the house in order.

Grandmother Miriam

As many Jews, we lived a more assimilated life. We spoke Hungarian and Romanian. Our home was kosher. I remember Father going to *shul,* synagogue, every morning. He was a respected member and sat at the right side of the rabbi. He was charitable and supported many worthy causes including the famous *yeshiva,* religious school.

I attended the secular school where I excelled and was the only Jewish child and was well accepted among the students. But I do recall that

157

the undercurrent against Jews was expressed by my teacher. She had asked a question which no one could answer except me. Her comment was to show the kids that a "Jew" could answer. I confronted the teacher asking her why she had to point out that only a Jew knew the answer. The teacher came over and slapped me. When I complained to my mother about this event, she went to school and challenged the teacher. My mother was a tough lady and even though she was the disciplinarian at home, she would not allow harm to her children.

My Jewish education was provided by employing a tutor from the *yeshiva*, while Rommy attended *cheder*, a Hebrew religious school. Many years later, he found his niche and talents by becoming a famous pastry chef. All my interests and achievements were encouraged by my parents.

Our social life was the usual enjoyments, but mostly I remember the excursions into the mountains where we climbed obstacle hills. This peaceful and good life changed when our part of Romania was allocated to Hungary in 1941. Before the partition, the total Jewish population of Transylvania was 200,000. Of these, over 164,000 lived in the territories given up to Hungary.

The newly established Hungarian authorities immediately implemented the anti-Jewish laws that had already been in effect in Hungary proper. The Jewish newspapers were suppressed, including Jewish clubs and associations. The discriminatory measures affected the Jews particularly, curtailing educational and civil opportunities. Jewish students were excluded from pursuing their education. Some businesses managed, for a time, to circumvent the restrictions against them.

A forced labor service system was introduced in 1939 by these new Hungarian rulers. In the beginning, the Jewish recruits of military age, though subjected to many discriminatory measures, fared relatively well. After Hungary's involvement in the war against Yugoslavia in April 1941, the Jewish labor servicemen were compelled to serve in their own civilian clothes; they were supplied with an insignia-free military cap and instead of arms, they were equipped with shovels and pick axes. For identification the Jews were required to wear a yellow armband; the converts and the Christians identified as Jews under the racial laws had to wear a white one.

Despite the many casualties and discriminatory measures, most of the Jews of Northern Transylvania at that time, like those of Hungary as a whole, lived in relative safety. They were convinced that they would continue to overcome the discriminations and hoped for the protection of the conservative aristocratic government. This life and hope was crushed almost immediately after the German occupation of Hungary on March 19, 1944, which included our area.

The policy of the Final Solution was beginning to be implemented with the cooperation of the local leaders by registering Jews and supplying lists.

Unaware of the sinister implications of these lists as well as the visibility of wearing the yellow Star of David. These measures were established to isolate Jews and ghettos of Northern Transylvania.

And so our suffering began. All intellectuals and the young were taken away. Valuables were demanded to be handed over; no supplies were given to the Jewish community, including flour for baking bread. All had to wear the yellow Star of David.

In the Spring of 1944, we were told to take small bundles of necessities because we would be relocated. Carrying our bags, we were marched to the nearby synagogue where we were imprisoned for a couple of days without food or water. Some kind non-Jews snuck some milk for the little children.

After this harrowing experience and inhuman treatment, we were glad when trucks arrived and were told that we were being taken to a better place. Some of our local neighbors ran after the trucks yelling, "Where are you taking our Jews?" But of course this protest fell on deaf ears. It was too late!

They drove us to an abandoned brick yard, where many more Jews were gathered. This structure had no roof; it was open to the weather. All were searched for valuables, humiliating all, by searching in all the body orifices, young and old. There were no facilities of any kind. It was heartbreaking to see the suffering all around. We slept on the cold ground, Mother, my brother and Grandmother, along with hundreds of others.

We received a meager bowl of watery soup, and those who had Gentile friends, sometimes had some food thrown over the fence to them.

We stayed there for about a month. Time became endless. Finally one day, I believe sometimes in May 1944, we were loaded on trucks. They drove us to the train where we were crammed into cattle cars about eighty into a car. Each car was chained and padlocked. Before embarking, again all were searched without consideration and with brutality. All personal papers were taken and torn.

They left in each car a bucket of water and an empty bucket to be used as a toilet. We traveled losing all sense of time, but I think for three or four days. Half of the people died by the time we arrived at our destination.

Finally the train stopped. This was Auschwitz. We were met by German soldiers with fierce German shepherd dogs glaring menacingly at us. There was no time to associate anything. We were ordered to get off and leave our bundles behind. We were starved, dazed, dehumanized from the arduous, suffering, long and gruesome journey. One thing that I noticed that there was a strange odor in the air, which I could not identify. We learned later that it was the crematoria burning humans.

We were separated by Dr. Mengele, the Angel of Death, from the old, the sick, children and invalids. Incoherent, confused, we lost our ability to think rationally after our suffering.

My mother, brother and I were selected to one side, while my grandmother went to the other. The other turned out to be death. We did not realize that this would be the last time we would see my grandmother.

We were taken to an area where we were shaved and sprayed with disinfectants. We were handed out dresses, either too big or too small, but fortunately I got my own shoes. We were then taken to Lager "C," the *Farnichtung Lager*, the annihilation camp. Again, a selection took place and, I was separated from my mother and transferred to Lager "B." I ran back to be with Mother and was accosted by a guard, who kicked and beat me mercilessly and left me bleeding. A couple of my friends who knew me from our town, helped me and dragged me to each *appel*, roll call, so that I would not be shot for not appearing. Thanks to my friends, I recovered but now in my senior years, I have repercussions from that beating. I never saw Mother again. In Lager "B" we were tattooed. I was in Auschwitz a few months.

As the Russians were getting closer, we were transported to Bergen-Belsen and housed in tents. Dead bodies were strewn everywhere. One could not tell the living from the dead. We had no food and the water was a trickle. Conditions and the suffering were beyond description.

I believe that I was meant to survive because I was chosen by an industrialist who came to select workers for his factory in Rocklitz, Czechoslovakia. When we arrived there, it was a miracle. Each had a cot and clean sheets and we were treated humanely. We were trained to work on machines which produced airplane parts. I worked there for a couple of months.

Again the Allied front was nearing and this time we could hear the roaring of the American planes. We were taken away to Graslitz together with criminals and we began the "Death March."

It was Spring 1945. There was no food and even the Germans had none. I became ill with typhus and did not have any strength to continue walking. An elderly German soldier, instead of shooting me, had my group hold me up and walk with them. He spared me and saved my life.

We stopped in a barn where Hungarian Gypsies were among the marchers. I cannot tell why, but a man, a German, told me and my *lager* sisters, camp friends, that he will take us to his house after dark. He and his wife's kindness I will never forget. They heated some water for us so that we could finally bathe and they fed us. The man promised that he would steal a chicken somewhere and make chicken soup for us and he did. In the evening, he took us to his attic and kept us there as the "Death March" continued. He assured us that we would be liberated soon.

A couple of days later, peeking out through a tiny attic window, we saw jeeps flying American flags. By this time, I was very sick with typhus. The three of us were taken to the Red Cross Center where the American soldiers ordered that I be cared for. I was placed in a hospital for contagious diseases, isolated. I was all alone and in a coma for a long time. Miraculously I survived.

The American Jewish soldiers filled up my room with all good things. I questioned where are my two sisters, my *lager, camp,* sisters. They took me with a jeep to search among the scattered survivors, but we could not find them. That night I dreamt about a town sign "Pernarec." The next day I asked the soldiers to humor me and see if there was such a town. Sure enough, my dream led us to my two friends, Helen and Agi, where we were reunited, but I had to stay in isolation for months because I had TB and was treated with penicillin.

The American GI's were kind to us but soon were reassigned to Japan. They gave us money and put us on a train to Pilsen where survivors gathered. From here, we were resettled in a DP Camp Lansberg in housing where the German army stayed before.

After a while I discovered that my brother survived. Our reunion was filled with tears and hope that maybe more of our family were alive. Rommy decided to return to Romania to search for any of our people. I could not go with him because I was still very weak from my illnesses. He found nobody, all were killed.

While still in Germany in the DP camp, I met my husband Aron and we were married in 1946. All refugees were looking for some place to go, which country would take them in to rebuild our lives. Because I had an uncle, my mother's brother, in the States who went to America in the 1920's, he found us and sponsored us to come to the States. It still took years until we received our visas and met the immigration quotas. Finally we arrived in New York in 1949.

I entered school to became a specialized technician to work in the garment industry and was sought after because of my specialty. Aron too acquired skills in the garment industry in the installation of special equipment and being a trouble shooter.

Our life was good. We settled in the United States with a feeling of safety and instead of our large families of Europe, we had many good friends and tried to forget our years of suffering.

We became active in the community and contributed to many charitable causes like, ORT, the State of Israel, American Jewish Congress, Hadassah and many more.

Aron and I moved to Florida in 1986 and enjoyed a few years of ease in our retirement. Sadly I lost my dear husband in 1994.

A few years ago, I discovered a group of Child Survivors/Hidden Children meeting in Boca Raton. I was very impressed with the work they do in witnessing about the Holocaust history and also developing books in order to leave our voices for the future. Frankly, I was not sure that I wanted to have my survival story recorded and now published, but I am convinced that this is necessary.

I became a member and although I am not able to attend all meetings, the correspondence and newsletters tell me what our group is accomplishing. While there, I met a wonderful lady, Helene Greenberg who befriended me and I her. We are like sisters, which is a great comfort that we have each other.

When I speak about myself, I speak with the voices of my family, my people who lost their lives to the hateful murderers. We have to remember and record. Our span on this earth is short, but these stories will become memorials for the future generations.

Hedviga 2012

With the strongest voice that I can emphasize, I state, "We Must Never Forget. We Must Be Aware and Weary. We Must Fight All anti-Semitism. We Must Fight Discrimination."

Hedviga passed away on July 17, 2013.
She was a wonderful lady and her passing is a great loss.

HERBERT KAMMER
IN SEARCH OF SELF

by Herbert Kammer

It came to public attention about a group of Jewish children who were brought to the United States during the Hitler era in the years of 1933-1945 and were placed either in foster or Jewish children's homes.

It is well documented about the *Kindertransport* children who were saved in England. The rescue of about 1,400 youngsters, including me, was not a known story. I am such a survivor.

Herbert Age - 9

It is very disturbing to me that my memory has been blocked. Was I so traumatized by the evil that befell the Jews of Berlin and Germany? I get angry that a piece of my childhood was not only abused but erased from my mind. Apparently the separation from my parents affected me greatly.

My memory begins in Milwaukee at the age of ten. Here I was able to piece together some of my previous life and occurrences with the help of my mother and some of my fellow children who were with me during our hiding and escape.

I was born to Rosa and Georg Kammer in Vienna, Austria in 1931. My mother was a loving woman, who was an excellent homemaker, cook and baker. We lived in an apartment building on the fourth floor and apparently our life was comfortable. My father worked as a clerk for the Cunard shipping line and my mother was trained as a dressmaker.

In 1939, after the takeover of Austria by Germany, Mother managed to get out to England on a work visa and was employed first as a domestic and then at her trade as a seamstress. At the same time, my father and I managed to escape to Brussels, Belgium in the hope that we too would be able to escape and reunite with my mother by fleeing to England.

When the Germans invaded Brussels in May 1940, my father was arrested and sent to Recebedou, a concentration camp near Toulouse, France. He remained there until August 4, 1942, on which date he left on a convoy, presumably to Auschwitz, a concentration camp in Poland. I was left alone but was lucky to have been placed in a home for Jewish children that was run by Alex and Elka Frank, along with one hundred boys and girls, ages five to sixteen.

The Franks and the one hundred children were able to escape on a freight train, at the last minute, to France where they were hidden on a farm in Seyre close to Spain. The living conditions in a barn were very primitive and harsh, especially in the winter. We spent close to a year in this area and then moved several miles closer to the Pyrenees Mountains into an abandoned castle, the Chateau de La Hille, France by *Secours Suisse Aux Enfants*, a sub-sector of the Red Cross of Switzerland. It was directed by Mr. Maurice Dubois. It was a very neglected building and the older boys and leaders worked to make the old chateau habitable.

Herbert - center with suspenders

In 1941, when I was ten years old, along with the nine youngest boys and girls, we were transported to the United States on the ship Mouzinho, under the auspices of HIAS and the American Friends Society, "The Quakers." During this time, I was able to correspond with my mother and learned why I was chosen to go to the United States. HIAS was able to get a signed consent from her for this move.

I was sent to Milwaukee to join my uncle and aunt and their young son, but since they too had recently arrived in America, they were not in a financial position to care for me. So the Jewish agency placed me in the Milwaukee Jewish Children's Home. Here I spent five years.

I began my studies starting with first grade. My curiosity, excellent aptitude and abilities, enabled me to progress, recapture my education and graduate grammar and high school in nine years. I also attended Hebrew school and was a Bar Mitzvah.

Mother Rosa

In 1946, when I was fifteen years old, I was happily reunited with my mother, who was able to get a visa from England. Our reunion, after all the years of separation, was satisfying. I regained the love and caring that only a mother can give. I left the Children's Home to live with Mother and rekindled a family life.

Throughout most of my life, I was curious and questioned my lack of memory. In 1998 I received an e-mail from Walter Reed, one of the children who was in the castle de La Hille with me.

In July 1998, this unusual group of child survivors, held a reunion where I reestablished my ties and recaptured some of my memory. They also held a reunion at the castle and farm in France in September 15-19, 2000. At that time a memorial to the children of de La Hille was placed at the entrance to the castle grounds.

Herbert 2013

I attended the University of Wisconsin where I earned a Ph.D. in microbiology and worked for thirty-four years for firms that manufactured human and veterinary vaccines.

My wife Betty and I have a melded family and seven children between us. We retired to Florida in 1996, and reside in Boynton Beach. We are happy in our community and are involved in many organizations including the Child Survivors/Hidden Children of Palm Beach County. We appreciate and support their dedication to Holocaust education.

IN SEARCH OF SAFETY HIDDEN IDENTITIES

by Ester Frucht Kisner

Busk, meaning stork, was part of Poland until 1772 and during 1918 to 1939. Now it is part of Ukraine (East Galicia). It dates back to the 11th century.

One of the most famous attractions is the Olesko Castle, which now serves as a museum displaying objects from the eighteenth and nineteenth centuries.

The town is built on a hill and is surrounded by brooks and rivers. The largest and famous river "Bug" flows through the middle of town. It is situated thirty six kilometers from the city of Lwow (Lemberg). The nearest railway station is in the village of Krasne, about six kilometers away, which was reached by horse-drawn carriages which were run by a few Jewish families.

The Jewish presence can be construed by an edict from the year 1510 by the Polish King Zigmunt saying that only Christians are eligible for election to the Town Hall. Other legal documents from the year 1500 tell that a Jewish area called Ghetto was located in this town. This is where

**Ester, Mother Feige, Father Isak,
Sisters Sala and Clara**

I was born on August 2, 1930.

During the 17th century, in the eastern provinces, Jews were targeted and many were killed. Research shows that at the end of the 17th century, about 400 Jews were living in poverty, hardly keeping body and soul together. However by 1772, during the Austrian occupation, conditions improved. At the beginning of 1860, Jews were permitted to buy land, deal in commerce and were able to buy lots and build houses in town.

A number of surrounding suburbs were populated by Polish and Ruthenian peasants, skilled craftsmen and other workers. A few Jewish families lived in each suburb as well. The Jews worked in agriculture, had small retail stores selling tobacco, groceries, dry goods; some traded in grain and cattle.

When the Austrian monarchy collapsed at the end of the WWI in 1918, Busk, as well as Eastern Galicia became a battlefield between the Ukrainians, Bolsheviks and Poles. Finally, it became part of Poland. All these battles affected and decreased the Jewish population causing emigration to America.

Busk population and percentages of Jews were:
1921 - 6,148 - 1,533 24.9%
1931 - 7,010 - 2,600 22.8%
Under German Occupation:
1941 - 1,800 Jews
1942 - 2,000 Jews
1943 - 7,494 Jews in ghetto

My maternal grandparents, Ita Landes and Favel Raubvogel, were successful entrepreneurs, dealing in lumber and construction ventures. They had four children, two boys and two girls, Jacob, my mother Feiga, Ester Lea and Mordesh. My mother was her parents' favorite.

My paternal grandparents, Rivka (Bochner) Frucht and Abram Frucht, had a family of seven children, two girls and five boys, Ruchel, Moishe, Hilel, Aron, Laizer, Baila, and my father Isak, the oldest. They were poor and had a hard time scraping together a living. It became my father's duty to help them.

My father, a tall, attractive man, with a self-assured air, found employment at my maternal grandfather's lumber business where he showed great talent, was industrious and creative in all that was assigned to him. My mother, a lovely, pampered, indulged girl, attracted Father to seek her hand in marriage. After finding no objections, they married with the blessings from my grandparents. They had three daughters, my sister Clara, Sala (Sara), and me, Ester.

My family moved to Lwow where Father established his own lumber enterprise and other businesses. We lived a comfortable and modern life with many of the most current advantages of the time. My life was full of exploration, mostly of the adult world. I had a constant companion, protector, guide and caregiver, our Polish maid Maricia, for most of the day. I waited with impatience for my sister Clara, six years older, whom I adored, to return from school. She took over my pre-school education and entertainment.

I started Polish public school at age seven and soon became aware of the anti-Semitism against Jews. I recall feeling punished and humiliated when my teacher expelled me, with contempt, from the classroom when the Polish children were learning their catechism. I could not understand why she was so hostile and mean to me. I was ordered to sit in the hallway as if I misbehaved to earn this punishment.

My parents warned me to avoid certain streets where the attacks on Jews were common. The biggest affront for my sisters was when they could not continue in the Polish Gymnasium because quotas for Jews were in effect. They continued their education by attending the Jewish gymnasium where they received Hebrew and a Polish education.

In September 1939, our peaceful life was suddenly torn apart by a German bomb falling just a few houses from ours. Father packed us onto a horse-drawn wagon and we moved away to an out of the way village to avoid this violence. After the Soviets marched into Lwow without any resistance and occupied our areas, we returned to our home. Thinking that we would be able to settle into a normal and peaceful life, we soon found it otherwise. Father's businesses were confiscated, and he was left without means to earn a living. This was our new world, our new order. We were under communist rule. We had to share our apartment with a Russian family and did not dare to complain.

We soon learned that Father and our family were in danger of being shipped off to Siberia, labeled as a *"burzhui"* class enemy, capitalist exploiter. This is when Father decided that we must return to Busk. We moved in with my maternal grandparents and changed our name to his mother's maiden name Bochner in order not to be found and sent away.

It was 1940, a new era of accommodating the new regime began. A new ideology, a new language, which was Russian and with hope for freedom from anti-Semitism. Father managed to support us with his back door bartering and kept us provided for. I started public school, third grade, where all subjects were taught in Russian. The indoctrination of Communism was at a constant pitch and set to marching songs.

When the pact between the Soviets and the Germans fell apart, Germany attacked Russia. On June 22, 1941 the Germans marched in without meeting any resistance. About 1,800 Jews lived in Busk when German forces entered. We had heard rumors from the arriving refugees from Western Poland of the evil that was happening under German occupation. Without delay, the Germans began their systematic methods of making life for Jews a state of constant unexpected chaos and fear. Many Jewish men were immediately snatched for slave labor. The free movement in public for Jews was restricted, and Jews were physically attacked.

After the German occupation, the ghetto was created in which all Jews of Busk and the surrounding areas were incarcerated. My grandfather's house became overcrowded with five families. Conditions became very dire and typhus spread affecting Clara, Father, and my grandfather, who did not survive this disease.

A *Judenrat*, Jewish Council, was formed, headed by Isak Margulis. They hoped to establish work details trying to make each person important and useful and avoid deportation. Father was invited to be part of this Jewish-appointed government but when he refused, a German officer slapped his face with force, humiliating him in public. Father was in shock, his complexion turned ghostly. I too was in shock to see my brave, clever, strong father, who could conquer anything, turn so pale with quivering lips. I was eleven years old and suddenly I was thrust to endure adult emotions and being brave.

Bronka

Father's keen insight and cunning insisted that I declare myself older and go to work with Clara, cleaning the castle, which became German headquarters and living quarters. He said we would be safer there then being exposed to selections. The Germans, with the help of the Ukrainian collaborators, carried out the first *aktion,* selection, on *Yom Kippur*, Day of Atonement holiday, September 21 1942, murdering about 700 Jews in a village near Zloczow. During this time, Father built a concealed hiding place in the attic for Mother and Grandmother while we were at work. Father became a broken man. He wanted to get away to Hungary, but Mother refused to abandon Grandmother. She was too old and frail to go on such a journey.

When Father was approached by an acquaintance, a *Volksdeutche* from the Gestapo, to provide false papers for Sara as a Polish girl and have her sent to work on a farm near Vienna, Germany, he grabbed this offer and scraped together some gold coins, which he had hidden and agreed to this deal. A while later, Clara too was sent off to do farm work near Hamburg, Germany.

Bronka, a friend and neighbor of Maricia, came to the ghetto one day and offered to take me with and hide me, but Father refused, saying that I was too young to be separated from family, so she offered to hide Mother, Father and me.

Parting from my grandmother left us devastated and like emotionless stones. We were torn but she insisted that we go with Bronka. On April 6, 1943, the three of us left for the village where Bronka lived with her indifferent husband and four children, the oldest my age, thirteen and the youngest six years old. Bronka saw an opportunity to help us and thus help herself after the war because she knew that my father was a successful man and would compensate her.

We moved into an attached, windowless storeroom where she kept some food stuff and had an oven where she roasted pigs and made whiskey from sugar beets, which she sold to locals and to Ukrainian collaborators. This lean-to room also had a cold storage dugout where fresh vegetables and more perishable goods could be kept. She provided straw and some planks for a bed for Mother and me and Father slept on the floor on straw. To this day, I remain in awe that the little children did not give us away even by mistake.

Father became stricken and restless. This turmoil drove him to escape and hide in the forest rather than be cooped up in this potential trap. After a few days, he decided to unite with some men from the ghetto and escape into the deep forest to stay hidden. This was the last time we saw Father. We were told by Bronka that a six year old kid spotted the men and reported to his father who returned with a rifle and killed seven of the men. It was on May 27, 1943. After the war, we met with the eighth man who escaped and who confirmed this event. The ghetto was liquidated on May 19–21, 1943. The Jewish population was deported to Treblinka.

On May 8, 1944, Bonka's house was burned down by the local Ukrainians who hated the Poles. Mother managed to run into the nearby bushes through an escape door from the dugout, while I was mistaken by the locals as Bronka's daughter Juzka. Bronka was wounded in her arm in this skirmish. She appealed to the town elder to stop this violence against her, but she was told to go to West Poland to live among her own and not on Ukraine land.

She managed to get some false identity papers for me and Mother, who now became known as my aunt. Maricia came to drive us in her wagon to Krasne, to the rail station, where we joined Bronka, her husband and children and arrived at a village Nowocielce near Przeworsk to her family. They seemed to recognize that we were Jews and screamed at her "Why are you bringing Jews to us?" Realizing the danger, Bronka gave me a small piece of bread and water and directed me to go to another village and declare that I was a Polish orphan and perhaps I would find safety there. At the next village, I did not know where to turn or what to do; I was on my own, hardly fourteen years old.

After much walking and being tired, I stopped to eat my meager rations and noticed a horse standing tied to a post next to a small tavern. Loving horses, I shared my piece of bread with this beautiful animal when a young fellow, Adam, came out and asked me what I was doing. I told him that I was an orphan. I needed shelter and I would work. For some reason Adam had pity on me and took me home to his parents' house. His father was the chief of this village. He took me to a woman who had a room and would let me stay with her. Seeing that this was a kind man from a kind family, I told him that I had an aunt who needed help too. Together we went to Bronka's and picked up Mother and so we were reunited.

Adam made arrangements that I resume my education and attend church. When our landlady became suspicious about our identity, Adam had me attend underground meetings of the resistors, the AKA, the Polish underground army, which made her understand that she would face repercussions if she harmed us.

We remained here until July 27, 1944 when the Soviet freed us. As soon as possible, we hitched a ride on a Soviet army truck to Lwow hoping to find some of our family and friends, but no one was alive.

Finally finding my mother's cousin who returned from Russia wounded, together we went to Busk, thinking that we could return to a normal life. There were a few Jews who returned from Russia. When we saw that we could not rebuild our lives here nor have a future, we decided to resume life in Pzerwosk where we were able to rent a room, and Mother cooked meals for people.

In the meantime, I heard that my benefactor, Adam, was arrested by the NKVD, the Soviet secret police, for his activities in the Polish underground, which the Soviets did not look upon with favor because Poles looked at the Soviets as occupiers. I went to appeal to the chief of the NKVD, creating a fuss when they would not let me see him. A soldier with a German shepherd dog, who turned out to be the chief of the NKVD, came into the room demanding what was the commotion, coming from a scrawny fourteen year old. I proceeded to explain to him that Adam saved me and my mother and was not an enemy. He looked at me with pity and admiration when I told him that I was a Jew and was saved by their prisoner. He promised to release Adam and that was the last that I heard about my savior. I never saw him again and did not want to return to his village. I was afraid that I might be killed by the anti-Jewish elements that were marauding with violence and killing the returning survivors.

Our life was in a constant state of limbo, living from day-to-day without direction. Like many survivors, we drifted to the larger cities of Poland and decided to make our home in Krakow. My sister Sala returned from Germany and joined me to help support Mother who was not well.

In the beginning of 1946, this precarious life, without a future, prompted my mother to send me with friends to illegally cross the borders into Germany, to the American zone DP camp near Munich, where I discovered that my sister Clara was already there. Mother and Sala followed a few months later. Like all survivors, we knew that the DP camp was only a stopping point in search of safety, permanence and rebuilding a life and trying to remember and yet forget the evil that we lived through.

Throughout all our lives, especially during our flight to live, Mother always imprinted into our minds that we had a great aunt Dinah, living on 899 Schenectady Avenue, Brooklyn and more aunts and uncles. We made contact with our two great aunts and two great uncles in the United States who immigrated in the 1920's. They sent us visas to enter the country.

With a sense of great loss and a part of our lives left behind in Poland, with aspirations of hope for a better life and rebirth, we sailed away on the ship Marina Flesher. We arrived thirteen days later, on December 13, 1947, in New York.

To express my feelings on seeing the outline of the skyscrapers and congested road with cars, at two in the morning, was a wonderment to me. Americans driving around in the middle of the night! And as the dawn rose, the Statue of Liberty's powerful and immense image was an awe-inspiring sight. Later learning the inscription on it, "Give me your tired, your poor, your huddled masses yearning to be free........." was an inscription that served me as a welcome. I finally reached a place where I was home.

We were welcomed by our American family with compassion and a sense of hope that we do have a future here and that we were finally free and safe. After about three weeks with Aunt Dinah, we

Ester Age - 12

moved to our own little apartment in Brooklyn. All of us got jobs and with haste tried to fit in with everything American. My job developed into costume jewelry designing and contributed to our household.

I met a kind and gentle young man, Benjamin Kisner from Bendzin, Poland who was also a survivor of the Holocaust from concentration camps. He never wanted to talk about it, even with me. We got married on September 24, 1950 and built a wonderful family, a daughter Pearl, who was named after Ben's mother. She married Bob, a tax attorney. They have two sons Daniel and Samuel. Our son Harold, named after Ben's father, has three daughters, Corrine, Rebecca and Nicole. This is my treasured family, my heritage invested in this new generation.

With great sorrow and loss, I continue my life without Ben who passed away fourteen years ago. Our children carry on our family with dignity and a love for their heritage.

172

To have lived five evil years during the Holocaust, and have lost my dearest family to cruel murderers, to have lost my childhood, one wants to forget and move on but, we cannot. We must fight against such evil to happen again. I must be the voice of my lost family, for the Jewish people who faced murderers and had no more tears to cry or words to pray.

I have seen with my own eyes hate and made myself a promise that I will not emulate the killers. I know that I must survive, hope, build a life no matter how hard, to build a future and do it all with humane acts and acceptance of all people.

Ester 2012

The Jewish people have carried a message of humanity, love of education and love for fellow men. This I hope will serve as my message too.

I SURVIVED TO SPITE THE KILLERS

by Edith Weissman Kovack

1st Row L to R: Sister Irene, Mother Fany, Edith (3 yrs. old), Sister Magda, Father Bernard. 2nd Row L to R: Brothers Isador, Howard, Lepot

The Jewish community of Uzhgorod, possibly goes back to the 17th century. Jews played an important role in the economy of Czechoslovakia especially developing the textile industry, produce, wood and paper industries. Many Jews owned craft shops and factories, were carpenters, cabinetmakers, tailors, shoemakers made a living and provided for their families. They managed woodcutting shops with every kind of wood products for in-country and export markets. The majority of Jews were poor. But a great number of doctors and lawyers were Jewish.

As the Jewish population grew, by 1890 Jewish schools, including a Hebrew school, a *Talmud Torah*, and *yeshiva* were founded. In 1904, an impressive synagogue was opened, including a Jewish hospital and home for the aged. In 1930, the community numbered over 7,000 Jews, about one-third of the total population.

Vojnatina, my hometown, is the village in the Sobrance District in the Kosice Region of East Slovakia, where I, Edith Weissman Kovak, was born on March 18, 1926. It is located a few kilometers outside of Uzhgorod, Slovakia (then known as Czechoslovakia). It had a small population of probably 300 people and about thirty Jewish families. In 1930, 65% of the Jewish population were living in villages.

My family were observant orthodox Jews. Mother Fany (Weinberger) wore a *shaitel*, wig, as is the custom of married orthodox women. She was an immaculate and caring homemaker, skilled cook and baker, who was applauded by many as exemplary. She never showed strain or complained of her responsibilities. She took care of our large family with love and respect, especially since she was widowed.

My parents raised nine children, five boys and four girls. The oldest Helen, was born in 1904 and immigrated to America, whom I never knew. She was followed by my brothers Lipot, then Howard, who also left for America before the war. Ignatz, Tobias, Irene, Magda, Isador, and I, was the youngest.

Our house was built by the young couple when they got married. It was appointed with lovely furniture, which was hand-manufactured by my two older brothers, fine wood craftsmen. Our large family was provided for and lived with comfort and a quiet elegance as the fashion and times in those days.

My father, Bernard, was a kind man with a serious demeanor, who expected much of his children. The children did not dare or want to disappoint him. He was a designer of shoes and produced patterns for shoe manufacturers.

The loss of Father when I was just a tot, left me with anxiety that kept me in fear for the safety of Mother. When I returned from school each day, I immediately searched for her. Seeing her about quieted me.

As in most Jewish homes, we spoke *Yiddish* in the house. I attended both the Slavic public school and Hebrew school and did finish two years of high school. I cannot recall any discrimination against me. I was a good student and was not differentiated by teachers or students. We lived in peace with our neighbors. Actually, one of our neighbors helped us during the tragic times of the German occupation and after liberation.

In 1938, Vojnatina/Uzhgorod was annexed by Hungary, which immediately implemented anti-Jewish laws, mirroring Hitler's plans. In the winter of 1939-1940, all Jews of Polish citizenship or Czech citizens who were originally from Poland were expelled to Poland. The edicts were shocking to us since we never felt not being a part of our country.

By 1941, we were not allowed to go to the public school, no kosher slaughter was allowed, and therefore we did not eat meat. A curfew was enforced, and we had to record all our property with city authorities. There was a curfew for Jews from 7 p.m. to 6 a.m. Travel was not allowed, yellow stars of David had to be worn, and we were not allowed to play with non-Jewish children. We lived in fear not knowing what to expect. Many of the Slovaks were too scared to help in any way and kept away from Jews.

The young, including my brothers, were drafted into forced labor. They were sent to work in Poland and on a couple of rare occasions, they were given leave (not together) for a couple of days, which of course caused joy and sadness to have them with us and then have to part again. Each would tell us that horrible things were happening to Jews in Poland. They encouraged Mother to pack and leave. She replied, "This is impossible! You must be dreaming. It is not possible that they are doing bad things to Jews. You always have bad dreams when you come home. And how could I pack it all and go?" And so we stayed.

In April 1944, the Germans announced that on the last day of *Pesach*, Passover, we need to come into the street, bringing only a loaf of bread for each person. Just before this, our good Slovak neighbor Maria Mayzova, offered to help us hide some valuables, which we buried. We were not allowed to lock our homes. As we were leaving, a mob of looters were waiting like vultures.

The guards led us to the synagogue where we had to disrobe and were humiliated and inspected, in every part of our bodies, for any hidden valuables. Then we waited in the courtyard for the horse-drawn wagons and were loaded thirty to thirty five people in each, standing. We were driven for about two hours arriving at a brick factory where each one grabbed a piece of space on the bare floor.

To describe the inhumane conditions is impossible for me. I have blocked some of my memories of our suffering. We stayed there for six weeks until the holiday of *Shavuot*, (the holiday when the Torah was given to the Jewish people in the dessert). Then, we marched to the train depot, packed into cattle cars, standing room only, without water, without sanitary buckets, without any food. We traveled for two and a half days. Some men, who had pocket knives, poked little holes in the boards to see where we were going, announcing that we crossed into Poland. Finally we arrived in the dark of night at Auschwitz. Now Auschwitz is known as a name of horror. To us then, it was a promise for work and better conditions.

After this torturous travel, the cattle car doors slid open to the screams and shouts "*Raus, Raus!* Get Out, Get Out." Nazi SS soldiers carrying machine guns and women guards with German shepherd dogs screamed and prodded us with blows at those who did not react fast enough. Inmates in striped uniforms greeted us with voices of resentment, as if we were disturbing their orderly day. As soon as we disembarked, we could see huge plumes of fire and smoke lifting to the sky from the smoke stacks. A smell of something burning made us question the Jewish inmates in Yiddish, *"Vos Brent Doo?* What is burning here?" They answered with indifferent voices, with cold faces, "You have been brought here - know where you are - you came through those gates and you will go out through those chimneys. Remember to say *Kaddish*, a prayer for the dead every day."

Women were separated from the men while the elderly and children were ordered into another line. My line was led before an SS officer wearing an impeccably tailored uniform and white cotton gloves with a riding crop in hand; it was Mengele "The Angel Of Death. " He was standing in the middle of the road pointing at the new arrivals indicating *links oder rechts,* to the left or to the right. Those sent to the left, roughly 10 to 30% of all new arrivals, had their lives spared, at least for the moment. Those sent to the right, usually 70 to 90% of the arrivals, were condemned to die.

As my mother and I approached Mengele, she was pointed to the right while I was pointed to the left. Not knowing what this separation meant, I did not want to be separated from my mother. I screamed uncontrollably. I tried to cling to her. I was beaten mercilessly by a *kapo* and I passed out. When I came to, Mother was not with me. That was the last time that I saw her.

The chosen line of women and girls were taken to a nearby barrack where we had to undress. All hair, including body hair were shaved. We were shoved into a shower and when we got out, we were thrown a striped dress, no underwear, no shoes. We looked at the gathering of women and could not recognize each other. They proceeded to tattoo us with a number on the left arm, mine is A-13794. Finally we were led to the barracks, which housed about 1,000 women. My barrack was Number 18 in the "A *Lager.*" We were instructed to climb into a wooden plank bunk. Twelve of us laid down, six at each end foot to foot. In order to turn, everyone had to turn as well. The *Lager altester,* overseer, was a young Polish girl Eris, a kind person who told me, "You have to watch yourself and listen." Having my long curly hair shaved, which was always my prideful mane, was shocking. I tore off a piece of the dress from the hem and wore it like a kerchief on my head. Two weeks later we got wooden clogs.

The next morning, we were awakened at 3 a.m. and told to line up outside for an *appel*, count, for three hours till 6 a.m. in the morning. We were given a slice of bread, nothing more, and taken to work. My group of women was taken to work on alterations of clothing for the overseers of the inmates. When we ran out of sewing, they had us collect the corpses or serve on a "*scheiss commando*." Our job was to scoop out the "shit" from the outhouse-like areas and pull a collecting wagon to a pit.

I was in Auschwitz until January 6, 1945. When the Russians were getting closer, we could hear the exploding bombs. We were taken out on a bitter snowy midnight, just in our threadbare clothes and taken to Bergen-Belsen in cattle cars. Arriving there, the barracks were full, there was no place for us. The camp was overflowing with decomposing corpses and walking skeletons ready to join them. Typhus was rampant and there was no help or order.

I spent two weeks in Bergen-Belsen and then was taken away on a "Death March" to Gallenau. We marched two days in bitter cold, without provisions, just in our striped dresses and clogs. They marched us in the ravine next to a road, which was a struggle. Many could not continue and died or were shot there. The factory in Gallenau was situated between two mountains, producing airplane parts. Many, after the exhausting travels, fell asleep while operating the machinery, and their fingers and hands were cut off.

After a couple of weeks, the bombing was reaching this area. At the end of April 1945, they took us by train to Mauthausen. As we were traveling through the Czechoslovakian area, kind people brought buckets of gritty soup and water which we gulped hungrily, passing around the handled container from person to person.

At Mauthausen, on a Friday, as the sun was setting, planes were bombing again. The German guards made us change clothes with them, locked us into the gas chamber and ran way. That Saturday morning, May 5, 1945 at 9:30 a.m. American soldiers unlocked the doors and we ran out like crazed animals into the farm fields searching for potatoes. We managed to contrive an outdoor cooking fire and boiled the potatoes. That was our first free meal. The American soldiers handed out chocolates and sardines which turned out to be a killer for many because this food was too rich for our digestive systems to handle. My sister Magda died the same day that we were liberated.

Sitting: Husband David, Standing L to R: Edith Mayzova Kudrik, Mike Kudrik, Edith, Sister Helen, Brother Isador and his wife Rose

Now being free, I along with some of my inmate girls, ran away from this place, not trusting anyone or anything. The Duna River was not too far and we were able to take a little boat across the river from Austria to Budapest. I managed to get on a train to return to Uzhorod. This journey took two weeks because the railroad tracks were bombed out and had to be repaired.

My sister Irene, who survived in Theresienstadt and brother Isador, who both survived hell, were looking at the arriving trains for survivors, hoping that someone from the family would turn up. They spotted me. Our reunion was beyond emotional belief. We were happy to be together, but to know that we lost the majority of our family was tragic. We cried and mourned and rejoiced. Just the three of us survived.

I was emaciated and sick with typhus. They took me straight to the hospital where I was treated and stayed for one year from the end of May 1945 to the end of May 1946. Thanks to my sister and our wonderful Slovak friend Maria Mayzova, a righteous person, who baked and cooked and came to the hospital to help rebuild my health. She opened her home to the three of us until we found a place where we could settle. Maria, who lived to age one hundred and three, even named her new baby girl after me, Edith is my dear lifelong friend.

Maria returned our buried valuables, Mother's wedding ring and a few other family heirlooms, a candelabra which casts a light now to remember our loving family. She cared for us like a mother, but we could not impose on her.

Since our home was destroyed, and the *Banderowcy* - anti-Semitic gangs, were marauding in the area, we left our hometown to go to Sobrance. We integrated into the non-Jewish community as non-Jews to avoid danger. A friend and I opened a small shop and were successful in producing ladies clothing.

In the meantime, I met David (Ickovic) Kovack in 1946, who changed his name not to be identified as a Jew. David fought in the underground as a partisan blowing up trains and transports, creating damage to the German forces. He was the only survivor of his large extended family of eighty five people.

We were married on November 21, 1948 and decided to leave for Israel in 1949. Our journey was sidetracked when I became sick in Linz, Austria. We were advised by my sister and brother in the States and Isador, who was already in Israel, that we should go to America. Life in Israel in those years was a struggle.

After living through what we did, we decided to come to the United States for an easier life. So we settled in a DP Camp in Linz for two years and waited for our quota. Finally we were approved and on December 23, 1950 we arrived to New York.

Our family met us with tears of joy. We lived with my sister Helen for six months, who treated us like a mother. Then we established our own apartment working at any job to earn a living. After a

Edith and David

couple of years of working and learning the American way, David and a partner opened a dry goods stores and I worked as a seamstress in an upscale store where even the Kennedys shopped.

Edith 2013

We were blessed with two wonderful children, a daughter Leah and her husband Steve Rocklin who blessed us with three grandsons, Mitchell, who is a rabbi and is studying for a PhD. He presented us with a great-granddaughter, Ruthie Gittel, and great-grandsons Zev and Mark. Our son Bruce and his lovely wife Annie increased our family with two boys Isaac and Arye. We retired to Boca Raton in 2000 and enjoyed our retirement with our families.

I lost my dear friend, my devoted husband, father, grandfather in 2007, which is difficult for me.

I share my life story and open up my wounds and painful memories not to feel sorry for me. My life and my pain is my burden, but what I want to share is the truth of what happened to me.

The world stood by silently.
We cannot forget.
We must fight the deniers.
I was there.

I speak for my family and for the Six Million.
My tattoo on my left arm is not a number
but my badge of survival, my strength.

A SEARCH TO BE FREE

by Selma Koltanowsky Lindenberg

*Belgian Jews, as in most of the European countries, were op-
pressed and discriminated as far back as the medieval times.
During this period Belgian Jews were expelled or killed, but
Jews began returning to Belgium in the modern era. Antwerp
became a center of northern Europe for the reawakening and
thriving economic activity that changed Medieval Europe. Jews
played a major role in this transition.*

*Belgium had a much smaller Jewish population than neigh-
boring Netherlands, because the Spanish had defeated the Protestant revolt in the 16th century and expelled the Jews again. The
legal status of Jews began to change with the French Revolution
and Belgian Jews were then given more rights. While the country
had only a small Jewish population, quite a number of German
and other European Jews in the years before the World WarII
looked for safety and a better life in Belgium.*

Elsa, Mother Helena, Selma

My father's family, the Koltanowskys,
settled in Belgium after finding accept-
ability and a good life in Antwerp. The
family were transplants from eastern
Russia. Here they found safety and with
the help of the resident Jews, established
an affluent life in Antwerp, one of the
diamond dealer families.

Father, Louis Alexander, one of sev-
en children (only three survived the Holocaust), presented a serious demeanor
with a sense of self-assurance and success. He was frugal and tough in his
dealings but he was honorable and fair.

181

He was tall, blond and handsome and could pass as a non-Jew.

He served in the Belgian army during WWI and wound up stationed in Koln, Germany. During this stint he met my beautiful mother Helena Kurtz, whose family had established roots in Koln, Germany. They were immigrants from Lodz, Poland and found stability in Koln where they felt safe. They established a business, which provided the family with a life unimaginable in Poland. Father and Mother got married in 1920 in Koln, where I was born on January 11, 1921.

As soon as Father was discharged from the army, we moved to Antwerp where Father established his business in diamonds, among the Jewish society of dealers, and life was good. My little sister Elsa was born four years later.

Although our life was intertwined with the Jewish people, the family lived a completely assimilated life, without religious observances. Jewish holidays were celebrated by getting together with family.

I attended public school. This is where I first experienced discrimination because I was Jewish. Traveling home by bus to our home on the outskirts of Antwerp, the non-Jewish kids would not let us near them, even if there was an empty seat. I saw how unfair this was, but I could not understand this behavior. I ignored this intolerance and built my youthful life in the Jewish community among the Jewish kids. We had many social gatherings and learned to appreciate our own culture. This is where I met Benno Lindenberg. We were just thirteen and fourteen. Benno and his family escaped Germany when Hitler came to power around 1933.

My focus was education, and I began to attend the university and practicing piano, which was my greatest joy and which was encouraged with enthusiasm by my mother. I learned to appreciate classical music and became proficient playing this instrument and, on many occasions, performed concerts especially music by Chopin.

As much as Jews had great opportunities in business, there were still glaring restrictions, such as Jews could not have a separate Jewish cemetery in Antwerp. It was stated that if Christian cemeteries were not good enough for Jews, they could not have a separate one. The Jewish community circumvented this law by having a cemetery in Holland which was only about ten miles across the border.

My parents had a great influence on my life and choices of a future so when I turned eighteen, they arranged a match with a young man, Simon Kool, who had his businesses and life in Amsterdam. He was successful, and financially secure, so that my parents' wishes for me to have all the best in life became my life. Simon indeed provided all comforts in life. But this soon was to come to an end when Germany attacked Belgium and Holland on May 10, 1940. It took only eighteen days to conquer this small state.

In the beginning months of occupation, thousands of Jews, especially foreign Jews, fled from Belgium or were deported to neighboring France. We heard many unbelievable reports of Hitler's reign of hate in Germany and Austria, and his hate began to spread to many countries of Europe. And so it came to Belgium too.

Anti-Semitic measures, between 1940 and 1942, began by separating Jews from the rest of the population. First came the prohibition of ritual slaughter in 1940. Registration of Jewish property began on October 18, 1940. Jews who had worked for the government were let go in December 1940. Jews were not allowed to practice or acquire professions or continue education. Jewish children could not attend Belgian schools by December 1941. The Nazis began to seize Jewish property. Curfews were declared for Jews. Jews living in small towns had to move to major cities into Jewish communities. They had to wear yellow bands as of May 27, 1942. The identification documents had to have the word "*Joden*," Jew, stamped in them. Impoverished and concentrated in cities, they were now ready for the next step, transport east and the death camps.

The killing of Dutch, Belgian, and French Jews began in July 1942 when the Polish death camps became fully operational. The Nazi anti-Semetic campaign, which began soon after the occupation, was not of concern to most Belgians. Yes, many Belgians did oppose the Nazis and saved many Jews. The most noteworthy priest, Father Bruno, saved hundreds of children. A higher proportion of Jews were saved in Belgium than in most other occupied countries.

The exiled Belgian government, the Catholic Church and the citizens remembered the German occupation in WWI and opposed a second German occupation.

At first, the Germans could not identify Jews because the Belgian constitution does not permit mention of religion on civil documents and most Belgians did not help them. In fact, many actually helped Jews. And after the war, almost all Jewish children were returned to their families.

Simon and I remained in Amsterdam, and when we saw that Jews were being loaded into trucks, we managed to get on a canal barge and fled to Antwerp to join my parents.

In 1942, we escaped the occupation in Belgium and went to France. We lived week to week in hotels in tourist areas as vacationing tourists. This enabled us not be identified as aliens. We managed to live comfortably for a time because Father had hidden diamonds in linings of his clothes with which we bought safety and passed the next couple of years in this way of life. He also managed to get us baptismal papers so that we were not identified as Jews.

On May 5, 1944, Simon and my sister Elsa went out to buy flowers to celebrate our anniversary. They were arrested by the occupying Germans because neither had French papers, only Belgian. Elsa was released and Simon was sent to Drancy where he was tortured, beaten and after many hours of interrogation and merciless beating, Simon gave up the information where we were staying. When we learned of his arrest, my parents and I ran to another town, Grenoble. While on the train, the SS stopped us and checked our papers. They had Father undress and when they saw that he was circumcised, they arrested him, Elsa and me. They said, "Leave the old woman alone." Mother was left behind and she hid out on a farm cooking for a farming family. We were taken to Drancy, a concentration camp outside of Paris.

When we arrived at Drancy, someone passed us a message to be sure to declare that we were not Jewish, and that I was only married to a Jew. Our baptismal papers in hand, we stood in line for questioning. We saw the SS guards pointing at us as one said in German, "Look at those two, they are two big fat Belgian cows." Our papers passed the test and we were taken to another detention barrack, not for Jews.

We were assigned to take care of two little Jewish baby boys, from early May to liberation, August 17. These two boys were the children of the banking Rothschild family. One was Edward Rothschild, who is now the head of the Shoah Memorial in Paris.

The night before liberation, when we were asleep, the babies were taken away by the Red Cross. We awakened to the surprise of the missing children and that we were now free. Somehow disorientated, alone, poorly dressed, without shoes, not knowing what awaited us, we could not decide how to use our freedom. We walked miles to Paris and were happily reunited with our parents. Our relief to find our parents alive was a moment of great emotions of joy and sadness. At this time, I found out that Simon was shipped to Poland, to Auschwitz, and later we learned that he was assigned hard labor in the coal mines and died there.

We stayed in Paris, and with the help of the Jewish Committee and other organizations, we revived. One day, while we entered the Jewish restaurant Flaumbaum, I looked around, and spotted a familiar face. He was looking at me as I recognized my childhood friend and crush, Benno Lindenberg. To find someone from our previous, secure life was like finding a witness who could identify and recognize that we were not aliens, not merely remnants of a destroyed Jewry; a validation that we came from a normal life of worth and dignity.

Benno, who was in a French army

Selma 2013

184

uniform, had overcome his torturous Holocaust experiences, which read like a saga of a fiction novel. He was glad to attach himself to our family and finally when conditions stabilized, we all returned to Antwerp where Father rebuilt his business and we all reestablished our lives. But the tragedy of finding that most of our family were jailed in Drancy and sent off to Auschwitz and murdered was difficult to bear, but we were not alone. Out of a pre-war population from Belgium of about 55,000 Jews, only 1,200 survived the concentration camps.

Like all young people, attachments were formed immediately and families rebuilt. And so did Benno and I. We were married on September 22, 1946.

Our first son Daniel was born in 1947. In May, 1950, we were able to immigrate to America and help our son in his development. Our sons, Lewis and Jay were born in the States and have enriched our family and lives.

We take comfort in seeing that our children were not marred by our Holocaust experiences. Their success and contributions for good and our treasured four grandchildren are our joy.

My journey from a good life to scenes of evil and having to live with deception has left me with unforgivable memories, but I must acknowledge that I also met good people who saved my family and me.

To win over evil, one must recognize and fight it in order to preserve the future for all good men.

TO RETURN TO THE LOVE
OF MY PARENTS

by Basia Israel McDonnell

The history of Jews in Krakow dates back to the 13th century. Records show a *mikveh*, ritual bath, a bathhouse and cemetery were established by the 1350's. But Jewish life was restricted by many laws.

By the end of the 19th century, Jewish schools, *cheders*, were also set up. In addition, elementary and secondary schools taught Polish and German.

In 1938, Krakow's and the surrounding villages' Jewish population numbered about 70,000, about 25% of the city's total population of over 230,000.

In 1948, the post-Holocaust Jewish population had been decimated to about 5,900.

Father Isaac and Basia

I often question how and why I should speak about the Holocaust or add to its history. After all, I was only one year old when WWII and the war against the Jews began.

Yes, I don't have those memories, not until I was about three and a half years old, but I feel that I must add to the story of the evil era because my life and my sorrow and my losses must count for something.

I was born to wonderful parents on September 29, 1938, in Krakow, and being the first born, I was lavished with attention and love by the large

Basia with Mother Theofila

186

extended family. My mother, Theofila, maiden name Gotesdiner, came from a religious home. She was one of seven siblings; only three, including Mother survived. One of her brothers got away to the Soviet Union and actually served in their army fighting the Germans. The other brother lived in London and served with the Anders Polish Army. My mother's parents, Grandmother Malka and Grandfather Yoel, were taken away in the first selection.

Father's parents, Grandfather Yoel, died before the war and his mother, Grandmother Rachel, was selected very early and sent away to be killed.

Father, Isaac Israel, had a successful business in plumbing, heating and dealing with water distribution and much more. We lived a good life with all the modern facilities and luxuries that our economic status could provide. I remember that I was an adored child and felt safe and indulged.

The German occupation began on September 6, 1939 and soon appointed a *Judenrat*, Jewish Council to administer Jewish affairs. From November 1939, all Jews aged twelve years or older, had to wear armbands. According to Jewish sources the *Judenrat* sold over 53,000 armbands bearing the Star of David.

Jewish homes and shops were looted. SS and the army troops even blocked off entire streets to do this. The best Jewish apartments were confiscated for German officers' and officials' families. The houses of the Jewish community were also confiscated. German soldiers moved into the modern dormitory of the Jewish Academic Society and the old peoples' home. Many young Jewish men were sent to forced labor camps. In April 1940, it was proclaimed that Krakow should become the "Cleanest City," meaning without Jews.

Basia with parents

Therefore, on May 18, 1940, the Nazis ordered the resettlement of a large part of the Jewish population, within four months, to the *Podgorze* area, a destitute section of Krakow. According to this order, only 15,000 working Jews were permitted to stay in Krakow together with their families.

The Jewish ghetto was created by the Nazis in March 1941. Jews who lived in Krakow had to move into the ghetto by March 20, 1941, which housed 20,000 Jews, including 6,000 Jews from neighboring communities. A wall, in the style of Jewish tombstones and part a wooden fence, surrounded the ghetto. All windows and doors overlooking or leading to the "Aryan" side were closed with bricks. Four guarded entrances were created.

Hunger became the biggest problem since the daily ration of bread for each person was 100 grams, with an additional 200 grams of sugar or fat given monthly.

Special workshops were established in the ghetto. German factories supplied the raw materials and issued production orders where most of the Jews worked in these workshops and factories. ID cards were supplied to many Jews. In this way, a great number of Jews were employed and thus saved from immediate deportation.

Deportations began in June 1942. Five thousand Jews were sent to the Belzec Death Camp. In October 1942, 6,000 more were deported to Belzec. Patients at the hospital, residents of the old age home and 300 children at the orphanage were killed in the *aktion*. Several hundred Jews were put to death in the ghetto itself.

In January 1942, SD (secret service) and Security Police (SIPO) officers entered the ghetto and announced by loud speaker that all Jews had to hand over their furs and woollen garments. Anyone refusing to comply with this order would be shot. As a warning, they executed one Jew who had concealed his furs.

Basia with parents and Jewish Ghetto police

From May 30, 1942, the Nazis implemented systematic deportations from the ghetto to surrounding concentration camps. Thousands of Jews were transported in the succeeding months as part of the *Aktion Krakau*, headed by SS Oberführer, Julian Scherner.

Jews were assembled on Zgody Square first and then escorted to the railway station in Prokocim. The first transport consisted of 7,000 people, the second, an additional 4,000 Jews were deported to Belzec extermination camp on June 5, 1942.

On March 13 and 14, 1943, the final liquidation of the ghetto was carried out under the command of SS *Untersturmführer* Amon Göth. Eight thousand Jews, who were considered able to work, were transported to the Plaszow labor camp. Those who were judged unfit, some 2,000 Jews, were killed in the streets of the ghetto on those days.

This is the background where my family and I wound up. When I shared my own memories with Father, he told me that on the fourth selection on October 28, 1942, all children were taken, which confirmed my own hazy memories. Father wearing a very large long coat engulfed me in it, and I was not seen by the guards. That is how, at the age of four, I escaped being taken away with all the children and I was told after the war that I was the only child who survived this selection.

The next night, Father devised a plan to get out of the ghetto. Somehow he, Mother and I were able to get out through the sewer system. I was supposed to go with Mother to hide with a Polish family, but as we were walking away in the street, because Mother wore high heels and walked slowly, she was spotted by a German soldier with a German shepherd dog. She was captured. Father and I managed to evade them and he brought me to a village Wieliczka to stay with a Catholic family Stefanik. I was told that they were my grandparents. He left me in a state of distress with these strangers, while crying, "*Tatush, Tatush,* Daddy, Daddy." The Stefaniks tried to quiet me and said, "There is a war outside."

I don't know how I was able to adjust to these strangers. Apparently they were good to me because I learned to trust them and be guided to find safety in prayer to the statue of Jesus, which was displayed prominently in their small bedroom. A large cross hung over the bed I shared with the lady. We prayed together morning and night to Jesus and Mother of God and kissed the statue. I was tutored to hide behind their oven, in a tiny broom closet from which I could observe when it was safe to come out.

One of the neighbor visitors was always questioning my grandmother Ela Stefanik why she did not heat the house using the oven. She answered that Mr. Stefanik instructed that they save the coal because they needed to have it for the ironing of the church linen. The truth, of course, was because I was hidden there during the day. And they did their ironing of the church garments for the priests and church at night.

One day when I was sick and coughing, they had to take me outside to get fresh air. There was a vegetable garden in the back of the house. I was sitting on the stairs and the neighbor across the garden came over to me and said, "You are not their granddaughter. You have such big blue eyes. You are a Jewish child." This incident happened seven months before the war ended.

The next night, after this incident with the neighbor, there was a knock on the door. We were all in bed. Grandmother opened the door and there stood two men. One spoke German and the other one Polish. Then one man came to where I was laying and uncovered me. He was a German SS man. I cannot forget this young, handsome man. I stared at this clean crisp dressed soldier with amazement.

The SS went back to speak with my grandmother and told her that tomorrow he would be back with more soldiers to check the house. The Stefaniks had to find another place to hide me before they returned.

In the middle of the night, Grandfather Stefanik carried me on his shoulders as I was hidden, rolled in a mattress. He took me to the partisans in the forest because his son was a member, and I would be safe there. Of course, the partisans were not happy to see a girl child entrusted to them. But there was no choice.

In the forest was a shed with an attic where I stayed for two weeks by myself. Then Stefanik's son's wife Halina came for me and took me to Krakow to live with her until the end of the war in the summer of 1945.

My father was in hiding, along with a number of other Jews, in an ice factory, which he had secured and equipped with survival needs during the time of the selections. He and the others did survive. He came to reclaim me after the war. By this time, I was already over six years old and my life had become adjusted to my Polish family and being a Catholic girl. Now, it is hard to admit that I did not want to go back with Father. He showed me pictures of myself with him and Mother and I was finally convinced that I had to be with my own mother, my beautiful mother and father.

A couple of months later, we discovered that Mother survived Mauthausen Concentration Camp and, of course, came looking for us. When I saw her, I was shocked to meet this emaciated ugly old woman. This was not my beautiful, elegant mother I saw in the pictures and remembered somewhat. I announced loudly, "You are not my mother. My mother is beautiful, and you are ugly, you cannot be my mother." I think that the sad look on her face made me regret these words then and until this day. Also, when my uncle returned from Russia, around 1946, he was putting on the *Tefilin*, phylacteries, and as he was praying, he informed me that this is the Jewish way of praying to God. I told him that I was going to the police to tell them that he killed my Jesus.

After the war, about 4,000 Jews resurfaced in Krakow. By early 1946, Polish Jews returning from the Soviet Union swelled the Jewish population of the city to approximately 10,000.

Pogroms in August of 1945 and throughout 1946 as well as numbers of murders of individual Jews, led to the emigration of many surviving Krakow Jews. By the early 1990s, only a few hundred Jews remained.

After liberation, Father abandoned his Jewish identity and melded into the Polish society. He opened a business where he manufactured sausages and alcohol. Our life was not in danger but hearing of the abuse and killing of Jews, who were still suffering in free Poland, he decided that we could not rebuild our life here. Most of the survivors were leaving Poland. We too managed to get out and through Italy, we came to the land of Israel in April, 1949.

My brother was born in Poland in 1946 and lives in Israel. He served in the

Israeli Army and became a general and an attaché to the Israeli Embassy.

Life was not easy for us in the beginning, but I had to adjust to be a Jewish child and forget about my Catholic rituals. At times, I would find myself crossing my heart when I felt stress. I felt guilty and angry that I could not abandon this habit.

I continued my splintered education and in Israel eventually graduated college. I built a very successful business in advertising and catering. I married Menachem and we had three children, Elan, Nir, and Ornit and now I have nine grandchildren. Menachem was injured and lost his legs during one of the terrorist attacks and lost all desire to rebuild his life. He gave up. He became an invalid. He passed away soon after.

In the meantime, in 1986 I came to the United States and rebuilt my life by establishing a number of businesses and teaching Hebrew. I did remarry a very nice non-Jewish man. Our differences and my sense of belonging strongly to my Jewish roots was a great obstacle to overcome, especially when he became very Catholic in his observances. It created a terrible dilemma of how to continue my Jewish connections and life. So we got divorced.

It is a double-edged sword my life. I was torn between two worlds of devotion and love of a family, and an obligation to pray to a non-Jewish deity. But now, in my senior years, I feel a complete sense of belonging, which is pulling me to recognize the little child that I was, accepting my own identity and to remember my family who were murdered.

Basia 2013

I am most grateful to be part of an organization that has taken on this painful obligation to remember and teach about the Holocaust. We the child survivors are the last witnesses. Some of us were very young and our lives were disrupted by an evil that tried and almost succeeded to destroy our own humanity.

I WANT TO LIVE

by Jay Rabunski

I was born in November 1938, in a *shtetl* Kurenitz, Poland to Wolf and Rose Rabunski. My maternal grandfather, Mendel Chosid, and his son Paul, a chemist, ran a business dealing in herbal medicines.

Mother was an exceptionally lovely girl whose burning aspiration and commitment was to the cause of establishing a Jewish state, as it was for many of the young at that time.

My father was an innovative man of action. He was handsome, with dark green eyes, blond hair and someone who was admired by many girls.

His father, Yitzhak Rabunski, whom I was named after, was the mayor of the town sometime before the war. My paternal grandmother's maiden name was Perski. She and her brother Getzel Perski, were partners in producing *kvas*, a root beer. My great uncle Getzel was the father of Shimon Peres, the former Prime Minister and the current President of Israel.

Grandfather Perski had several brothers and sisters scattered all over the world. One of them was the father of Lauren Bacall whose name was originally Betty Jane Perski.

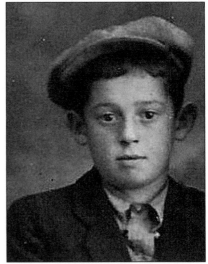

Jay Age - 7

Times changed in 1939. As the partition of Poland between the Germans and Russia became a fact, the Soviets entered our area and enforced the Communist dogma. The working class became the "ideal people." They were rewarded with good political positions while business people became outcasts and many were sent off to Siberia. By this time, we lived in a rustic little house in a distressed section of Kurenitz.

192

On June 22, 1941, Germany broke the treaty with the Soviet Union and attacked. They entered our village with tanks. The soldiers pushed, shoved and screamed at us in a foreign language. Immediately, the inhabitants of the village were divided into groups. Families were separated.

After a couple of months, the police took Father away, along with many other men. They were sentenced to be shot for being Communists. Many of the men were killed together with their wives and children in a mass grave that they dug with their own hands. This *"aktzia"* action, was later known as the "Killing of the Fifty-Four." My mother appealed to the Germans and somehow was able to save Father. My grandparents were killed when I was four, but I have no information how and when.

Later, professional people were taken to a labor camp in Vilejka, a nearby town, and soon their wives and children were able to join them. We were among them. The Germans also chose people who were capable to work hard labor, and they too were taken to other camps in Vilejka.

We were housed in wooden barracks. One could see through the gaps between the boards. We slept on wooden plank beds without mattresses.

Life in the Ghetto Vilejka was unspeakable. The men were taken every morning to small factories where they made uniforms, shoes, medicine, and war products. The 5:30 morning head count was daily, in all kinds of weather. Breakfast was handed out before work. It consisted of bread, a smear of pig fat and a mixture of hot water that had the color of tea.

Horse-drawn wagons took the people to their work. Some women, including my mother, worked in a hospital for wounded German soldiers and some cared for the SS soldiers' families. Some pretty women were taken for experiments in a hospital.

The children worked. We were crowded into one huge room where we were forced to grade buttons for uniforms. Some children were putting medicine into bottles according to color, which would then be sent to the German front for the soldiers.

You learned very quickly that it is futile to ask questions. You learned to keep quiet, to stay in your corner. You learned what is pain, horror, and death. You learned to wait for the little bit of food, the little bit of bread and water. You learned to watch your few belongings, especially your shoes. You noticed that people you knew disappeared without a trace. The constant fear for one's life made you numb and blind to the brutality that invaded our lives.

One cold day in November, Father led me by the hand, joining a group of about fifty men and their children. We were driven by horse-drawn wagon outside of the ghetto to a field. Soldiers with machine guns and automatic weapons surrounded us. We were told to undress. The soldiers viciously were beating the men to hurry, using their weapons. In the distance, there was a large crowd of young women standing nude.

I can remember the sound of the machine guns. I could see pieces of human flesh scattered all over. Our group of men with children were forced to identify their loved ones. Soldiers were hitting and pushing the men, shouting, "Filthy Jews, you'll be next." Father vomited as he identified parts of his sister Channa. I grabbed him and held him tight. He trembled and his eyes bulged as he returned my hug. No one cried.

The Germans told us to get dressed. The men were taken back to work and the children were taken to our work room. That day, a female supervisor began to hit me with a soldier's belt. I was not putting the right colored buttons into the right place. I was numb from the day's events and could not feel pain. I could hear her screaming but it sounded like an echo coming from one hundred kilometers away.

Days went by. A Christian man brought in fresh vegetables for the SS soldiers daily by horse and wagon. The wagon had two layers. The top layer held vegetables, the lower layer hid weapons that the partisans smuggled in. We were aware that one day we would be killed. These weapons were paid for with personal possessions. We were smuggling out bullets for the partisans that were stolen from the Germans.

Sometimes in February 1943, the vegetable wagon came as usual. We saw an SS man stop the wagon, and everyone thought that he discovered the layer with the weapons. Panic spread and could not be stopped as the women ran screaming that the SS had found the weapons. German soldiers ran among the Jewish crowds shooting everyone in sight. Mothers and children, husbands and wives were separated. Children were left all alone. My father, who had a pistol, left my mother and me alone. I understood what was happening. I started begging my mother, "Do not leave me. I want to live." We later learned that an SS officer stopped the wagon to take his pregnant wife to the local hospital.

My mother's chances of survival with a four-year-old were almost impossible. Mother ripped off the Jewish stars we all wore, put on an old Russian shawl, and covered me as she cradled me in her arms. I could feel her trembling heart. She started to run toward the hospital. An SS man stopped us saying, *"Sind sie eine Jude?* Are you Jewish?" He was screaming, shouting, and pointing his machine gun at us. Mother replied in Russian, "No, my baby is sick, I live in the village, and I am in need of a doctor." She opened her scarf and showed him that she had a baby in her arms. She showed him only my face. I guess because of the panic and commotion, he let us by.

My mother hid in a section of the hospital she knew well, since she worked there. At nightfall we switched to an old Russian schoolhouse that had a double-layered floor. There was snow on the ground, and we had to find a way to cover our tracks so that the SS would not discover where our hiding place was.

Railroad tracks divided the constantly-patrolled German side of Poland from the area in the forest where the Russian partisans had a base. The Germans had machine guns placed every sixteen meters, about fifty feet. Anyone who attempted to cross the railroad tracks would be shot down immediately. For five days and four nights, all we ate was snow. My mother had courage and snuck out at night to a couple of local farmers with whom my grandfather used to do business. She brought some bread and sometimes some boiled potatoes.

Mother was superstitious about dreams. A dream of her dead mother told her that we had to leave our hiding place at once because one of the farmers was going to inform the Nazis where we were hiding.

Quietly, we made our escape by crawling out that night. We hid in the bushes next to the railroad tracks. She placed me down in one of the bushes. I feared that she would not return for me. I looked into her eyes and begged her not to leave me. Even though I had no concept of life and death, but seeing the daily fear in people's eyes, I feared it. I wanted to be with my parents, my safe place. As young as I was, I looked at my mother and said to her, "Mom, I want to live, don't leave me." I did not cry. Mother did walk away a few steps, turned around, took me back into her arms, covered me up with the shawl and said nothing but hugged me tightly.

We hid in the bushes for several hours. There was a full moon that night which would show footsteps and shadows in the snow. But we knew we could not stay until morning because the Germans were searching the entire area with dogs, looking for escapees. Despite the risk, we had to move. Miraculously, we met with Father later that night and together we successfully crossed over to the forest controlled by Russian partisans.

The thick forest had icicles hanging from their branches and the ground was covered with snow. As the snow melted, swamp areas became obstacles. We proceeded to walk north to the area controlled by the partisans. Our progress was slow. We were cold, hungry, and tired. Father and Mother took turns carrying me. Periodically, we would lie down on the cold ground to rest.

In the morning, we heard sounds of armored cars, trucks and barking dogs. The Germans were looking for escapees from the camp. To get away, Mother and I, without Father, went into a swamp to hide. She reasoned that the Germans would never follow into the swampy area. We waded in and we sank into this muck up to my neck. Mother had to hold me up to keep me from drowning. We stayed submerged for four days and three nights. The frosty mud ate our flesh. After four days my mother finally pulled us out of the mud. We had very little feeling in our bodies; we were frozen. Mother carried me because walking was too painful. I suffered all my life from the affects of this experience and frost bite. It left scars on my childhood memories.

Eventually we did join up with my father who took me in his arms and carried me. I was frozen and unable to move. He attempted to remove my wet boots which were stuck to my scrawny bony legs. He cut the leather with his pocketknife. The boots were filled with frozen muck that ate away the skin and flesh from my legs and open wounds were all the way up to my knees. My hands were numb, and there were several parts of my upper body that also had wounds. Apparently the sores became infected and I developed a very high fever. Though I had begun to thaw out, I did not react to the pain. Somehow at this very young age, I learned that I could not acknowledge fear or pain.

Father ripped the lining from his leather jacket and dipped it in water puddles to gently wash and cover my open sores while mother applied herbal remedies, which eventually helped heal my open sores. She also gathered wild mushrooms and tree roots and boiled them in the melted snow to make a mixture for me to bring down the fever.

A few days later, the partisans appeared and warned us to leave the area because the Germans would soon be returning. My parents devised a makeshift stretcher using branches and my father's leather jacket. I weighed very little; I was skin and bones.

My fever worsened. My parents knew that I would not survive if we traveled any further in this condition. At this time we had joined with other escapees who resented the burden of protecting me. They resented the danger that I represented to all of them. They were afraid that the delay would result in all being caught. None wanted to watch over me while my parents were away searching for food and medicines. If my parents didn't return, I would be a burden to the group. So my parents made a critical decision not to burden the others and left me hidden in the forest. They tied my hands so that I would not scratch or pick at my wounds. I whimpered that I did not want them to leave. I was afraid that they would not return. They gathered small stones to mark a trail as markers for the way back.

To share my distress and fear cannot be described in words. I was a little boy left in the wilderness. My parents were gone a long time. Finally, on the following night, they came back bringing food and aspirin for my fever. Father traded his pistol for me. After they rested and I got some food and aspirin, we continued our search for safety going north.

Luckily, we found a kind and a very special Christian family who took a huge risk by taking us into their home. This was the first time we had a roof over our heads since we went into the forest. These extraordinary people washed us and allowed us to rest in their home. They fed us chicken soup that warmed our souls. As we readied to leave, these kind people provided us with supplies of food, ointment, and bandages and told us about a path that would lead us safely away from the village. These people literally saved our lives.

After liberation, in 1945, my father went back to Poland to find these people so that he could express his gratitude properly. He discovered that they had helped other people and were eventually caught, and their home was burned to the ground. The Germans executed them as an example to all those who dared show humanity and help the "enemies" of the Third Reich.

We left the village again going north, looking for the partisan camps. Father knew that they would help us cross the border into Russian, our only hope for survival.

As we continued on our search for safety, we came across more villages. We discovered that the people in these villages were more willing to help us. There were over 200 people living in these forests at this time, and the villagers near the forest edge were accustomed to having people ask for food during the night.

Groups of escapees began to form. It was the best way to beg for food, in order to coordinate the effort and reduce the number of people going to the same house for food. Because of my situation, it was difficult to join a larger group. I was practically one of the youngest children living in the forest, and I was still unable to walk. I would be a liability to any of the groups.

My parents, to feel safer, went together to search for food. Sometimes people would give them food, sometimes they had none to give, or they had already given so much that they resented being asked yet again. Some villagers were unsympathetic and complained to the Germans. The threat of German soldiers coming into the forest was constant.

As we got closer to the Russian border, we met up with groups of partisans. They advised us to walk on a safer path. They gave us extra food if they had any, and told us of any news from Kurenitz and the surrounding area.

The partisans, including many Jewish escapees from the ghettos and camps, were fighting a guerilla war against the Germans. They damaged roads, blew up bridges, railroad tracks, telephone poles and any outposts of Germans. They also attacked the appointed local collaborating police and the collaborators. They added a great effort in slowing down the German advance toward Russia.

In the forest, we lived in *zemlankas*. *Zemlankas* were pits in the ground which were covered with branches as a roof and camouflaged with dirt, twigs, and moss. They were difficult to spot from a distance, and kept us out of the severe weather and provided a hiding place from the Germans. After gaining strength, we began to move north again. Eventually, we came to a place in the forest near Riga, where hundreds of Jews were waiting to cross into Russia. This area was well protected by partisans. We were able to light fires at any time.

Father built a *zemlanka* that was larger than the one we lived in previously. At night, Mother would sing me to sleep. The song she sang most often was "*Chorna Wrona*" black crow. Her voice was soothing and made me feel loved and secure. The muscles in my legs began to regenerate and I learned to walk again. I began to develop a little flesh on my bones.

Finally the partisans told us that we would be liberated within a matter of days and we would be safe to leave the forest.

Shimon Perez and Jay

Our three-year absence from Kurenitz made us feel that we were worlds away from our old home. The journey back took less than a week. When we arrived in Kurenitz, we went directly to our former home. A Polish family occupied it. My father hired a horse and wagon, and we returned to the labor camp in Vileyka. The barracks were gone. All that remained was the hospital. The Polish people did not want a ghetto forming for refugees.

It was very difficult to decide where to go. We could go to Russia to try to find members of our family or to Germany where the Americans were setting up refugee camps.

We decided to go to Russia, getting a lift from an army truck. We traveled for two days to Minsk, stopping only to eat. The ravaged scenes of the destroyed towns were a confirmation that we survived hell.

My father befriended a Russian who found us a place to live. Adjusting to life in Russia was difficult. Food was still scarce, but we were able to get food through the black market. Fish, pork meat, and vegetables were readily available.

We did not feel safe here even after the war. Anti-Semitism was widespread. There was always the danger of falling out of favor with the Communist party. If that happened, one was exiled to Siberia.

My parents hired a man with a small truck to take us out of Russia. With luck, we managed to cross over into Poland safely. We spent three days on the road, stopping at night to sleep in small cottages that farmers rented out to travelers.

Eventually, we made our way into West Berlin. We discovered that some Jews were finding ways to smuggle into Palestine since the quota for refugees was small. Getting into Palestine this way was difficult. The best option for us was to go to a displaced persons' camp that the Allies set up in former German army barracks. There, refugees waited for visas to enter the United States, Canada, or other countries that would accept them.

We were able to settle in a DP camp in the town of Esvege, which was about a two-day drive from West Berlin. We stayed in Esvege for a while.

One day we received a special delivery letter from Palestine. Getzel Perski, my father's uncle, living in Palestine, had discovered that we survived the war. He arranged visas for us and we sailed to Palestine in 1947. I was nine years old and finally found a place we could call home.

I loved Israel and we were happy there. I had friends, family and we had a nice home. Father was in the construction business. In 1956, the war with Egypt was looming I was to be drafted, so my parents decided that they did not want to take a chance to lose their only child, the "apple of their eyes," so we immigrated to the United States.

The transition and adjustment to the American way of life was difficult. We settled in the Bronx, New York, in a little apartment under the L-train. Father, because he was an accountant, became a representative of Holocaust survivors to get German restitution for them.

In the meantime, I attended city college and studied engineering and also helped Father in his work. For my 24th birthday, Father gave me an incredible gift, a partnership in an apartment building on East 10th Street. That began my real estate career. I expanded my interest into hotels and construction as well as other buildings such as the Alamac Hotel on 72nd and Broadway. I also was the general manager there.

Rabunski Family

It was in the lobby of the Alamac Hotel in March 1965, where I met the love of my life, Tova Farkash, an Israeli and survivor. We got married in July 1965.

We have three daughters, Sharon, Michelle and Jacque and five grand-daughters, Samantha, Nicole, Wendy, Alexandra and Daniel.

The German killers wanted to wipe us out, but I survived and raised a beautiful family.

Jay passed away on June 4, 2008

CHILD OF LATVIA

by Edith Kahn Rhodes

The History of the Jews in Latvia was first noted in 1571. They became more established in the 18th century by the influx of Jews from Prussia. They were important contributors to the economic life by engaging in a variety of occupations and professions including business, manufacturing, craftsmen, workers, teachers, physicians, lawyers, and engineers.

Before WWI there were about 190,000 Jews in the territories of Latvia (7.4% of the total population). By 1935 it had declined to about 93,00 (4.8% of the total population) as Jews were resettling in other countries.

My mother's family was well established in small communities. Grandmother, Zippa Perman, married my grandfather Mendel. He, with his sons, owned lumber businesses and flour mills. One of the mills was in Indra, about 150 miles from Riga. My father, Israel, was assigned to manage and run it after he and Mother got married.

Father Israel and Edith Age - 13
Berlin, Germany

Mother was one of nine children, six sisters, Paula, Riva, Vera, Ema, Milia, Sonia and three brothers, Grisha, Herzel and Jafim. Only Riva, Sonia and Jafim survived the Holocaust.

My father's parents, Fanny and Joseph, passed away before I was born. They had four children, my father and three sisters, Hannah, Lina, and Liba. All were killed in the Holocaust.

After my parents were married, Father was invited to run his uncle's business in Germany. That is why I was born in Germany in 1934.

As Hitler came to power, life for Jews became tenuous, especially for foreigners, which included my family. We returned to Latvia, Indra. Soon, after my birth, my sister Aga was born in 1936. She was a very sunny, playful child, while I was more serious and quiet. I loved my baby sister and enjoyed having a playmate that filled our house with laughter.

My parents came from orthodox and even a couple of chasidic backgrounds. The younger generations chose to be more modern. They identified themselves with their Jewish roots, customs of celebrating holidays, and were educated in the Torah, Yiddish and the Hebrew languages.

Mother was a striking, stylish woman. She was an accomplished home-maker, loving and gentle. She always dressed in tasteful fashions and dressed us in pretty attire, which pleased her to see her little girls admired.

Father showered me with special attention being the first born and I tried my utmost to always please him. He was genuine in his ways with people and was liked by all. On many of his trips to Riga, he took me along and I remember attending the opera with him and his sister. We were a happy family.

The year 1940 brought many changes and challenges. The Soviets (Russia) marched into Latvia on June 17, 1940. Everyone had to learn new ways. We had to adjust to a different life, both politically as well as the struggle of daily existence. Commercial enterprises were nationalized. Officials of the previous administration lost their positions and the educational curriculum was changed to fit the Soviet system. Religious education was prohibited.

By December of 1940, Jewish community institutions and non-communist organizations were not allowed to exist. Any anti-Soviet expression was not permitted and usually punishable by exile to Siberia. The *bourgeois,* as the rich were referred to, were exiled to Siberia, which turned out to be a blessing. They escaped the Nazi killers, if they managed to survive the difficult conditions of hunger and hard labor.

When Germany invaded Latvia on June 22, 1941, everything changed. I was six and a half years old, my sister, Aga, was about five. I didn't really understand what was going on, but I could see my father and mother were upset and worried. They tried to protect us and hide from us what turned out to be a tragic reality.

The Jews suddenly became hunted people. They had no rights. Anybody could do anything to them. They lost their jobs. They had to turn over their positions and property to the Germans. Jews had to wear the Star of David so they could be identified. I can't remember if my sister and I also had to wear the Star.

In no time, the Germans mobilized a cooperating Latvian Auxiliary Police. These forces began persecutions, theft and killings of Jews. Mutilations and unspeakable evil was done by this willing police force, who initiated unimaginable acts against Jews. When Jews were directed to relocate to other towns or streets, Latvian guards terrorized and shot those who fell behind. Many were mugged and robbed by the local peasants.

Mass killings began. My five aunts, their husbands and my cousins were all killed at that time. Somehow my parents were able to hide us and themselves. We were not found by the Germans or Latvian policemen. Besides us, some other Jewish families that weren't killed in the first mass killings were with us. Aunt Riva, her husband, and their two little boys also managed to survive that slaughter.

I don't recall how it happened, but we wound up in the Riga Ghetto. A workshop was established outside of Riga. The adults were assigned to different kind of work, repairing, cleaning uniforms and other jobs. This lasted for about a year or a year and a half. My sister and I, my two little cousins and some other children still survived.

Our daily existence was full of deprivation and fear of being killed. One of my terrifying memories is when Aunt Lina was accosted by her building's janitor who wanted to kill her for her apartment. She ran away and melded into a group of Jews in the street. They were all taken to the outskirts of Riga and shot.

One day a truck with Nazi soldiers arrived and announced, "All children are to be taken to a children's camp and get them ready." People knew this was a lie. The head of the workshop, a Jewish man and a friend of my father, noted that the number of children that were to be picked up was one less than there actually were. He quickly realized he could save one child. Of course, it couldn't be a small child, it had to be one who was old enough to hide and not to cry. He picked me and hid me in an industrial size clothes dryer.

Parents tried to hide their children, but the soldiers didn't leave until everybody was found. My aunt tried to hide her two little boys, but they also were found and put in the truck along with my sister, Aga. As one can imagine, this was a great heartbreak for the parents. They knew they would never see their children again. After the truck left, it was safe for me to come out. I was very sad and felt very bad and uncomfortable that I was the only one who was still with parents.

Shortly after that the ghetto was closed. We were taken on a boat to a concentration camp near Danzig.

When we arrived, the men and women were separated. Then came the selection process. People were separated into two groups. As we learned, one to work and live and the other to be destroyed, to die. Those who were young and healthy were to be used for slave labor. Those who were old and weak were directed to the group that was to be killed.

My mother and aunt were selected to the work group. When my turn came, the young soldier who had to decide where I should go didn't seem to know into which group to send me. He told me to stand there and he would ask his supervisor. My Aunt Riva, who was nearby, quickly grabbed my hand and pulled me into her group. In all the noise and confusion, the soldier didn't notice. Because of her quick thinking and brave action, she saved my life. Among many, my mother, Aunt Riva, and I were now in the Concentration Camp Stutthof. Mother and Aunt Riva were always with me and somehow their presence and caring protected me and I felt safe. They shared whatever little food they had.

Mother Paula   **Aunt Riva**

About Stutthof
A gas chamber was built in the autumn of 1943. At first it was used to disinfect clothes but in June 1944 they started to murder prisoners in it using zyklon-B. In Stutthof's small gas chamber where Jewish transports of Hungarian, Greek and Czech Jews were mostly transferred from the Auschwitz-Birkenau Concentration Camp complex.

Newly arrived prisoners sometimes waited a whole day or longer, regardless of weather or season. Prisoners were prodded, beaten and subdued. They were forced to strip and had to hand over all personal possessions. This was followed by the shaving of both men and women, then the body-search for hidden valuables. They were issued camp uniforms and assigned a number. They were quarantined for about two to four weeks. After that they were assigned to a barrack and a work group. The three level bunks had paper mattresses filled with wood shavings, similar pillows and cotton blankets.

The sick, especially those with tuberculosis, were murdered by injections of phenol into the heart, or drowning in the bath. The camp doctor had the right of selection to the gas chamber.

With the approach of the Russian army, the Jewish barracks were set on fire with people inside and burnt alive. Stutthof was liberated by Red Army soldiers of the 48th Army under the command of Colonel S.C. Cyplenkow.

One day I was separated from Mother and my aunt. Some, including me, were taken to another place. That was an extremely difficult time for me being only nine years old. I didn't know what to do. There was a woman who knew my mother and that was a comfort and great help to me. When a soldier came and said to all, "You're being taken to another place. You can stay here or come with me." I didn't know what to do. I couldn't decide. I asked my mother's friend for advice, and she said she didn't know which was better, to stay or to go somewhere else, to the unknown. Somehow I decided to go; I don't know why. The soldier said, "If you are strong, you will be picked to go." I stood on my tiptoes to appear taller and I was taken with the group that looked young and healthy. As it turned out we were taken back to where my mother and aunt were.

Every day Mother and Aunt Riva had gone to search among the new arrivals hoping that I would somehow be among them. When they saw me in the group, they thought it was a miracle, and it was. I couldn't have survived on my own. People all around us were dying of starvation and typhoid. My mother also became sick with this disease.

We didn't know it, but the war was coming to an end. Germany was losing the war. The Russian army was surrounding this part of Germany.

We were ordered to line up to be taken somewhere else. My mother was too weak to walk and I couldn't decide if I should stay with my mother or go with my aunt. Mother insisted that I go with my aunt. After all these years of suffering and escaping death together, it was tragic to tear away from my mother. The camp was discovered and freed on May 9, 1945. More than 85,000 victims were murdered in the camp, including my mother.

We were led away from the advancing Russians by guards and German soldiers. Many people who were too weak to walk were shot. During January 23-24, 1945, the Russian army advanced close to Stutthof. The last two groups left on the 26th of January on the "Death March" to Lebork some 140 kilometres from Stutthof.

Twenty five thousand prisoners, in nine columns, started the march. The march was expected to last seven days, but it actually lasted ten days. The issued food was only for two days. The columns marched on through snow drifts with the SS guards murdering anyone who fell behind.

We were taken to a barn for the night where we slept on straw, grateful to finally rest. The next morning we had to continue the march. It didn't make sense since the Russian army was surrounding the area. But then, nothing made much sense. Some Jews who tried to run away were shot and killed.

One day we noticed that the guards were gone and we saw Russian soldiers. They told us we were now free. To be free? How does one realize this and how does one find freedom within oneself?

People entered abandoned German houses, found clothing, cleaned up and got whatever food that was left. We too, my aunt and I, entered one of these houses and rested for a day. The next day a few men with concentration camp uniforms came to look for clothing. As they were talking among themselves in German, Aunt Riva heard the accent like Jews from Riga. She dared to ask, "Do you know Israel Kahn?" They answered, "Yes, he is staying with us not far from here." They led us to that house. Father was there. Our reunion was full of tears and joy. At this point my aunt could hardly walk. She had become sick with typhoid. When my father saw us he couldn't believe his eyes. This was another miracle. He was sure that no one survived.

After he settled us in a place, he began to search for my mother and learned that when the Russians freed Stutthof and the ghetto, they took the sick to the local hospital. Sadly, it was too late for Mother. She had died there a few days later. This information was difficult for me. After seeing and experiencing all the evil and killing, somehow I hoped for another miracle that Mother would survive.

We found a little apartment that was vacated by a German family. Aunt was very sick but luckily she fought it through. In the meantime Father and I walked around in the little village and talked to the other survivors. Father realized that going back to Latvia would not be a good or safe decision. Father and Aunt Riva decided to apply for visas to either the United States or Palestine. Israel then was still under the British mandate. They realized that we needed to be in a big city in order to be close to the administrative offices to register, to know of what was happening. We managed to resettle to Berlin where we found a place to live.

Because Father spoke perfect German and Russian, the Russians hired him as a translator. He worked for them for a while until Father's friend, a Russian officer, advised him that we had better leave for the American sector of Berlin. The Russians were beginning to think that Father was a spy because he was able to speak such good German and Russian. They were planning to arrest him and send him to Siberia. So, of course, we left and found a place in Berlin, on the American side. At that time Berlin was divided into Russian and American sectors.

I was then about eleven years old. My father and aunt decided that I should start school and found a student who tutored me for a year and a half to enter public school into seventh grade. I was very well received by the German students and even made friends with whom I kept contact for a number of years.

During this time, we saw many survivors leave Germany. A friend of my father's persuaded his relative in Cleveland to sponsor us to come to the States. We arrived in the summer of 1950.

I was almost sixteen when we came to Cleveland. To give me the best opportunities, my father asked around where was the best high school. They told him it was Shaker Heights. We rented a tiny apartment in that area and I started tenth grade.

Even though I learned some English in the German school, I found using the language and talking to people was still very difficult. With a thoughtful teacher and kind students, in about three or four months I spoke fluently. I must admit that it was not easy to learn all subject, but with time I succeeded and it became easy. I was fortunate to get a full scholarship from Ohio State University where I earned a degree in education. I made friends and built a social life where I felt comfortable to leave my past behind.

At one of the gatherings in Cleveland, I met a young man who became my husband, Jess Rhodes. He was a very kind and good person and of course love grew. Jess started medical school at Ohio State where we got to know each other. Eventually Jess proposed marriage and I accepted. I'm glad I did. I received my teaching degree and Jess received his medical degree. He specialized in psychiatry.

When all studies and residency were completed, we settled in West Palm Beach where Jess opened his practice. Our children Paul and Steve and daughter Ava have filled our lives with affection and gifts of grandchildren, Samantha, Jessie, Stephanie, Hannan, Lola and Nina.

Edith 2012

A few years back, I heard about the Child Survivors/Hidden Children group meeting in Boca Raton. I was curious to meet other children (now adults) and feel a commonality of memories, confirming some hazy memories, recapturing the lost child within each one, and to find a way to remember the Six Million.

I am very pleased to be part of this vital group who add to Holocaust education efforts in Florida by witnessing and developing books to become our voices for the future.

In spite of all the suffering and what I experienced, as did many others, one should not lose faith in people or become haters. We need to remain good human beings and show a better way through our contributions of charity and service to the world. I have seen evil. I chose to be a good human being.

TO BE HIDDEN — TO BE SILENT SILENT NO MORE

by Edith Rosen

The Jewish presence in Belgium in the Brabant province was as early as 1200. Anti-Jewish measures can also be traced back to the 13th century when they were expelled from there. Many measures against the Jewish population were hard, but the crusades of 1309 were catastrophic. Jews who refused baptism were massacred.

Father Moishe, Edith, Brother Albert and Mother Rywka

Under the protection of Duke John II, the Jewish community was able to rebuild and grew even larger when expelled Jews from France began settling in different parts of Belgium. However, about thirty years later, this improvement was destroyed because of the Black Death (1348-49). The Jews, who did not die from sickness, were murdered by the populace or the authorities. They were blamed for poisoning the wells to cause the plague. Only a handful of families survived, most of whom were burned at the stake in 1370.

When Austria took over the rule of Belgium in 1713, it established a more open society, attracting Jews from France, Germany and also from Eastern Europe. But even so, Jews were burdened with special taxation. Things did improve under the French and later under the Dutch rule.

When Belgium became independent in 1831, the Jewish population grew significantly when Eastern European Jews began fleeing the pogroms and hard life in their homelands. At the outbreak of WWII, about 90,000 Jews were living among the Dutch population of about nine million people.

Brussels, Belgium, was my city and country of birth, where I, Ida Schajnfeld, Edith Rosen, was born on November 13, 1930. My father, Moishe and Mother Rywka Wajsman, were married in Warsaw and to escape pogroms, they came to Belgium from Poland in 1926.

Father, an intelligent and gifted student of Jewish studies had exceptional talents in the production of fine leather goods, especially excelled in the design of fine pocketbooks. His intuitive nature endowed him with the ability to adjust to unforeseen conditions with which, in the ensuing days and years, saved his life on many occasions.

Mother was mild-mannered yet exuded authority. She was willing to overlook and overcome with fortitude, a trait that saved us all. She was an excellent seamstress of fine clothes and helped supplement the family's income. As immigrants, they lacked the language and of course many rights.

In 1932, my brother Albert was born. He became the "apple of the eye" of my parents' and at times mine, as I grew older.

As a child, I never understood or sensed the hardships that my parents had to overcome to keep our family provided for. Yes, life was difficult, but regardless, my life was full of love and contentment, provided by my warm and generous parents. I was even sent to summer camps to benefit from the fresh air away from the big city.

At the beginning of World War II, more than 100,000 Jews were in Belgium. The Belgian people were mostly tolerant of the Jews, but one still could sense anti-Semitism from some and even from the leadership especially to those that were not Belgian citizens. Yet, my life continued with a sense of belonging and I felt as a Belgian.

On May 10, 1940, Nazi Germany invaded Belgium. Within two and a half weeks, Belgium was under the German rule. Anti-Jewish edicts began in the fall of 1940. The first edicts were barring ritual slaughter and barring Jews from professions. By 1941, they started to confiscate Jewish property. Curfews were established and Jews were restricted to live only in cities, not villages. In early 1942, they ordered Jews to wear yellow Stars of David and in September started rounding up thousands of Jews and deporting them, mostly to Auschwitz. Very few Belgian Jews survived concentration camps.

My father immediately understood that danger was lurking for Jews, and that we were no longer safe in our present surroundings. His pessimism was confirmed when letters from my mother's sister in Poland reached us with sad and fearful news that Jews were being rounded up into ghettos. My father said: "They will come and slaughter us all, no one will survive." This news depressed my mother and kept her in tears much of the time.

> *After the war I discovered that my grandmother had been murdered together with her son, wife and child in their hometown in Lukow, Poland during the German occupation. My parents had a large family in Poland. Eighty eight members were murdered.*

Father's keen mindset of survival made him arrive to an immediate decision to leave Belgium. And so on May 16, 1940, we took a train from Brussels to Southern France that lasted six days and nights.

Southern France at that time was not occupied by the German military. This part became known as "Vichy France." Father's plan was to escape to Spain, but unfortunately it was too late to cross the border. The French officials, dealing with this large exodus of people from the North, intercepted us at the Pyrenees Mountains and placed us with a farmer family, the Verdiers. Suddenly my parents became farm workers.

Edith in Communion attire

Ponlat-Teebourg, near St. Gaudens and Toulouse, was the town where we settled for six months. The farmers of the community treated us well, with respect and provided us with good food. We felt safe and happy surrounded by the beauty and serenity of this mountainous region. But this was not to last. The Vichy government passed new laws, which made it mandatory for all refugees to return to their country of origin.

And so our wanderings and struggles to return to Belgium brought us to a French detention camp where we were kept along with other refugees. We were helped by the

French underground, resistance fighters, and again did not feel any threat or danger, nor felt any discrimination. However, after five weeks, the situation began to deteriorate.

My brother, age eight, became seriously ill. He was taken to the city of Toulouse to be operated on and thankfully he recuperated to continue with the family. Father had the feeling that it was not safe to remain in this camp so he bribed a French policeman, who was known by the French resistance. We were able to escape in the middle of the night, joined by another family, and were taken by a rowboat across a river, which divided the occupied zone and Vichy France. We were now on our own. We, children, were warned to remain absolutely quiet and well-behaved. We walked through the night and dodged German soldiers on patrol, shining beams of search lights.

Father as a blind man

Our journey back to Brussels was full of fears and danger, but we found our way on foot and by train back home where we found our apartment intact because my mother's sister, who remained in Brussels, had taken care of it in our absence.

Not having a choice or really knowing what the future held for Jews in Belgium, we remained there for one and a half years. Luckily, my father was able to find work as a salesman. When it became too dangerous for him to be in the open, he had to find a way to conceal his identity.

Being a creative man and since he had poor eyesight, he decided to take a bold step and disguise himself as a blind man. He approached the director of the Brussels home for the blind, Mlle. Stercks, who assisted him to establish his new identity. She outfitted him with a white cane and dark glasses. He completed his disguise by wearing tattered clothes, which enhanced his appearance as a beggar. Being a child of about ten, it embarrassed and upset me seeing my father in this role and being among other blind people, many of whom were facially deformed and extremely talkative.

My brother was placed with a Catholic parish who hid him together with other Jewish children in Brussels. In the summer of 1942, my brother became very ill and had to return to my parents. This was a lucky move because soon after the Gestapo stormed the parish and twenty five Jewish children were taken and sent to concentration camps.

In December 1942, I was placed with a blind Catholic Belgian woman for whom I was to cook and clean house. Being only twelve years old and completely inexperienced in household chores, I became terrified. On the following morning, a bitterly cold day, I slipped out and took a streetcar back to my parents' apartment.

The conditions in Brussels were unsafe, too dangerous to remain. My father again contacted the Institute for the Blind. In January 1943, Mlle. Stercks placed me in a large Catholic orphanage.

The orphanage, known as Notre-Dame des Anges, was located in Mouscron, near the border of France. In order to stay at the convent, I studied catechisms, and in March 1943, I was baptized and given a new name. I now was known as Mlle. Gabrielle Stercks. There were a few other Jewish children here. Conditions were austere; we suffered hunger and were abused by the strict hand of some of the nuns.

In May 1943, I received communion, which included a feast that lasted two days. During my stay at the orphanage, I constantly lived in fear, not only of being discovered as a Jewish girl, but also because I told a lie that my mother was deported. I now felt totally abandoned and terrified. The fear of losing my family was always on my mind.

In June 1944, the Allied invasion of France had begun. There was now fighting in Normandy.

Again my father considered my stay at the orphanage too dangerous so he sent me to a second convent in July, 1944, known as Don Bosco in the town of Grand Bigard, outside of Brussels. I now was given a second new name and was called Gabrielle Pieters. I stayed at that convent from July 1944, until November 1944. At that time my parents and brother were hidden with the Pieters family. They were living in Berchem St. Agathe from August 1942, until September 1944. My brother Albert had also been baptized and attended a Catholic school during this period. He would also tell me how frightened he was in this environment. He too was in constant fear of being discovered as a Jew, especially when dogs would bark late at night.

In the fall of 1944, the Germans fired rockets, buzz bombs, towards England and Belgium. The cities in the area such as Brussels, Antwerp and others were hit.

I remember one afternoon, when we heard warning sirens shrieking, a buzz bomb landed about two kilometers, about one and a half miles, from the convent. The nuns yelled to us that we should quickly get under the desks. The bomb made a terrifying sound, continued to travel and turned towards the convent walls. When it finally exploded and burst into flames, it left masses of shattered glass, debris in the classrooms and courtyard. It was a miracle that no one was hurt. That evening all the children were evacuated. I went back to my parents and was delighted to be reunited with my family.

On September 3, 1944, the Allies liberated Brussels. Now we finally felt that we did not have to hide anymore and that we could be together, but still my parents sent me to a Catholic school for six more months. By now I was fourteen years old and understood my parents' motivations to help me have order in my life and an education. I attended high school from 1946 to 1947 and continued my education preparing with secretarial skills.

My father was able to resume his earlier occupation as a maker of pocket books and slowly, slowly normalcy returned. My immediate family had survived. My parents remained in Belgium, and my brother became a prominent scientist in Belgium.

In 1946, my mother's sister from New York visited us and made arrangements for me to come to the United States. It was very difficult to leave my parents and brother, but I wanted to leave Europe, forget the past and make a new life. However, it was difficult for me to discuss my experiences with my family or anyone else. It was painful to recall our suffering. I was especially ashamed that I hid my Jewish identity and was baptized. I even hid my communion pictures for fear that my children would not understand my shame and confusion.

I arrived to New York on November 10, 1948, rebuilt my life and met my wonderful husband Sam Rosen. We were married in 1955 and raised two sons, Richard, who died in 1982 and David who enriched our lives and has given us joy with a grandson Jeremy.

For many years I could not speak of my life during the war. It took much searching and anguish for me to be able to share my life survival.

We need to become more accepting of each other and appreciate the difference of all people. I will never forget the kindness

Edith 2012

and safety given to me by my godparents. The Pieters family, who hid my parents, were honored by the Belgium government for their brave sacrifices in helping the helpless and hiding Jews at the risk of their own lives.

ONE OF ONE THOUSAND CHILDREN

by Henry Rosenthal

Henry Age - 5

I am writing my story as a testimony of how it was for a Jewish child to live under the Nazi evil and my miraculous, yet fortunate escape to America.

My maternal family, the Auerbachs, had long established roots in Germany. They lived in Telgte in the same house since 1612. We know this to be true because they paid a "Jew Tax," *Juden Steuer,* that year.

My mother's father, Simon Auerbach, married Julchen Stern from Wilbadessen. Before or maybe during WWI, my grandparents moved from Telgte to Erkenschwick where they opened a hardware store for my mother.

My grandmother's only sibling that I knew personally, was her much younger sister, my Great Aunt *Tante* Rosa Stern, who never married and lived in a farm house in the village Wilbadessen. She shared this home with a brother Herman, whom I never met alive and his non-Jewish wife and two boys.

In 1985, two students of the Telgte "Real Schule", school, wrote a book about the Jews in Telgte and particularly about the Auerbachs. The students' research indicated that the Auerbachs, an upper middle class family, supplied food to many people in town who did not have money to pay for it. Records show that after WWI, the citizens of Telgte bought food on credit but never paid for it. Records also indicated that those debts were forgiven. The students could not believe how shabbily the Jews, and particularly the Auerbachs were treated by the citizens of the town during the Third Reich. The book is titled, The Story and Fate of the Jews of Telgete *1933 to 1945. The book is written in the German language.*

(Telgte the 1933 population was 8,757 and in 1938 there were fourteen Jewish families living there. The synagogue that served as a place of worship for the Jewish families of Telgte, was burned and the homes and business of these families were set on fire.)

My paternal grandparents, grandfather Louis Rosenthal was from Herte. He married my grandmother Hedwig Ransenberg from Wennemen.

The Rosenthal's claimed to be *"Sephardim," (Jews who were expelled from Spain during the Inquisition).* I know that he served in the German army prior to WWI because we have a photo of him in uniform. He died in 1915.

When my grandparents married, they moved to Oeventrop, a village of about 2,000. Three other members of the Ransenberg family lived in town. The village is very beautiful, surrounded by forests and mountains and the Rhur River flows through the middle of town. They bought a house on the main street of the village. It was a two-story house, with an attic and basement. They had a small stable with chickens and several goats. The vegetable garden and a wonderful orchard included many apple, plum and pear trees, and two trees with the most delicious white and red cherries.

Mother Hedwig

This house today is a national monument, not because the Rosenthal's lived there, but because of its old architecture. The Rosenthal's had seven children, two boys and five girls. Four siblings, including my grandmother, were sent to a concentration camp where all were mur-

dered. Three survived by escaping to England.

The Jewish Holy Days were celebrated in a small synagogue in Arnsberg, about five miles away and was located near the big church. It accommodated about fifty people. No sign indicated that the building housed a synagogue. The interior showed signs of age but had a feeling of a peaceful meditative quality, especially since the sanctuary overlooked a spectacular vista of the mountains. The ark, situated on the eastern wall, held fifteen Torahs, which were very old and some had been chewed by rodents in their long survival. All were decorated with silver crowns and breastplates and were cherished because they were the connection to the Jewish history and traditions.

The services were conducted by a *chazzan*, cantor, in the Sephardic style, which gives a hint that the Jewish history of the area dates to the time of the Spanish Inquisition and expulsion of Jews from Spain. Jewish history and Hebrew were taught once a week by a volunteer. I had to come by train to attend the classes. A rabbi/cantor was hired for the High Holidays only. It was great fun to accompany the family to the services, dressed in our best. Since we did not own a car, we walked.

My parents met at a party where Father, George, tried to play a joke on Mother, Hedwig. This first meeting and mischievous beginnings, both having a good sense of humor, did not stop them from binding their future together. Even the mismatch in height, mother was about 5' 10 inches tall, and Father was at best only 5' tall, did not hinder this match. There was always a lot of banter between them.

I was born in Erkenschwick, a dirty coal-mining industrial town in Germany, on October 5, 1926. The house we lived in was owned by my grandparents. There was a hardware store on the first floor and our living quarters on the second. The hardware store was a wonderland of all kinds of pots and pans, hammers, saws, shovels, cages, small farm equipment and anything that was useful for this rural community. In back of the house was a small stable where we raised chickens, ducks, rabbits and two goats.

Our apartment was nicely furnished, and I recall the large living/dining room with dark heavy furniture. To this day, I see my grandfather sitting at the table playing cards. He was very old and could not hold the cards in his hands, so Father made a device that held the cards for him. I have the fondest memories of him, perhaps that was because he showered me with love and attention, especially since I was the only grandchild at that time and was treasured by all.

My father was caring and kind and intervened on my behalf when Mother, who was the disciplinarian, punished me. He was an extreme extravert. Even though he had only an eighth grade education, he was very intelligent and well read. He devoted his time to his friends, politics, and family, in that order. My mother took charge of the business and the family.

In 1931, I started kindergarten, where the teachers were nuns. In the fall of 1932, I began public school, which was like a Catholic parochial school of today. Some of the teachers were nuns, and every classroom had a crucifix hanging on the wall. The days started with a prayer and the students crossed themselves. I was the only Jewish student and was excused from crossing myself. The others looked at me as if I am being punished.

In 1932, my maternal grandparents sold the house in Erkenschwick and moved to Recklinhausen, so we had to move, including the business, to a new address, an apartment building in Erkenschwick. The store was on the ground floor of the building, and we lived several stories above the store. No more back yard, no more stables, no more animals. Times were tough in Germany at that time. Unemployment was rampant, and money was tight. That was the time when Hitler made his presence felt. There was a lot of unrest among the German people.

Because of my gregarious father's involvement in politics and being a social democrat, he was persecuted by the Nazis, which forced us to flee from Erkenschwick in May 1933, in the middle of the night with some of our belongings. We ended up in Oeventrop in my grandmother's house. There was no room for us in her house and having no options of where to live, we made a kitchen in the basement while my parents' bedroom was in the third floor attic. I slept in Uncle Willy's bedroom, Father's brother.

It became my job to buy sacks of coal from the dealer and drag it home in my little wagon. The dealer no longer delivered coal to Jews, and once a week I went into the forest to scrounge for small pieces of wood to use for kindling. It was fun because I loved the fresh pine smell of the forest and enjoyed the tranquility. I also helped with our food shortages by picking blueberries, blackberries raspberries and mushrooms and was an expert in discerning good mushrooms from poisonous ones.

On the way to school, I had to pass a *kiosk*, newspaper/magazine stand, which displayed a sign, "Wann das Juden blut from dem messer spritzd alles wird besser werden." When the Jew blood runs from the knife everything will be better. Below this statement were posters with caricatures of Jews with long noses, side curls, long black coats and skull caps. This anti-Semitism reinforced hatred against us.

Our situation became desperate. Father could not get regular employment and we could not continue to live off the generosity of my grandmother. He found work in a quarry and as caretaker of the Jewish cemetery in Arnsberg and worked there in the years 1936, 1937, and in 1938. I helped Father in the cemetery pulling weeds, raking the walks and other chores. Each night he came home exhausted and disgusted, and the hunger became a constant because the food rationing was much lower for the Jewish people than for the non-Jews.

Father's pay was not sufficient so mother found a way to help. She went to a Jewish non-kosher butcher in the next town where she bought two large suitcases full of sausages. Carrying this heavy load she traveled by train, about one hundred miles, to a larger town, Elberfelt. My educated, proud, and aristocratic mother was forced to peddle the sausage to sympathetic Jewish customers. She had to rent a small room in the town because she could not come home every night. When she did come home, she was exhausted, depressed and crying. Both my parents were very unhappy but tried to mask their emotions. They showed me love and consoled me about my daily problems in school. My life and the life of my parents deteriorated little by little for the next few years. Food rations were cut, my schoolmates hated me more. The walk to school became more dangerous, being threatened with harassment and assault. I must boast that I never let them beat me; I stood my ground.

Between 1933 and 1938 many Jews, including members of our family, emigrated out of Germany. They left for Palestine, South Africa, South America and the United States. I am not certain why my parents did not move. Was it fear of the unknown or was it lack of money? Or perhaps they would not leave my old grandmother? I know they did not have a visa for the States. I do not even know if they applied for one. And perhaps my father's stoic ideas that because he was a WWI veteran and a proud German citizen, yes, a proud decorated German veteran, nothing will happen to him. He was convinced things would improve. Why intelligent persons like my mother and father could not see the writing on the wall, I'll never know, but of course in hindsight it is easy for me to judge. Who could ever envision the horrific future that became the lot of all Jews in Germany and all of Europe?

Then came November 9, 1938, *Kristallnacht*, the night of broken glass. No matter how old I get, this horrific day will remain etched in my memory and still gives me nightmares. I have questioned my beliefs that a God, a loving God would permit this to happen. No clergyman of any faith has ever explained this to me to my satisfaction. And above all, I question how can a town of 3,000 people, who knew my family, attended school with them, attended social functions, fought WWI on the same side with them, celebrated new births, and mourned deaths, how can this town's total population stand by, not protest, or lift a finger, while my family, including myself, a twelve-year-old boy, were physically abused, kicked, hit, spat on and humiliated. Was it latent hate for Jews, fear, cowardice or what other beastly rage and insanity possessed all? Surely I cannot find such hate in my soul for anyone, how could an entire educated country become a tool of hate, abuse, robbery and murder?

We learned that on that day my father and all Jewish men in town were arrested and placed in a jail-cell located below the public school. My mother, my seventy-five-year old grandmother, my aunts and myself were pulled, pushed and kicked out of the house. We were shoved into the middle of the street by a gang of about eight or ten men, screaming and cursing Germans. It was in the late afternoon, just getting dark. The local policeman stood by unaffected and did not lift a finger to intercede in this vile abuse. Was he acting on government orders not to interfere? Yes, it was an entire society that went mad together with their leaders.

218

The crazed gang proceeded to destroy the inside of our home as well as all of the other Jewish homes in town. Our front door was pulled off its hinges and splintered. Every window, including the frames, was thrown into the street. Everything was thrown into the street. A lifetime of memories, mementos and all those things that make a house a home were destroyed and were now laying broken in the street. Our home was not the only home destroyed. The other five Jewish homes in town met the same fate. An eighty-year-old widowed woman living alone and whose house was located directly across the street of the Catholic Church was also destroyed. Was the pastor of the church blind and deaf?

During the destruction, a man kicked my mother, and I went after him to protect her. It was at that point that the policeman took me to the jail for protective custody. I joined my father and the other Jewish men there.

After the destruction ended, the cowardly bystanders went home. I was released from jail, but Father and any of the other men were not. They were sent to the Oranienburg Concentration Camp, near Berlin, and were held until around December 20th. I helped my family to put some of our belongings back into the house. We salvaged the bedding but not the beds. We found some pots and tableware but all the china, plates, cups and drinking glasses did not survive. I cannot remember the next few days. I do not remember eating or sleeping. I cannot even remember if I, or any of my family cried. I cannot tell you who fixed the windows and doors. From time to time, at night, some kind person or persons left some food at our back door. Who left that food for us?

The century-old synagogue in Arnsberg was also totally destroyed on *Kristallnacht*. All the furnishings were broken up. The pipe organ was either destroyed or perhaps stolen; I don't know. The holy Torahs scrolls were rolled down the hill and then burned together with all the prayer books.

The change in the law did not permit Jewish children to attend German public schools so in early 1939, my parents enrolled me in a Jewish school in Cologne. Cologne is about 150 miles from Oeventrop. I had to live in an orthodox Jewish orphanage. The teachers and counselors did their best to keep us busy and content, but it was not a happy place. About thirty boys, aged ten to fifteen, slept in one room. The girls were also accommodated the same way. The orphanage also cared for around thirty infants. The Jewish school was about a mile from the orphanage. To attract less attention to ourselves, we walked two by two about one hundred yards apart. But that did not prevent the German kids from beating us. Sometimes a grownup would intervene and sometimes a grownup would encourage violence. I learned that my best defense was to kick the abuser.

During this time, Germany was at war with England. Almost every night, the English planes flew over Cologne. Many times they bombed the city. The German antiaircraft defenses answered with their weapons. All of us spent nights in the cellar. Besides fragmentation bombs, the English dropped incendiary bombs.

While in the orphanage, I turned thirteen. I was prepared by the staff to recite the blessings and read from the Torah for my Bar Mitzvah. My parents came to Cologne for the day. No one else from the family had the money to make this trip. My parents celebrated with me with a small cake and left right after the ceremony.

About a year later, the house that my grandfather bought, the house that my father was born in, the house that all my father's sisters and brother were born in, was forcibly sold. It was sold to an old family friend, a Christian. His attitude changed immediately after he acquired the house way below market price. My whole family now lived together in the attic in extremely crowded conditions.

In the early spring of 1941, my parents informed me that they had made preparation to send me, by myself, to America and helped me get a German passport, complete with swastikas. It was very difficult to obtain. We had to produce a myriad of documents. They included a certificate that I was never arrested, a birth certificate, a document stating that I paid all my taxes, that I would not take more than ten marks out of Germany and many, many more requirements. The passport lists my name as Heinz Israel Rosenthal. I was given a new middle name "Israel" as it was given to every Jewish male as of August of 1938, and all females were given the middle name of Sara. My German passport also has a large red "J" to make sure, at a speedy glance, that whoever looks at this passport cannot miss the fact that I am indeed a Jew.

Henry's documents, travel pass

I traveled alone from Cologne to Frankfurt to get my American visa. In Frankfurt I was received in someone's home, apparently a prearranged plan. Over the next few days, the American consulate had me examined by a dentist,

220

a physician and then I was interviewed to make sure that I was mentally healthy and physically fit. After a few days, I was issued an American visa.

Once I was destined to leave Germany, I left the orphanage, the *Kinderheim*, and was sent to visit my *Tante* Rosa in Willbadessen. I could not understand why my family sent me to Aunt Rosa rather than to be with them. Perhaps they did not want me to see them sad or to see them suffer under these difficult and harsh conditions that Jews in Germany were forced to live in.

Returning from *Tante* Rosa's to my parents, we spent the last two nights talking about the future. My suitcase was packed. The same suitcase my mother used on her honeymoon. I still have this old suitcase. Old and useless, but how can I throw it away? There was very little clothing to pack. Mother gave me her damask tablecloth, and matching napkins embroiled with her maiden name initials and three silver tablespoons with her initials. My mother felt that these items are negotiable and can be turned into cash in an emergency. All of her treasured items. She also included my silver Passover cup. Some of the other things in my suitcase included a notebook with addresses and a few photos. Unfortunately, they did not include photos of my parents.

June 15, 1941, was our last day together. Before going to the train and while still in the house, we hugged and kissed and cried. Father put his hands on my head and gave me the priestly blessing even though he was not an observant Jew. My parents walked me to the railroad station arriving just in time to board the train. I stepped aboard with my suitcase. Our goodbyes were as if it would be only a short trip and I would soon return. A fast handshake, no crying, no kissing, no long goodbyes. Not even waving goodbye from the train window. We were told to make the departure look routine. And that was the last time I saw my beloved parents, my gentle father, my caring mother. It is my hope that their unselfish act of sending me away for a better future gave them peace of mind because they did the best to save their son, the life of their only child. My feelings still dwelt with this question, when would I see them again?

I was met in Berlin by someone at the station and taken to a stranger's home. The next few days I was coached on how to act, what to do, and what to expect. I was also introduced to ten other children of this *Kindertransport* and an adult escort. All of us left Berlin together on the same train, but we were split up, two children per compartment.

After spending most of the day on the train, we reached the German Belgian border where our papers were examined, suitcases searched. Next we were interviewed by the German authorities. Again our papers were examined, our suitcases were searched and interviewed by the Belgian immigration personnel. Then a Belgian physician examined us before we got a series of inoculations.

Early the next morning, we boarded another train and traveled a few hours to the French border where we went through the same routine that we experienced at the Belgian border, the same interrogations, and we received exactly the same inoculations. We were than guided to an empty railroad coach, which

Henry is first on the right - front row

was then attached to a train. This train took us to Paris where our railroad car was sidelined in a vast Paris railroad yard. The window blinds were drawn making the coach semi-dark; too dark to read. This now being the end of June, the weather was very warm. We spent several days in this hot car. The sanitary conditions left much to be desired. We had little water for drinking and none for washing. Every morning someone opened the compartment door and delivered food and drinking water.

After five days in the railroad yard, our coach was finally attached to another train. The next stop was the French Spanish border where again we were interviewed, this time by the Spanish authorities, examined by medical personnel and given the same inoculations we had in Paris and at the Belgian border. We entered Spain at San Sebastian and proceeded to Madrid where we spent a few days in a hotel. Then we were taken to Barcelona, a port city on the Mediterranean Sea and spent a few days there.

Finally we embarked the 10,000 ton, *Ciudat de Sevillia*, ship that was to take us to America. My assigned cabin was furnished with four rows of bunk beds, each was four bunks high. There were about a thousand people on board. We were given one meal a day. The food was spicy and greasy, but it sated our hunger. We spent three weeks on this ship. No bathing, no showers. I escaped from the human din and smells by staying on deck as much as possible. The ship's route to the United States was from Barcelona to Tangiers, North Africa, through the Straits of Gibraltar, then to Lisbon Portugal and on to the Canary Islands. We were docked next to a German naval ship, flying the swastika flag. Because the Canary Islands were neutral, the German ship was safe in port but outside the harbor several British ships were patrolling. I don't think that this ship made it back to Germany. On the way to the US, we had a lot of older people aboard the ship. Because of their age, a few died during the voyage. At that time the US did not permit the entrance of corpses. The captain was required to perform several burials at sea.

August 20, 1941 was a beautiful, sunny morning. The Statue of Liberty was off our port side. Yes, I was impressed by this enormous statue, and it gave me a sense of finally being safe but not of joy. I was here alone. I missed my parents and I am sure, my parents missed me. Looking over the side of the ship, I saw what really amazed me was the never-ending stream of cars on shore. All these cars, America must be very rich. This was a sight which I could not have even imagined.

The ship docked and most of the passengers were pressing against the railing. It seemed that thousands of people were standing on the dock. All of them cheering, screaming, and holding flowers. Most of the passengers recognized someone they knew. Passengers and crew were leaving the ship; no one was left on board except two frightened boys, me and another boy. It is not until the afternoon that a second cousin came to pick me up and delivered me to a HIAS, Hebrew Immigrant Aid Society, person Mrs. Lotte Marcuse. She spoke German and took me to dinner and then to the Roosevelt Hotel where I was given a large beautiful private room, just for me. What luxury! She returned in the morning and took me for breakfast and spent the entire day showing me New York. In addition, she bought me a Timex pocket watch which overwhelmed me with excitement and pleasure. My own watch!

The following day, I was put on a Pullman train and sent to Atlanta, Georgia where I was met by Mrs. Armand Wyle, from the Jewish Children's Bureau. After a bit of small talk, she introduced me to my foster parents, Mr. and Mrs. Sam Rosenberg. The Rosenbergs were immigrants from Russia but had arrived long before the war. They were pleasant and had a family of four children, the youngest was six years younger than I and with whom I shared a room. He did not care for that idea but eventually we became friends. They spoke very little English. Most of our conversation was in Yiddish.

I started school right away, day and night school. I did have a problem with the students in the day school because I was "the Goddamned German." In Germany I was "*Der verfluchte Jude*," the cursed Jew. When the students were informed about my status, the problem disappeared. I did have trouble with the English language, but geography, history, and mathematics came easily to me because I learned that in Germany.

Early 1943, I was summoned to the Atlanta main post office. I was escorted to an office where I met a naval officer. The officer seemed to know a lot about me. He informed me that I was considered an enemy alien and could not be drafted. However, he advised me strongly that I should volunteer and enlist. Frankly, I could not wait to join the armed forces. I did have an ax to grind.

In 1943, at the age of seventeen, I entered the United States Army Infantry. At first my job was to interview German POWs. I must admit that I was not too successful in this assignment because I lost my temper too often. So after basic training, I was sent overseas to the Philippines. I was glad to do something useful in the war.

Besides my regular duties, I served as an assistant to a Christian chaplain, reciting *Kaddish* when a Jewish soldier was killed. I served for two and a half years, including one year in the occupation of Japan.

After the service, Uncle Willy, my father's brother, urged me to settle in Montreal. I attended school there, working towards an engineering degree. While in Montreal, I met my wife Millie Black. We moved to New York and got married in October 1947. Both of us worked and I continued to study and became a mechanical engineer. We have three daughters, Heather, Gail, and Hope, six grandchildren and three great grandchildren.

Henry 2012

A good opportunity came my way, and I started my own business designing and building machinery. I moved my business and my family to Florida in 1979. I added two partners, and we incorporated under the name of MIMA Inc. We were successful and after ten years, employed 165 employees. We sold the business to Illinois Tool Works in 1986, and my partners and I retired in Florida that same year.

After my retirement, Millie and I spent our life enjoying the fruit of our labors and hosting many visits from our grown children and grandchildren and our friends. Sadly, my dear wife passed away in 2002.

After the war ended, I inquired about my family in Germany and found that no one survived. The only survivors of my father's family are two sisters and one brother who immigrated to England. However, they have passed away since. On my mother's side, all were murdered.

I did return, by an invitation from the local government, to Arnsberg and Oeventrop in 1972. I visited the grave of my grandfather. Since no one knows when and where my father, my mother my grandmother and two other aunts were murdered, I added their names on my grandfather's grave site.

Ten other survivors also attended as well as several hundred town's people. My question to the town's people was, "Where were you when we needed you?" An attending rabbi refused to say Kaddish because we did not have ten Jewish males present. Over the rabbi's objection, I said Kaddish. Since I do not know what date my parents were murdered I say Kaddish whenever I find myself in a synagogue.

In all the years, I never considered myself a survivor. I knew I was one of the OTC children (One Thousand Children) who were brought to America during the war years. I never spoke German again. My family heritage is not connected to Germany anymore.

Now in my eighty-sixth year, I question why Jews had to be the victims of such bestiality, an evil that cannot be imagined and now again we must fight against it being repeated.

The deniers and ignorant are spreading the untruth that the Holocaust never happened. We, while we are still here, must speak, must write, and must record. It is difficult for most of us, but we must speak of our own survival and suffering and, most of all, we speak for our lost families.

This photo is of a monument in the Arnsberg cemetery. In 1970 when I visited the cemetery, my grandfather's name, Louis Rosenthal, was the only one inscribed.

I commissioned an engraver to add my grandmother's name, Emma Rosenthal, below his. I then added an additional stone and the names of Georg Rosenthal, my father, Hedwig Rosenthal, my mother, Klara Rosenthal my aunt, Emmi Rosenthal, my aunt, Elly Rosenthal, my aunt. Below that is the inscription,

"Killed in a concentration camp, but not forgotten."

A LIFE RENEWED

by Joe Ross

My name is Joseph, Josef Rozenzweig, Ross. As I am trying to record my Holocaust experiences, I cannot just start with the evil. I must start to share about my life in the town of Skarzysko, Poland, where I was born on February 28, 1930.

I had two sisters Dora, six years older, and Lidia six years younger. We lived amid a large family and a Jewish community that contributed to the fabric of all aspects of life for all people who lived in and around this town.

In the 1890's, Jews settled in Kamienna, which was known as Skarzysko. This town established the manufacture of steel and leather tan-

Joe after war - Germany

ning. In 1924 the production of munitions for the army provided an increase of employment for many, although not for Jews, which in turn increased the population to about 19,000 people, including about 2,800 Jews.

The town of Skarzysko on the shores of the Kamienna River, with distant mountain views, grew to become an important railroad junction leading to Kraków, Warsaw and other places.

Jewish community life included a number of *shtibel*, prayer houses, serving different followings of Judaism. There were two Jewish religious elementary schools and a number of organizations of different leanings

Father Itzhak

227

My father Itzhak was one of seven children, most of whom and their families were murdered. His father and mother passed away before I was born. They left a legacy of about twenty acres of land, which eventually became part of the town where the family owned a building, housing four stores: a bakery, a shoe store, a cabinet maker, and a wholesale grocery. They also ran a lumber yard. Father's siblings used the properties and Father got compensations, a share that was generated by this building. His own business interest was in forestry trading and in the manufacture of lumber building materials.

Father was a modern man, very much connected to Jewish history and an ardent Zionist. He even applied and got visas to immigrate to Palestine, two weeks before war broke out, which we did not get a chance to use.

People valued him for his fair dealings, outlook and sought him out to head organizations. Even the rabbi came to confer with him.

He was not a playful man with his children because his intense focus was always on the political and Zionist interests. Yet there was a feeling of safety, warmth and pride knowing that he was our father. He was a great provider; we lacked for nothing. We were in awe of him and I wanted to emulate him.

Mother, Mindle (Feldman) was also one of seven children, of whom five and their families were murdered in the Holocaust. She came from an orthodox family, not affluent, one of dignity and influential in raising their children with a connection to orthodoxy. Although our home was modern in all ways, Mother ran a kosher kitchen and was the one who made each holiday important, keeping her connection to the orthodox upbringing.

My grandfather, Abish Josef Feldman, passed away before I was born. But I do remember my grandmother Rochel. She showered me with affection, with warm hugs and many kisses planted all over my face. She was a special lady. She was sought after in the community because of her healing talents, ability to set broken bones and assist with other ailments to help many.

I attended public school, walking three miles each way every day. I must admit that I did not like school and made no effort to excel. Perhaps it can be attributed to the bullying and beatings that I endured, especially at the end of the school year, which made me a reluctant student.

When walking by the church, one had to take off one's hat and of course, that was not acceptable for Jews. I learned to avoid beatings by making a wide circle around. Discrimination against Jews was, at times, without fairness or reason. If one was proven to have called a Pole, "Polish swine," a two year jail sentence was not an unusual punishment.

At first we lived at the outskirts of town, but being away from the family and hardships with school, we moved to the Jewish neighborhood in town. This too was not a safe place. Hooligan gangs periodically attacked the community creating havoc, robberies, destruction, accosting and beating Jews. On those days, the Jews stayed off the streets not to become targets of this hateful group and their attacks. Truth be known, it was not easy to be a Jew.

On September 1, 1939, Poland was attacked by the Germans and by September 8, they captured Skarzysko-Kamienna using flyover bombings and strafing, avoiding damage to the three munitions factories. This attack created a state of confusion, and fear was on everyone's face.

The Germans took over the ammunition factories to support their own war effort, and from 1940 it was controlled by the company Hugo Schneider Aktiengesellschaft or HASAG for short, which ran it as a subcontractor for the German home defense forces.

They immediately initiated anti-Jewish edicts. Everyone had to wear the yellow Jewish star. All Jewish students were forbidden to attend public schools. Countless decrees and restrictions repressed and oppressed our lives.

At first it seemed that eventually an order would return. A *Judenrat,* Jewish Council, was formed, which became the intermediaries for the Germans to do their bidding.

Working groups had to report for sweeping streets, and in the winter for clearing the railroad tracks off any debris and snow. On one occasion, I reported for this work instead of Father. A trainload of German soldiers stopped as we were clearing the tracks. To show off, a Polish guard began to yell at us. A soldier got off the train and accosted my friend, forced him to kneel and shot him in the head. This shocking scene was my first encounter witnessing the evil that was upon us. I managed to sneak away, ran home and reported this incident to the *Judenrat*. They complained to the Mayor of town but nothing was done.

The ghetto, for the town's Jewish population, was established by the Germans around May 1941. The Jews were incarcerated in the ghetto, and for two years were constantly tormented by the Nazis. It was enclosed with barbed wire fencing and entry in and out was restricted and guarded. We lived in two rooms and managed to survive with Father's connections outside the ghetto by bartering any valuables for food.

My sister Dora worked as a bookkeeper in the office of the headman of the factories. She was able to get me in to work in the factories as a messenger boy. Eventually I worked in the tool department. I think I was their youngest worker. She also had connections where she learned about the liquidation of the ghetto and about the rumored killings in Treblinka. With bribery of gold and valuables, she succeeded in having our family move to the factory camps, out of the ghetto.

During this time, Father managed to have my little sister hidden by a Polish family, claiming her to be a niece, his sister-in-law's child from Warsaw. However, after one month, because the Polish lady was afraid that she would be discovered, Father smuggled her into the working camp by bribing the camp commandant with some gold and jewels.

When searches were conducted of our labor camp by the Nazis, my little sister, who was alone in our barrack, only six years old, understood to hide. She crawled in under the straw mattress and avoided being taken away. The Skarzysko Ghetto was liquidated in October 1942. About 500 were selected to move and work in the factory while the rest, about 2,500 people, were taken to Treblinka and murdered there. We felt fortunate to have escaped the deportation to Treblinka. But our existence hung on a straw and at the whim of our overseers.

Those who were fit worked in the ammunition factories of the HASAG conglomerate, where they suffered severe hardship and hunger. The work was grueling, dealing with extreme heat from the metal smelters. Those who worked in Factory C, where the explosive powders picric acid were used, the people turned bright yellow. This acid was used in the production of the detonators. If any damaged bullets where discovered, the entire department was beaten with fifty lashes. Assignment to work for the HASAG was almost always a slow road to death.

The factory and living quarters were surrounded by forests. Some that managed to escape the captivity were intercepted by the Polish underground and turned over to the Germans.

We worked twelve-hour shifts. One night, one of the workers from the night shift tried to escape. He was shot. To teach all a lesson, the entire night shift was lined up in rows and had to count off by threes. The third person had to step forward and was shot. As this process was going on, my father shoved me into another row, and so I avoided being the third number in the previous row where I would have been shot.

On another occasion, someone stole a rubber production belt, which was used by the inmates to make soles for shoes. He was captured and hung from the water tower as the entire camp was called out to stand in the *appel* field to watch. This was their methods of keeping order and instilling fear into everyone.

Between August 1942 and the summer of 1943, Jews from the surrounding areas were brought to the three factory camps. The German records show that over 17,000 were brought in with fifty transports. About 6,400 managed to survive long enough to be evacuated to other camps when the Germans closed the factory in 1944.

When the Russian front was getting closer, the Germans transferred us to Czestochowa, Poland. This is where my mother and sisters were liberated by the Russians.

In the summer of 1944, the camp was liquidated. The remaining prisoners were either killed or transported to the Buchenwald Concentration Camp in Germany.

The factory workers, including my father and I, were put on a cattle car train, about one hundred men in a car. For three days, we were transported without food or sanitation. We arrived in Buchenwald in the winter of 1944, where we were met by guards with growling dogs, ready to attack.

We disembarked, marched to a large hall and were told to undress. Our hair was shaved, and we were inspected in every orifice looking for any hidden valuables. We figured that we were headed to the gas chambers, as it was rumored. Instead, we were immersed into disinfectant baths. Uniforms, with a yellow triangle designating that we were Jews, were issued along with wooden clogs, and were assigned an identification number. Mine was 114810, Father's was 114809. We lost our names.

At first I was housed with my father in the men's barrack, in deplorable conditions, crowded and overrun with vermin. Every day, early in the morning, an *appel* was called. Father gave me his clogs, while he stood barefoot in the snow, so that I would appear taller standing on them and would be able to stay with the men. After a couple of weeks they separated me from Father and I was transferred to the children's barrack. I did not know if he was alive. After the war the records showed that he was killed about five days before the United States army liberated this camp.

We were abused by a number of *kapos,* who made our lives more miserable. An amazing event and somewhat of a relief from these abusers happened when some inmates got together and killed these torturers. The Germans did not miss them or make an issue as to what happened to them.

We were starved and many were worked to death. They took us in trucks to clear the rubble in Weimar.

In Buchenwald, there was a secret barrack where they performed medical experiments on prisoners. Another ghastly event happened when the commandant's wife, Ilse Koch, saw a tattoo that she liked. She had that person killed and made lampshades from the skin.

When the Allied Forces were getting closer to Buchenwald, the Germans chose to evacuate the non-Jewish prisoners. I wanted to get away even not knowing where we would be taken. I removed my Jewish triangle and replaced it with a red one in order to pass as a non-Jew. We were in Buchenwald for six months.

Three thousand men were packed into cattle cars and were taken to Theresienstadt Concentration Camp. We traveled locked up without food or water for three weeks. Once in a while, bread was thrown into our car. Any time we stopped and were let off in the fields, every blade of grass, every bark and leaves were stripped off the trees and eaten by the people. The stops would be used also to get rid of the dead and unhook the empty cars.

One time, Allied planes flew over us. The train stopped. All the German guards and some inmates jumped off and ran to the fields. I was too weak to get off the car. The planes mistook us for German soldiers but did not shoot when they discerned that this was a prisoner train. They flew over low and tipped their wings as if to say hello and give us hope. As soon as the planes left, the guards herded everyone back into the cattle cars.

When we arrived in Theresienstadt, only 399 men were left alive. I was suffering from bleeding dysentery. On May 8, 1945, all the guards disappeared. The gates were opened and we were liberated from our hell. The Russian soldiers took over this part of Czechoslovakia.

One of my camp companion took me to a hospital where I was cared for over three weeks.

Luck was with me, when my sister Dora discovered me in Theresienstadt. Our reunion was filled with tragic laughter and tears, which we could not control; an expression of all the years of suffering. She took me out of the hospital and took me to Czhestochova via Prague, where I discovered that Mother and my younger sister survived. Our meeting was full of joy and sorrow.

Mother and my sisters remained in Poland until 1957, when Jews were permitted to enter the United States. One of my sisters studied medicine and became a doctor in Poland. Dora became an x-ray technician and Mother cared for the house and my sisters.

We were warned not to go back to our hometown, Skarzysko, but I had to see for myself if there was someone of our family alive and to see about our homes and property. This was the week of the Kelce Pogrom in 1946, where over forty survivors were murdered by local Poles.

I was fifteen years old and did not know how to find myself or how to create a life again. In Czhestochova I joined a *kibbutz,* which tried to get us out of Poland illegally. We were caught at the border and taken to jail. The court had many legal cases represented by many lawyers. There was a big disorder and confusion, so when some of the lawyers walked out of court, I just walked out with them, melding in among them. Our next attempt to cross into Germany succeeded and I settled in a DP camp in Berlin. From there I went to the DP Camp Eshwege near Kassle where I decided to learn a trade by attending the ORT technical school.

All refugees were searching for how to relocate and establish a normal life somewhere. I too applied for a visa to go to the United States, especially since my mother had a sister there. The HIAS helped me to qualify and on December 25, 1949, I sailed on the ship SS Sturgis, landing in Boston.

The HIAS sent me to Flint, Michigan to work for General Motors. After visiting the factory, I decided to investigate opportunities in New York and got a job there in a garment factory. Getting used to the American ways, I changed jobs and worked in a luggage factory. The pay was small but after changing to work from an hourly wage to piece work, I produced more than a team of workers. The owner valued my motivation and hard work and promoted me to be a foreman. In the meantime, I learned the luggage business and industry.

In 1950, I met my wife and best friend Roz Mazor, and we were married in 1951. We were blessed with two daughters, Gail and Lisa and four grandchildren, Sarah, Melissa, Adam and Josh. Eventually, we settled in New Jersey where I established a successful business in the production of luggage.

Remembering my beautiful community of Skarzysko and my father's example of being involved in work for good, my commitment to Jewish causes became very important to me. I had a drive to revitalize and help by joining boards and enabling many charitable and worthy causes.

After I retired from the business, we found ourselves enjoying the easier life in Florida. Here I found the organization, the Child Survivors/Hidden Children of the Holocaust, who have inspired me to support the work they do, especially speaking at schools.

Joe 2013

SANCTUARY AND SURVIVAL IN SHANGHAI

by Evelyn Rubin

Evelyn Age - 4½

I was born in Breslau, Germany, now Wroczlaw, Poland, at the onset of the Nazi era, to an orthodox, Zionist-oriented family who had been in Germany for many generations. On my maternal side of the family, I am descended from Ezekiel Landau, *Naude B'Yehuda*, who was also chief rabbi of Prague 1753-1793. My maternal grandfather was a Talmudic scholar and a follower of the Gerer Rebbe.

My mother was the youngest of seven children. Two of her brothers established businesses, and two became rabbis and two sisters married. My mother founded a successful paper and twine business in 1916 and married my father in 1929.

My father served in the army in WWI. He was wounded at the Battle of Verdun, captured by the French, and awarded the Iron Cross Second Class by the abdicating Kaiser Wilhelm II.

In 1935, as a Jewish child of a veteran, I was able to attend public schools, however, my parents enrolled me in a private Jewish School.

When the Nuremberg Laws were promulgated in 1935, my parents started looking for countries we could immigrate to.

Besides signs posted all over, "*Juden Verboten,*" Jews not allowed, pleasure travel outside Germany was also forbidden to Jews. A big red letter "J" was stamped in our passports.

We attempted to go to Brazil, Palestine, Cuba, England, America, all to no avail. My one remaining, widowed grandmother, my father's mother, moved in with us after Hitler came to power. She tried to get her sister, living in New York at the time, to send us an affidavit. With the help of the HIAS we received it in 1938. We were in shock when the American Consulate informed us that we were not eligible to be placed on the German immigration quota, which guaranteed almost immediate immigration, but were placed on the waiting list of the Polish quota with a very long wait. The reason for this was that Jarotschin, Germany, the city of my father's birth, had become Jaroczin, Poland, under the Versailles Treaty. The fact that we had German citizenship, were born in Germany and that my father had been a German soldier, did not help.

In the spring of 1938, right after the *Anschluss,* Hitler's annexation of Austria, we had to turn in all our valuables to the Nazis. And then we heard about Shanghai, that was established as an Open City under the Japanese, and that no visa was required. All that was needed was the price of a steamship ticket. Austrian Jews had already been departing for Shanghai in droves after the *Anschluss*, and now German Jews were thinking about doing the same. My parents, however, decided to put the idea of going to Shanghai "on the back-burner," still hoping to get an American visa in the near future. With that in mind, we dismantled our beautiful seven-room apartment, and moved with my grandmother into three furnished rooms, with bags packed.

November 9, 10, 1938, *Kristallnacht,* the night of broken glass, was the beginning of the end for European Jewry. My mother was in Berlin at the time hoping again to persuade the American consulate to place us on German quota but to no avail. The consulate had closed their doors at the start of the *aktion,* as the Germans called it. When she returned to Breslau, she found that my father had been among those arrested and sent to the Buchenwald Concentration Camp.

Evelyn with parents

During his incarceration, she went to Hamburg to purchase tickets on the *Hakozaki Maru* to leave for Shanghai the following February.

My father came home from Buchenwald three weeks after his arrest, one of the first to be released, due to the fact that he had received the Iron Cross Second Class. He had to sign in with the *Gestapo* every morning declaring that he and his family would be leaving Germany within two months.

On February 9, 1939, we took the train to Naples, Italy to board the ship for the month-long voyage to Shanghai. At the time, my grandmother refused to leave Breslau. However, she did follow us to Shanghai the following year.

We arrived in Shanghai on March 14, 1939 – a teeming city of approximately eight million inhabitants, which included many foreigners; White Russians, Russian Jews, who had fled the 1917 Revolution, Baghdadi Jews, who had come to Shanghai in the previous century, and business people from all over the world administering branch offices of their respective firms.

We were welcomed by American staff members of the American Joint Distribution Committee, under the direction of Laura Margulies, to help the refugees settle in what was thought to be a temporary refuge. Refugees were put up in *Heime*, dormitory-like establishments, and soup kitchens were made available to those who couldn't help themselves.

The French administered the French Concession, the westernized residential area, and the British administered the International Settlement, the business sector. The Japanese, who effectively controlled the city, administered Hongkew, a mostly-slum area, much in ruins, the consequences of the Sino-Japanese war of 1937.

Aside from the tremendous culture shock were the horrific unhygienic conditions, which produced epidemics. We had to get inoculated three times a year against cholera, typhoid, para-typhoid and smallpox once a year. All drinking water had to be boiled at least five minutes past its boiling point, and the same had to be done for all fruits and vegetables.

With the proceeds of the personal possessions, which my mother had the foresight to bring along, my parents purchased an apartment in the French Concession and then established a typewriter business. My father did the repairs and my mother took care of the business end.

I continued my interrupted schooling at the Shanghai Jewish School, learning English rather quickly, as well as French and Hebrew, which were part of the British curriculum that the school followed. We sang "God Save the King" and "*Hatikvah*", the Israeli anthem, every morning at assembly. This school had been established in the early 1900's by the Kadoorie and Sassoon families. With the arrival of the refugees, many of whom settled in the Hongkew area because housing was very cheap there, Sir Horace Kadoorie purchased land, built a school and staffed it with refugee teachers.

The subtropical climate, with cold, wet winters and monsoon rains that constantly flooded the streets, which had a very poor sewer system, coupled with the summer temperatures measured by today's humidity index reaching sometimes one hundred and forty degrees Fahrenheit in the shade, wrought havoc for the western Europeans. By the time the refugee population had reached approximately 18,000 in 1941, the attrition rate was tremendous. Sadly, it hit my family. My father kept getting fevers, which the doctors were unable to diagnose and treat properly. He died in March 1941, at the age of forty three. I was ten, my mother was forty nine and my grandmother was seventy two years old.

On December 8, 1941, as Pearl Harbor was attacked, we woke up to a tremendous explosion in the harbor of Shanghai as the Japanese dynamited some ships that had been docked in the Whangpoo River.

The Imperial Japanese Army and Navy were in power now. Soon thereafter, we were considered enemy aliens of Japan and Germany and were interned in camps where we were remained for the duration of the war.

A tremendous food shortage developed. The American staff members of the JOINT were repatriated to the United States, and no financial help was forthcoming to help the stranded refugee community.

My mother now ran the typewriter business by herself, bringing in very little income. Her American and other foreign customers were now interned, and she had to depend on her few remaining German and French customers.

On February 18, 1943, the Japanese issued a proclamation that all "Stateless" people, (the word "Jew" was never mentioned in that proclamation), who had come to Shanghai after 1937, had three months to "relocate to a designated area," a section of Hongkew. This took into account all the refugees, for we had all lost our respective citizenships soon after our arrival in Shanghai. My grandmother died two months before our move. She was seventy four years old and had never recovered from my father's death.

With three other families, we moved into a four-room house, really a hovel down a narrow Chinese lane. We had one flush toilet for all and also, sinks in each room for cold running water. There was no heat. We did our cooking on a little Chinese stove on the rooftop, forming egg-shaped coals from coal dust mixed with cold water. The stove had to be constantly fanned to keep the flame going. We purchased our hot and boiling water from the hot water stand at the entrance to our lane. Vermin, rats, large flying cockroaches, mosquitoes were all over the place. Dysentery was rampant.

When food shortages became even more acute, and refugees were not just dying of disease but also of starvation and despondency, my mother decided that we were going to survive, no matter what! She used her imagination to put food together in many different ways. She would mix one ounce of peanut butter with about six to eight ounces of syrup and that would be a "great" spread. Little Chinese boys chased grocery trucks, slit the sacks, noodles would fall into the gutter, then swept up and be sold very cheaply. We would then separate the debris from the noodles which we would eat with some cinnamon and sugar. We still received our ration tickets.

Japanese Ghetto administrator Kan Ghoya handing out passes

For *Shabbat* and *Chanukah*, my mother fashioned metal into shapes that would hold some oil and then made a wick out of cotton threads. One ounce of butter would last a whole week for us and salami could be bought by the slice from the refugee grocer. Two slices would last about a week.

Mr. Ghoya, one of the Japanese ghetto administrators who promptly proclaimed himself "King of the Jews," issued a *T'ung*, special pass, to leave the ghetto area during the day and return at 6:00 p.m., which was our curfew. My mother received a pass by applying as a typewriter mechanic. However, she used her pass for a different purpose. By visiting Chinese peddlers in parts of the city that Westerners did not often frequent, she purchased sundries, which she brought back to the ghetto peddlers, who sold them on a consignment basis. It did not bring in much money, however, it kept us about one step above starvation.

The Shanghai Jewish School was now very far away from Hongkew. Our British teachers were all interned, but we still had our British-trained Russian teachers. Our parents wanted us to transfer to the school situated in the ghetto area because it would take us up to two hours each way to continue going to that school. Also, we had to obtain a special pass from Ghoya. However, most of us did not want to transfer.

While the ghetto regulations were sometimes annoying, inconvenient and aggravating, they were not impossible to follow. Mr. Ghoya gave us most of the problems by deciding who would and who would not get a pass to leave the ghetto.

By approximately 1944, money came to the beleaguered refugees via the efforts of Laura Margulies of the JOINT and was handed over by the Japanese to the *Juedische Gemeinde,* the Jewish Council, in the ghetto area. Soup kitchens were again established.

American planes constantly strafed us, and the favorite pastime of the children was to bet with marbles, as to who would shoot down whom, as we watched the American and Japanese fighter planes up in the sky.

The Japanese had instituted a fantastic air raid warning system, so that we always knew when we would be under attack. Unfortunately, Germany's surrender on May 7, 1945, did not end the war for us in the Pacific. And then we heard the horrible earth-shattering, incredible, unbelievable news. What we had escaped by coming to Shanghai was now our "paradise" as bad as it was. We felt lucky indeed. No one knew, of course, the complete impact because there was no way of finding out at that time what had happened to family left behind. We found out soon enough. Of my mother's siblings and their families, only two survived, a brother in England and a sister in Tel Aviv, Israel.

When we heard about the two atomic bombs that were dropped on Hiroshima and Nagasaki, we were really frightened, hoping that the Americans would not drop this bomb on us.

On July 17, 1945, American fighter planes bombed the ghetto. Some thirty refugees were killed and hundreds more were wounded. Scores of Chinese inhabitants also were killed that day. One of their targets was the radio station located on the outskirts of the ghetto.

Our liberation came six weeks later with the arrival of American Liberation Forces from Chungking under the command of Major General Claire Chennault, accompanied by Generalissimo Chiang Kai-Chek.

It was only then that we got the full news of the horrors that had taken place in Europe. We couldn't believe that we had escaped that nightmare, even as the realization had set in that we had actually survived the Holocaust. This was a new word for us, Holocaust. It took a while for it to sink in. We were approximately 18,000 lucky survivors who had escaped the Nazis' diabolical clutches.

The JOINT arrived very quickly and so did UNRRA with army k- rations for us. Finally, "real food." The American hospital ship HOPE docked at the Bund, river front, and the sailors were very generous allowing us kids on board to drink Coke, eat popcorn and watch an occasional movie. My mother got a job as typewriter mechanic with the US Quartermaster.

When we wrote to my uncle in Manchester, my aunt, his wife, contacted her nephew living in Lakewood, New Jersey, who sent us an affidavit. We were placed on German displaced persons quota and received our American visa in February 1947. The trip to San Francisco on the SS "General Gordon," an American troop transport ship, took two weeks.

I will never forget the ship passing under the Golden Gate Bridge at 4:00 a.m. as we all stood on the deck crying. I cried for my father and also my grandmother.

During the Cultural Revolution all western cemeteries were destroyed. There are no graves to visit.

We were welcomed by members of the JOINT and were put up in a hotel where we savored our first bath in four years. A volunteer couple was put in charge of us. They took Mother and me to their home for dinner and then showed us around San Francisco. The JOINT then put us on a train to New York and then by bus to Lakewood, New Jersey to meet the Heinrichs, the couple who had so kindly sent us the affidavit. We stayed in their home for about two weeks and then made our way to New York.

At first, we lived in a furnished room and Mother went to night school to improve her English, working days in a camera factory. Subsequently, we moved into a small apartment in Queens and she got a job as forelady in a powder puff factory.

While still in Shanghai, I taught myself shorthand and typing. As soon as we got to New York, I was hired by Mark Cross Fifth Avenue as secretary to the manager of their Credit Department. In 1949, I got a job at an import/export firm in downtown Manhattan at the grand salary of $65.00 per week.

In 1950, I met the man I was to marry. Harold Pike, born in Brooklyn, had just been accepted at the *Ecole* de *Medecine* in Geneva, Switzerland and was leaving to go there within four months. He proposed within six weeks of our meeting. We got married and my husband left in August, while I applied for my American citizenship. I was only going to go back to Europe with an American passport. I became a citizen in February 1951 and promptly left for France on the *Ile de France.*

I needed a job to support us while my husband was at school. I had never wanted to speak German again, yet I found speaking the language came in handy for I was able to get a secretarial job rather quickly. At the same time, I perfected my French, which also helped considerably. The small checks that my husband got from the government under the GI Bill, supplemented my earnings. The years in Geneva were very pleasant. In 1955, I gave birth to our first daughter Marilyn. My husband graduated medical school five months later and we returned to New York.

Evelyn 2013

My husband started his internship, while I took part-time jobs, working two days a week to supplement the meager income from the hospital. When he started his residency in psychiatry, the pay was better, and in 1958, we had our second child, Sheldon. We moved to the suburbs in 1959.

My husband worked at Creedmoor State Hospital and also opened up a part-time practice from the house. I worked as his secretary and took care of all the appointments as well as the bookkeeping. We were prospering, and in 1961, I gave birth to another daughter, Doreen, followed by Sheryl in 1962.

In 1975, my marriage broke up. I was now a single mother with three children still at home. My oldest daughter, Marilyn, had gotten married in November 1975. My years in Shanghai would help me cope with this hardship. I was going to survive this crisis too.

I rented out two rooms in my large house, arranged single parties at my pool, started a typing service from my home and registered with a temp agency for jobs. I also obtained food stamps for a year. With much difficulty, I managed to get college loans and grants, to send three children to college, Sheldon to medical school and Sheryl to law school. Marilyn had gotten her college degree six months after her marriage.

In 1983, I met Len Rubin, who had recently been widowed. Our friendship evolved into love, and we were married in my backyard in 1984.

Just two weeks prior, I had become a grandmother for the first time when Marilyn gave birth to Jocelyn. My mother was then ninety two years old. She was so thrilled to attend our wedding and become a great-grandmother. She died ten months later, just short of her ninety fourth birthday.

I am fortunate to be the mother of three daughters, one son and step-mother to two daughters. I also have eleven grandchildren, one great-grandson and six-step-grandchildren.

In 1994, I published the first edition of my book *Ghetto Shanghai*, followed by a second edition in 2000. I have been featured in several documentaries, the best of which is *Shanghai Ghetto*. I have devoted much of my time to lecture, volunteer at our temple and other causes, including the welfare of Israel.

I am honored to be included in this book and to add my story to the Holocaust survival and events.

COMMUNION FOR SAFETY

by Janine Gimpelman Sokolov

My mother, Irma Werthheimer's family claimed their roots for many generations in Germany. The Klipstein family, Father Leo, on the other hand were more current transplants. Grandfather, Chaim, came from Poland and established a good life for his family. We all resided in Plaun, not far from Leipzig. My parents, Leo and Irma were a compatible couple who started life together and in Plaun is where I, birth name Ursula, an only child was born in 1930.

To secure a better living and income, the young couple moved to a small village, Frankenhausen, in 1932 and resided there until 1938. They established a dry goods and haberdashery business and lived in a comfortable apartment adjoining the store.

Janine Age - 4

Father was a tall, slender man with good appearance and manners, who ran the business with cordiality that invited the customers back. My mother was attractive, short, a bit plump and someone who was all business. She took upon herself the responsibility of the store and subordinated the house and childcare to a housekeeper.

I entered school and recall that my experience and friendships were not unusual. We lived a modern, assimilated life and enjoyed the fruits of our labors without disturbance. Regardless, my family applied and were waiting for visas to go to America where many of the family were already resettled.

As the Nazis manifested greater influence and the anti-Semitism started to surface, my family liquidated our store and possessions in Frankenhausen and managed to ship to America crates of goods to await our arrival. In the meantime in 1938, we moved in with my mother's parents in Plaun where my grandfather owned a number of properties and a large store dealing in ladies' and men's suits, coats and clothing.

By November 9, 1938, the date of *Kristallnacht*, my grandfather already did not own the store and the properties and although we were not maltreated personally, a desperation and terror set in to get out of the country. On Christmas Eve, my father and a friend crossed the borders illegally to Belgium to escape the gathering Nazi storm.

In February 1939, I was placed on a train which was going through Belgium to the South of France and then to safety. The railroad platform was a scene of tears and tragic crying. The separation from hundreds of children by tragic figures of mothers and fathers and the quizzical and shocking big eyes of the children was a scene of sorrowful suffering.

My mother remained in Germany to care for her elderly parents. I remember the hurt and feeling of abandonment to this day, although now as a mature adult, I understand and realize my mother's heroic act. I still pine for the protective embraces of my mother.

The train chugged along for hours under the supervision of the Red Cross caregivers and stopped at Brussels where we were placed into a Jewish orphanage. I continued school and found some order to my life. My father came to visit on Sundays, which gave me a feeling of some security by his weekly presence. In 1939, when Germany marched into Eastern Europe, Mother was smuggled into Belgium, hidden under the back seat of a car.

I remained in the orphanage from February 1939 until May 1940, when the German army invaded Belgium.

In 1940, when the orphanage children were being transported to France and then to England, my parents decided to keep me with them. They lived in squalid, tight quarters and not being citizens, were not able to get work. They stayed alive by Mother selling anything she could get a hold of on the black market and by cleaning houses.

The flow of refugees to the French border motivated our own resolve to escape. The border crossing was a chaos of humanity. People stayed in tents with few resources, only a hope of saving themselves. While in this locale, on the night that the Germans invaded Belgium, unbelievable shelling and bombardment lasted the entire night. To this day, any major storm becomes a flashback that brings a child's fear into an adult's heart.

Because we were stateless, we were unable to cross into France and so we had to return to Brussels. At this time, the Belgian government sympathized with the refugees and was helpful in issuing temporary papers. I was able to resume school unharmed until 1942, when the edicts and the first roundups began of Jewish men followed by families.

My father was able to relocate us to an undeclared residence with a family who hated the Germans and Nazis. We lived in hiding there from 1942 to 1943.

One day, when I was playing in the courtyard, two Gestapo appeared and spoke to me in German, looking for the Klipstein family. Having presence of mind, I replied in French that I did not speak German and ran upstairs warning my parents of the intruders, as they followed me upstairs. My father spoke to me in French, "You go down to your parents!" not claiming me as his own, and thus they were led away while I escaped the arrest.

I wandered about in the streets for hours in a distressed state not knowing where to turn. Finally I decided to return to our residence and appealed to the landlord asking what to do. The landlord kept me for that night but told me that I needed to find another place. They could not house me anymore.

The next morning I remembered friends of my parents, a wealthy highly-cultured family, who helped many to conceal themselves. They helped me to be placed in a small convent in a secluded, out of the way, countryside locale.

Four nuns cared for twenty five children among whom half were Jewish and of all ages. This was a daunting experience, but knowing my helpless state, without parents, without any support, I took on the role of a good Christian and studied for Communion. I was baptized, knowing that this would give me a greater degree of safety.

The convent facility was austere, with limited food supplies. The dormitory with little cubicles for each child was to keep modesty for each. Because I was one of the older children, twelve and a half years old, I cared for the little ones, performed any chores and was sent on errands, which on many occasions I feared being discovered, although I did not look Jewish.

After my parents' arrest, they were taken to a gathering compound where most of the Jews were sent to Poland. A Jewish staff, under the supervision of a German commandant, ran this camp. As a recreational diversion, the camp had a talent show in which my mother entered her own poem, which she read in German. The commandant was enthralled by the poem and the dialect of her German and asked to see her since he was from the same area. He was an un-usual overseer because my mother's appeal to help her and Father to remain in Belgium resulted in them working in the camp for one and a half years, until they were liberated. My father worked as a carpenter on different projects and Mother cleaned the soldiers' barracks, polished their boots and assisted in their laundry and general cleaning.

In September 1944, they were liberated by the Allies. As the Allies approached, the commandant opened the gates and announced to the inmates, "Get away from here. You are free. Now it is our turn to run."

The family that was instrumental in placing me in the convent retrieved me. I lived with them in luxury for about a year. The beautiful surroundings, butlers, maids, opulent settings and foods were beyond belief. I luxuriated in this comfort and was glad to remain with them for as long as possible.

In 1945, I was reunited with my parents in Brussels. Of course I was happy to be reunited with them, but somewhere in my child's mind, I had a certain resentment and estrangement that took many years to overcome.

Once again, I resumed school where my father encouraged me to also learn a trade. Pattern and dressmaking was a needed occupation wherever one lived. I worked hard to achieve normalcy after all the years of upheaval of the years 1938 through 1945.

We soon established contact with our American family who reissued the affidavits for us to immigrate to the States. In December 1947, we crossed the Atlantic and landed in New York. The relatives arranged for us to board with families in Washington Heights, while another cousin employed my parents in his factory of purses and bags manufacture. We soon rented an apartment of our own. We all went to night school and resolved to meld into the American society. We discovered that all the crates of be-longings that we shipped in 1938 disappeared because there was no one to pay the storage fees and, most likely, it was taken for granted that we did not survive the Holocaust, and so, all the goods were auctioned off.

Janine 2012

I finished school and became a sample maker for custom ladies fashions. I fell into the fast step of American life, reached for goals, and married Kenneth Gimpelman in 1959. We had two sons, Peter, who is an accountant, and Alex a civil engineer. I also am overjoyed with our three grandsons, Jonathan, Brandon and granddaughter Morgan.

I married Irving Sokolov a few years after Kenneth passed away. I enjoy the opera, ballet, and concerts and keep my body and mind in shape.

In 1991, the call for Hidden Children to assemble in New York prompted me to join the others who were hidden. It was "Mind Boggling." I experienced validation and an awakening that my memories and hurts were real and that I was not the only one who always felt different and wanted to remain inconspicuous.

I reside in the summer in Long Island and am a member of the Long Island Hidden Children's group. And in the winter months, I am delighted to be part of the Child Survivors/Hidden Children of Palm Beach County. I appreciate the good work they do in speaking about their experiences and fighting the messages of the deniers. I am pleased to support their cause.

MANY COUNTRIES, MANY BORDERS, MUCH SUFFERING

by Joe Spindel

Cewkow, Poland is located about twenty five kilometers from Yaroslav. It was a small village of about 300 residents. A rural community, where moder-nity was a far-off dream. It supported about thirty Jewish families where life, although primitive by any standard, was rich in tradition with a thirst for learning. This little community supported a synagogue, *mikva*, (ritual bath) and served as the spiritual hub where the Jewish community found comfort and security in their own dedication and belief of the higher power, God. The adjoining cemetery displayed a history of Jewish life for years.

Joe Age - 14

Our family, as most of the Jews in town, followed the strict traditions of orthodoxy, which was always exemplified by pious good deeds and prayer. As were the biblical dictates, my hair was styled with side-curls, *payes*, as were the rest of the Jewish boys.

This is where I was born on October 16, 1931. My father, Shimshon, a tall man with a shock of red hair, had a quiet demeanor, slow to anger and actually left all disciplinary actions to my mother Feige. She was the one that provided a loving atmosphere with educational guidance for me and my sister Gitel, who was six years older.

Mother was one of thirteen siblings, ten brothers and three girls. She excelled in many subjects and biblical studies because she was a constant observer and absorbed the tutoring of her brothers. All had moved away and were

246

dispersed all over Poland; only one sibling, Lipa, lived in a nearby town Oleshyce. Actually he was expelled by the Nazi takeover from Hanover, Germany where he had been settled for many years.

Our thatched-straw roof wooden house served as our living quarters for us, my maternal grandmother and mother's two younger sisters. They used their sewing skills to produce clothing for the farming community. A section of the front room served as a general goods store, where the local farmers could buy or trade with their farm products such as chickens, geese, eggs, flour. We got milk from a local farmer who milked the cow directly into our own container, in order to assure that our milk was kosher.

The preparations for the Sabbath brought the women of each Jewish household into almost a frenzy to get all ready before the onset of the holy day with special foods. In order to have a hot meal on the Sabbath day, a crock pot dish, the *cholent*, was readied for the slow cooking in the sustained heat of the brick oven. Earlier, the *challah*, braided bread, and other delicacies were prepared with care and a sense of obedience to the commandment of honoring the Sabbath. The lit candles cast a rich aura in our humble home, and it felt like a palace transformed into a feeling that uplifted all. Accompanying Father to the synagogue, nibbling on a treat given to me by Mother, made me feel that I was special and transcended some unsaid connection to something mysterious and important. It made me feel that I was living in a special time and feeling close to God.

My earliest memories, from the age of five years old, are when I started *cheder*, a religious Jewish school, where a teacher, a *melamed*, was hired and whose wages were paid by a group of parents. Normally, only boys attended. Girls were educated by their mothers in their homes. About eight boys, of all ages, were tutored in the Hebrew alphabet and memorizing prayers.

Walking home from *cheder* was like running a gauntlet of taunts and abuse by the Polish and Ukraine hoodlum boys. To this day, I can recall the fear and pounding heart as I ran to avoid being accosted and beat up.

At the age of seven, I started first grade in the public Polish school. My excitement of being an official student brings back a painful scene, which still haunts me today. As I was walking home with a group of non-Jewish boys, we passed a church. The Christian boys genuflected and crossed themselves and expected me to take off my hat. I was told by Mother that my hat had to stay on at all times, demonstrating respect and reverence for God. My refusal to obey the boys brought on a brutal beating, and I was called Christ killer. Besides being hurt physically, to be called a killer devastated me. I knew that I could not hurt anyone and to be called a killer was most wounding to my soul. I came home crying. Mother comforted me with tender hugs and loving words and said that those boys were cruel and stupid and not to walk with them anymore.

In September 1939, all changed. Germany invaded Western Poland, and the Soviets came in from the east as was agreed by the Ribbentrop-Molotov non-aggression pact.

We heard planes flying at a distance dropping their load of bombs into the nearby forests with loud explosions and flashes of fire. A few days later, German soldiers arrived in our town, riding on three-seat motorcycles with attached sidecars. They did not encounter any resistance or fighting. We knew that we were under German occupation.

Our first occurrences that our lives changed was when our Ukrainian neighbors, emboldened by the German takeover, came into Jewish homes or businesses, and with threats, helped themselves to goods without paying. The attitude of the long-standing anti-Semitism was exhibited in the open with words and acts. We had heard of the cruelty and discrimination that befell the Jews of Germany, but we could not fathom that this evil would reach all the way to our remote little village.

A short time after the Germans came into our area, on a Friday, when Father was walking home from the synagogue after the evening prayers, he was shot and killed by a German soldier. The tragedy of having to bury our father in the cemetery made us realize that we were in the grips of evil that was even worse than our local anti-Semitic population. We never were able to return to place a tombstone over his resting place.

By this time, my grandmother had already passed away and my two aunts had moved from the village. Mother decided that we could not remain in this town among enemies, so we managed to escape to the neighboring town Oleshyce to join our extended family and Uncle Lipa, who gave us a room in his small apartment. This Polish town was under the control of the Soviet army. We tried to adjust to the Communist ways. And although it made the community feel safer from the local discrimination, following their dogma of atheism made many Jews resistant to this call. We could not abandon our heritage and spiritual and historical connection to the *Torah* and God.

In the spring of 1940, the Russian government raided the homes of immigrants, non-residents, in towns under their occupation. Tens of thousands of Jews, who refused to become citizens of the Russian might, were detained and sent off to Siberia to serve hard labor. We were among them.

One Friday night, we, along with many Jews, were put into cattle cars for this long journey. Uncle Lipa escorted us to the train and told Mother that she should leave me with his family. My protest and tears were two-fold. I did not want to separate from my mother and sister, and being only eight years old I also did not want to miss my first experience of riding on a train. This childish tantrum and Mother not wanting to leave me behind actually saved my life. My uncle, his family and all the Jews that remained were killed by the Germans in the Holocaust.

And so our many weeks of journey finally brought us to our destination, sometimes in May 1940. The camp consisted of a number of barracks and was situated in a remote pine forest near the Mongolian border. The barracks housed us without any type of furniture or even straw mattresses. Our beds were the cold floor. Each barrack had a pot belly stove which was our only source of warmth and did not manage to supply enough heat for the entire barrack. One had to stand near it to revive the frozen hands and feet. The lice were an enemy, which we could not rid ourselves from since we had no facilities or soap to maintain a healthy hygiene.

Mother was fortunate to be assigned to be a cook for the common kitchen where the residents got some meals. The meager rations were never enough to quiet the constant hunger. The adults became the slave laborers extracting pine oil from the thick, abundant forest. This product was apparently needed for the Russian industries and the war effort.

With the onset of the Siberian winter, conditions became dire. People got sick and could not get any medical treatment. Many suffered severe frostbite and many succumbed to this ordeal not being accustomed to this rigorous life. During this entire time, children were just left to their own devices. School was not provided and our only resource of keeping occupied was exploring nature. Another activity in the winter was skiing on makeshift skis, which the kids made from slats of an abandoned barrel.

Even in this remote area, where following religion was outlawed, men gathered for *minyans*, a quorum of ten men, to pray and follow the rituals of Judaism.

We were kept there until July 1941. When the Germans attacked Russia in June 1941, we were told that we were free to resettle out of Siberia. The emaciated and depleted population and families decided that the best place to go to was the Asian part of Russia where the climate was warm. We were fortunate to get ox-driven wagons and traveled for three days to the nearest train station. There we had to wait until available cattle cars were designated for us. We traveled for about six weeks and finally arrived in Uzbekistan, where people disembarked at different towns where the train passed by.

We got off in a large town called Kermine, where we found a Jewish community of Persian Jews and stayed there for the next five years, surviving mostly on black market dealings. Even though I was just ten years old, I was the man of our house/family and learned how to earn a few *rubles* by being involved with adults in the art of bartering, selling and avoiding arrests by bribing the local government officials and the police. Nothing was legal in Russia. Here I contracted malaria and had a severe bout until Mother was able to procure quinine, which cured me.

In 1945, my sister got married and I was displaced as the man of the house by my brother-in-law. I felt hurt and yet I was a bit relieved that I did not have to carry this burden and responsibility anymore.

We returned to Poland one year after the war, not finding a single relative alive. Arriving in 1946, we found that housing and livelihood was not available. Children homes were established for the orphaned surviving children. My mother decided to place me in *Bnei Akiva Kibbutz* home where I could be cared for better than she could provide. I had mixed feelings about having to leave our family, but it was a good decision. Because there I found that I was still a child and learned to enjoy youthful pursuits of fun, songs and rekindled a desire to be part of the movement of returning to our holy land, Palestine, now Israel.

A valiant effort by *Bricha*, an organization which from 1944 to 1948 facilitated Jews to illegally immigrate to Palestine from Poland, Hungary, Czechoslovakia, Romania, Yugoslavia and the Soviet Union, from countries where we were tortured and killed and lost all our families and homes.

Our illegal journey through Europe took our group one year to finally board an illegal ship for Palestine from the port of Marseilles, France. Being a religious children's home, it was of course *kosher* so our nutrition was mostly bread and peanut butter, which to this day represents for me a bread of affliction and a symbol of leading to freedom.

The ship, manned by a crew composed of American Jews and Israelis, was the "Exodus 1947." Four thousand five hundred refugees of all ages including families with small children, were crammed into the ship

Within two days from casting sail on the Mediterranean, the British navy started to shadow us. After five days at sea, the shores of the Promised Land were visible. Our ship tried to run the blockade, when two frigates rammed the ship on either side causing the upper deck to edge away and almost was torn off from its position. We were angry at this rough attack and tried to defend ourselves by throwing potatoes at our captives. And actually we suffered two fatalities caused by the British.

Helpless and with force, we were towed into the port of Haifa. With the beautiful sight of *Har Hacarmel*, the Carmel mountain in the background, the British forcibly removed all from the Exodus unto three troop carriers and sailed us away back to France where all refused to get off. We spent two months in port on the ship. We sailed again from the Mediterranean through Gibraltar into the Atlantic Ocean, north to Hamburg, Germany. We were forcibly escorted, without any exception, to trains secured with barbed wires on the windows and locked doors and were taken to Hamburg Germany. My group was taken to Camp Peppendorf, near Lubek, which was a concentration camp during the war. We were virtual prisoners, and this time, our guards carrying rifles were the British soldiers. This action caused a world outrage, and the United Nations condemned this act.

We remained in the camp till 1948 when we were given permission to enter Palestine legally this time. Arriving to ongoing warfare in Palestine, we were

Joe - Israeli Army 1953

taken to a transit camp and then, I was taken to a youths' school, where I finally started my formal education. I finished high school within two years and enlisted in the Israeli Army. I served for two and a half years and earned the rank of sergeant.

On May 14, 1948, Israel declared its Independence. The joy and sense of finally having our own country was celebrated in the streets with singing and dancing. This joy was short lived as the attacks of Jordanian planes bombed the refineries in the port of Haifa and the war for our existence raged. At the same time, the Egyptian army and the Sudanese volunteers attacked from the south. Syrian, Iraqi and Lebanese forces attacked from the North. The beginnings of Israel were very difficult for the Holocaust survivors and yet, there was a heroic stance and stubbornness that we will not be led to slaughter ever again.

In the meantime, my mother and family left the DP camps, immigrated to the United States and settled in Brooklyn, New York. They begged me to join them. In 1954, I came to this country and started my American life. Once again being with my mother, sister and her family I created roots and a sense of belonging.

I made a decent wage in retail, managing stores and after about two years in the country I met the love of my life, Erica who is also a survivor from Austria and the Shanghai, China ghetto. We got married and were blessed with two great sons, Barry named after Erica's father, Baruch Mendel. He is employed in a government job, married Deborah and they enhanced our family with two

Erica and Joe 2009

grandsons, Michael and Jonathan. And our younger son Steven, named after my father Shimshon, became a physician, married Jana and added to our family with two grandchildren, David and Cara.

Dealing with health difficulties since 1990, and overcoming them, we decided to move to Florida in 1995, where we established a good life with friends, community and the wonderful visits of our children. We enjoyed extensive travels, which included Poland and Shanghai, China.

We joined the Child Survivors/Hidden Children of the Holocaust organization and have found a circle of lovely friends who have added to our pleasure and purpose.

We have been active in witnessing about the Holocaust and adding our own stories to the total of the Holocaust history. My own sacrifices of a lost childhood, taking on adult responsibilities and fight for the Jewish nation has been a history that I cannot relinquish. It is part of my fiber, my heartbeat.

The message that I leave with you is that we, the Jewish people, must prevail. We have a great heritage, a great past for which we must fight and establish a bright future for us and the world.

Joe passed away on May 18, 2010.
He was a wonderful man and his passing is a great loss.

MY PARENTS' GIFT "BASIA MUST SURVIVE"

by Beatrice Sussman

Beatrice Age - 12

It has been sixty-six years since I left my birth town of Krivichi, Poland, now Belarus. It was a *shtetl*, a small town, of no great distinction where only about fifty families resided. A census showed a little over 400 Jews lived and thrived under difficult conditions and governments.

In its more current history, Krivichi was governed by Belarus, Tsarist Russia, Poland, Soviet Russia and by the killers of Nazi Germany. The nearest large town, twenty one miles northeast of town, was Vileyke.

Krivich, as the Jews called it, had one synagogue, *a mikva,* ritual bath, where Mother and I enjoyed the luxury of a hot bath every Friday. Also a *"shochet,"* a kosher religious slaughterer, served the community.

I, Beatrice, Basia Poliskin, Sussman, was born in 1933. I believe that I was named Basia after a maternal great grandmother. My baby brother, Avremel, was born seven years later in 1940.

My father, Sholom Poliskin, was one of four

Mother Libe, Beatrice Age - 7, Father Sholom

253

children. Brothers Morris and Harry came to the United States before the first world war, and a sister Libe, lived in town with her husband and three children. They were killed in the Shoah.

Father's parents died when he was a young boy. Somehow he managed to establish a life on his own, became a dealer in lumber and provided a comfortable living for us. He was a respected, good and kind man. He was charitable and generous to the needy to the point where Mother complained that his generosity will drive them into the poor house.

Mother Libe 1930

His work took him away on business trips often. I awaited his return home with pleasure and expectation of a gift for me. I remember a special gift was a large bouncing ball peeking through a woven net bag.

Mother, Libe, was one of four daughters in this order, Hane, Mother, Haske and Basie. They were raised by my widowed grandmother, Asne Leahe Weisenholz. Only Chane and Haske and children survived. All were married with children. My cousins were often my playmates in games of hopscotch, jumping rope or jacks, which were played with small stones. My grandmother, whom I called Bobie, spoiled me with her treats, especially potato pancakes, which I love to this day.

My parents married, introduced by a matchmaker, and even though their temperaments were opposite, they were a good match. Father was easy-going and followed rules, while Mother was full of spirit and stood her ground when necessary. She was the disciplinarian.

Mother was religious, ran a *kosher* home and followed the traditions of Judaism. She was always working at something. She did not employ any servants to assist her. She did all the housework, cooking and baking herself. She added to our income by cooking *kosher* food for the Jewish sellers, who came once a week from the nearby little towns, to sell their wares at the *"mark,"* market.

Our house, situated in the market square, was a single family four-room home, with an enclosed porch. It was nicely furnished with essential pieces of furniture, but the nickel bed was a showpiece and mother's pride and joy. Mother did have a sense of style and embellished our surroundings by painting the walls with a template to create a wallpaper look.

As in those times in most small towns, we did not have electricity. We had to bring water from a well. The sanitary needs were located in the back yard. We did have a cow, housed in her own small barn, where often I would come with Mother to get the rich, warm foamy milk, milked into my enamel cup.

Our life, like all other Jewish families, was stressful not knowing when the display of anti-Semitism would be directed and at which window or house. My baby brother barely escaped injury when a stone thrown at our window shattered the glass over his bed, just missing him. That is why most Jewish families did not place beds near windows.

The taunting of *"Zhidy do Palistiny,"* Jews to Palestine, became a slogan that was dreaded and was virtually a daily occurrence. This is the picture of our town and our life until the Soviets occupied our part of Poland with a declaration of war against Poland on September 17, 1939. Nazi Germany invaded Poland from the west, the Soviet Union from the east where we lived.

The control by the Soviets brought both freedom and relief from the anti-Semitic abuse, but on the other hand, those who had businesses or were considered *bourgeois,* capitalists, were taken away in the middle of the night and sent off to Siberia. Mother trembled every day and night that Father too would be taken.

Life became difficult because Father was not able to continue his business. Jobs were scarce and hard to come by. Thankfully, we had our cow and garden in the back of our house, which subsidized some of our food needs. Bribing or trading became a way of life. Despite all this, the small self-contained Jewish population, maintained, even if in a clandestine way, the traditional Jewish way of life.

In the meantime, many refugees arrived in town, escaping from the Germans, and bringing tales of evil against Jews. People could not and would not believe that such evil could exist. It was difficult to absorb and believe since many had the experiences of living under the Germans in WWI and stated that they were not so bad then.

I began school and found joy in being able to learn and be with children. This lasted till the spring of 1941.

On June 22, 1941, as I was playing jacks in the yard with my friends, a number of German planes flew overhead with thundering noise from their engines and zoomed down as if crashing, dropping bombs and pulling up into the sky. I ran to Mother in fright, not understanding what just had happened. I was hardly seven years old. The Russians retreated and we were left without any order or knowing what to expect.

The next day German soldiers entered our town. They confiscated all horses from Jews and non-Jews and had Jewish men take these animals to the front lines of the war. Father escaped this selection by hiding in our little cooling cellar. Most Jews had secret hiding places to hide from the Germans. Our hiding place could accommodate the four of us, standing up.

Our life was at the whim of the *Gestapo* or the non-Jewish hoodlum collaborators, who came and robbed us of our possessions. We had no option to refuse. They had gained courage under the Nazis and were encouraged to attack Jews without restraint.

As a young child, I only knew that everything was different, everyone was worried, no one smiled. The children did not play anymore, and everyone stayed out of sight as much as possible. Life under the Nazis came with all the edicts and hardship against Jews; to separate, demoralize, rob, use as slave labor and destroy. Our areas were the testing grounds of what the killers could get away with and if the populace would not object and even would collaborate.

One day Mother noticed the *Gestapo* in the back yard. By this time we had learned of the massacres "*shchite*" that occurred in a nearby town, executed by the *Gestapo* and collaborators. In a determined and frantic voice, Mother said, "This is it. We must go to our hiding place." We got into the cellar, but my little brother was crying frantically and, of course, would expose us. Mother, in command, declared that because of Avreml all of us will be killed. She demanded that Father and I stay in place while she carried my brother out to go to a neighbor's house. She was accosted by the *Gestapo* who shot her and wounded Avreml. She dropped to the ground dead, still holding my wounded little brother. The Germans kicked at Avreml with their boots until he was dead.

Father and I, peeking out of a crack in the cellar, saw this brutality which made me open my mouth to scream. Father grabbed me and squashed my face against his chest to stifle my crying. He said, "Basiele, you must live, stay quiet." I was eight years old.

That day we heard screaming and shooting all day long. The Belarus hooligans returned to our house and discovered us in our hiding place. They demanded valuables or they would turn us in to the *Gestapo*. Father paid them off with some gold coins, which he had hidden, and they left without disclosing us.

During this day of massacre, Grandmother and my aunt and cousins survived in their hiding place.

Searching for safety for us, Father got away to the woods to a farmer whom he knew and with whom he had business dealings. He asked him to hide us. He agreed. Father returned to get me, and we snuck away, along with a couple of Father's business buddies, to this farmer. We stayed in the forest swamp during the day, and the farmer let us sleep in his barn, in the hay, at night. When it became dangerous for him and his family, Father arranged that I be taken to Kurenets to my Aunt Chane who escaped to be taken because she was hidden in a wagon with hay. This town soon also was destined for the massacre. They shot the Jews that they gathered.

Aunt Chane's family and I hid in her hiding place, which was a space camouflaged by a false wall in a grain storage room. To get to it, one had to crawl through a narrow space. We heard shooting, screams, crying all day. The bestiality against the captured Jews was not to be described. Murder was not enough. They had to face death stripped of all dignity, naked they were shot and fell into a pre-dug pit. At night it stopped. I led Aunt Chane, her husband Itche and cousin Judel, (Jerry), to the swamps near the farm. Father was still there. Again we hid in the barn in the hay at night and back to the forest swamp during the day.

We learned later that my dearest grandmother was burned in her house by the Germans. Aunt Haske and family managed to get away to the forest and joined the friendly partisans.

During harvest time we could not go to the forest. It was dangerous because of being spotted by the workers. We all hid in the attic of the barn and lay flat, not getting out day or night. The farmer provided minimal food, and the men created a pipe from the pliable bark of a tree to use as funnel as a toilet. After a time, because we were so many hiding at the farmer's, he told us that he could not help us anymore because he was putting his own family in jeopardy.

The one hope to escape with our lives was to get away from the fighting zones and get to a safer area, deeper into Russia. Father, I, Aunt Chane's family and the others began our desperate journey. We walked under cover of night and rested hidden in the forests during the day. Some of our escapees became sick and could not keep up so they had to be left behind. All of us were infested with lice. I was covered with boils and swollen from the mosquito bites. Father carried me on his shoulders. He was told by others to leave me behind, but he would not be separated from me. His reply always was, "Basia must survive."

We wandered about for miles, begging for food from the locals. Some had pity on us, and others chased us away with a warning that they would get the Germans after us. Our goal continued to be to get away from the Germans and away from the fighting front.

Winter came and that was an additional enemy, no shelter, no winter clothing and being more visible because the footprints showed in the snow. Father had to carry me because my feet were completely numb from frostbite. The boils, not treated, were oozing and sticking to my clothing. They finally healed, leaving scars that to this day serve as a reminder of those days.

We met with a Soviet partisan, wearing white covers to blend in with the snow. He agreed to help us across the German-Russian front. We walked for over 900 kilometers until we got in the region of Stalingrad.

The Germans succeeded in bringing the fight to Stalingrad. This battle raged close to six months; we could not stay there. We traveled by cattle cars and were taken on a long hard journey, which brought us to a city in Siberia. The area was west of Novosibirsk. This is where Father was conscripted to work in a factory.

Right off the train, Father was taken to a hospital because he was sick with pneumonia. I was placed in a children's home. The home was mostly for orphans. The care was minimal, not sensitive to children, starving and filthy. We had one set of clothing for summer and one for winter. The school had no books, no pencils and no paper. We had to work in the fields planting and picking potatoes. After the winter thaw, we scrounged for frozen potatoes in the fields and ate them raw.

When Father got well, he took me out from this home. For a short while we were together, hungry and struggling, but still together. This did not last long because soon they drafted him into the army and sent him away. Again I was alone and placed in another children's home, which was not any better. Children died from a variety of diseases, but typhoid was the primary killer.

This was my home, my childhood, growing up without a feeling of safety love or hope. Education was neglected. Somehow I just barely survived for two and a half years there. What kept me going was the periodic letters from Father, which were brought to me by my father's lady friend Shimentchuk. She was sent to Siberia earlier just because she was considered a *bourgeois*, being educated and a pharmacist. The last letter told me that he was fighting somewhere near Berlin. That was the last time I heard from him.

Before Father left, he asked Mrs. Shimentchuk to look in on me. When she sent her daughter Malke to visit with me, I begged her to take me away from this home. She took pity on me and took me to her mother, who really did not want another mouth to feed and take care of.

Many years later, I appealed to the Red Cross to help find what happened to my father. Some years later I received information that he died on March 7, 1945 in Riga and was buried in a mass grave.

This village had a number of Jewish families who had been shipped here in 1939. Life was difficult for all, but they agreed to take turns giving me a daily meal, taking off the obligation from Mrs. Shimentchuk. I was an outsider, alone, and everybody looked at me with pity. I was depressed and felt a burden to myself and had often wished that my mother would have kept me with her and be killed with her, rather than live in this constant suffering and loneliness.

Even though I was away from the misery of the children's home, my life was difficult. I was treated like a maid and a burden to the family. I scrubbed floors and carried pails of water a distance away from a frozen-over lake, drawing the water from a chiseled hole.

On June 22, 1944, eastern Belarus was liberated by the Soviet Red Army, pushing the war westward to the Vistula River across from Warsaw by August 1, 1944.

I received a letter from my aunt Haske telling me to be patient, they are working to bring me back home. A family friend, Hazkel Gelman, who worked for the KGB (Russian Secret Police), made false papers for me and pulled string to have me return home.

Traveling for a few weeks across Russia in a cattle car train, the end of WWII was announced to shouts of joy and tears; this was May 8, 1945. I was now twelve years old, a child, yet an old soul who suffered a lifetime of pain and sorrows.

My aunt Haske and uncle Boris greeted me with embraces. They represented the family. They looked at me, as a stranger, but understood that the years did not stand still for me. I had grown. I was still a child but with eyes of an old person.

Krivich was a changed place. Our home was taken over by strangers. Only a handful of Jews survived. Every street, every corner of this town rang with screams and pain. We could not remain here. With the influence of my uncle, we were able to get to Lodz, where anti-Semitism was rampant. Abuse and pogroms all around Poland against Jews was an occurrence that drove all the Jews to get out of Poland.

My uncle connected me with an acquaintance to get me out of Poland. They were to follow shortly. We traveled on a train full of German repatriates who were turned out of their homes in Poland. At the border I was detained, but managed to talk my way back on the train. I rejoined my companion travelers on this journey, which brought us to the Russian Zone of Berlin. Soon after, I escaped into the American Zone to the DP Camp Schlachtensee.

Beatrice Age - 13   **Beatrice and friend**
DP camp Eschwege Germany

A few months later I was joined by my aunt, uncle and cousin. With the influx of survivors to the camp, we were transferred to Eschwege near

Frankfurt/Am/Main. I started school, Hebrew school, and finally had the opportunity to learn, study and grow.

My hopes of a future, although uncertain, were rekindling slowly. The spirit of establishing a Jewish state was ingrained through songs and indoctrinations by the representatives, *shlichim*, from Palestine, including Ben- Gurion, who came to visit and speak to us. We were awakened that we are not just remnants of an evil that almost erased all Jews of Europe. We are the future, the country's backbone and strength.

I registered to go to Palestine, but at the last minute, I found my father's oldest brother, Morris, in the United States, and he sponsored me. I decided to come to a family and find my roots again.

We boarded the ship the Ernie Pile, a battle ship that served in the Pacific. With cheers and hope, we set out on our journey to the land of dreams and opportunity. After just a few days at sea, the ship was damaged by an iceberg, and we had to transfer with hoists onto another ship, the Marin Martin, in mid sea. After a horrendous seasick journey of three weeks, I arrived in New York on April 1, 1947.

I was met by two uncles, Morris and Harry. Harry took one look at me, said hello, and I never ever saw him again. Uncle Morris took me to their home in New Brunswick, New Jersey where I was greeted by his wife with a look of resentment in her eyes, relaying a message "Here I have to feed a *greene*," newcomer. Regardless of the cold welcome, I remained with them for eight years.

I managed to attend school and graduated high school. I worked two jobs until nine in the evening as a sales girl and helped the Aunt with all that she demanded of me. I can honestly say that I was no burden to them.

In 1954, my aunt Hane's married son, Abe, who lived in Connecticut, invited me to move and live with them. I was glad to get out from my drudgery of a life. I met many young people and developed a social life. Here I met my husband Bernie. After a short courtship, we got married and worked hard together to build a financially comfortable life. We worked long hours in our grocery store, together with Bernie's two brothers. I spent many hours at the register while Bernie cut meat in the back of the store. Yes, the work was hard, but I was determined to learn to live the American dream, enjoy life and appreciate my survival.

After a few years we started our family. Our wonderful children, son Marc and daughter Laurie and four grandchildren, Ian, Nicole, Josh and Matthew, have been our treasures and pleasure of our lives.

We tried to establish a good life and opportunities for them. I did not want them to have regrets and difficult childhoods. Our tragedy and sadness to this day is losing my little daughter, Rosalynn, at the age of eight, to cancer.

Bernie and I moved to Florida in 1987. We enjoyed our life away from the cold north. Our home was a welcoming winter getaway for our children and many guests. My life partner and dear husband died in 2002 after many years of illness.

Through the years, Bernie and I saw a need and were determined to work for the Jewish people and for Israel. I served as a chairperson for Israel Bonds and was honored by the State of Israel in1981. I am a life member of many Jewish organizations that work for the good of Israel, Jewish people and all people.

I joined the Child Survivors/Hidden Children of the Holocaust, Palm Beach County because I always needed to be connected to Jewish causes. Remembering the Holocaust was most important to me. I admired the group's dedication and found a connection, a commonality of memories, which brings me close

Beatrice 2012

to my lost Mother, Father, brother, family, and our Jewish people.

I cannot and must not escape my roots and the Jewish people.

I am sharing my story and recording the names of my family who were killed with brutality so that here, in these pages, through these words, they will be remembered. I hope that my story will serve as a memorial. With pride and appreciation, I am sharing a poem written by my grandson Ian at the age of twelve, which shows the family lives in my children.

GRANDMOTHER

by Ian Brownstein
2005

She was born in Poland
She had a good life
Two parents and
A baby brother
Uncles and aunts
But her life crumbled
Her mom and brother die
In front of her face
But she survived
With her uncle, aunt and father
Hiding by day
Running by night
Heading for Siberia
Her uncle got shot
But he held on
When they reached Siberia
Her father was sent to fight
She was alone
In frozen Siberia
Without money or food
But a friend of her uncle

A policeman made fake papers
She went back through where she had come
Through Poland
To the coast
From orphanage
To DP camp
Until she made it to America.
My grandma
Might have been murdered
She had three kids
Four grandchildren
Had she died, they all would be lost
A branch cut off
The family tree
But she was saved
By her uncle's friend
So her family lives
I am one of them
Because she struggled to live
To keep the tree alive
I live.

TOO YOUNG TO REMEMBER ALL YET THE PAINFUL FEELINGS LINGER

by Alan (Abraham) Wainberg

Where does one begin to describe the pictures of my life? Today, in my senior years, it is still as vivid as if I was just there yesterday. Seeing the images through a child's eyes of my happy days among a loving family, surrounded by a community of good people, makes me feel a pining for those loving people. But the devastating images that make me shudder are remembering the horrible years of the German occupation and the slaughter of my dear ones and our Jewish people.

As I reached adulthood, I learned to understand the pictures in my mind and decipher the details of the tragic history of our town. I had to explore and put a meaning to what I saw. Now I can share what my family and all Jews had to face. A few survived but the majority were murdered.

Alan - Costa Rica

Zelechow, Poland, a typical *shtetl*, town, situated about eighty kilometers from Warsaw, had a Jewish presence dating back to the 17th century. Jews were invited to settle there by the feudal landlords. They needed and appreciated the Jews' business knowhow, trading abilities and their talent to develop commerce in order to enhance the landlords' incomes.

At the end of the 19th century, Jews opened several factories in Zelechow. The largest was a sugar factory. They also owned a few carpentry workshops, a brewery, a whiskey distillery, and a soda-water plant, which served the entire region. A large majority of the craftsmen in town, such as tailors, locksmiths, carpenters, blacksmiths, cobblers, and leather-workers, were Jews.

At the time of the outbreak of WWII, September 1, 1939, Jews were the majority population in town, 5,800 Jews and 2,700 non-Jews. The Jewish community followed the customs of Torah teachings, observing the laws, the traditions of Jewish life, and of charity, *mitzvot*, good deeds. The local welfare organizations helped the poorest by providing them with food, especially before

Taken in the year 1939
Top Row - Left to Right: Cousin Hershel, Cousin Rivka, my Sister Rivka, Cousin Berl, Brother Sholom
Front Row - Left to Right: Alan, Sister Sara, and Cousin baby Berl

Passover, and fuel for the winter.

The cultural and social life was vital between WWI and WWII. The Zionist movement was influential in awakening a yearning for Zion, the return to the land of Israel.

During the 1930's, anti-Semitism was occurring more and more often. Jewish businesses were boycotted, picketed and demonstrated in front of Jewish stores. Incidents of stones thrown at synagogues and Jewish homes became a great worry for the Jewish citizens.

At present and very often, I am pleased that my memory is clear, even though I was a very young child at the beginning of the war. There is a lingering pain and fear. I wish that my memories would be of a more pleasant and peaceful childhood and a peaceful world.

My family had deep roots in this town of Zelechow. My father, Chaim Meier, was born and raised in Maciewice, Poland, a village in Garwolin County, located about seventeen kilometers southeast of Warsaw. He was the oldest of three children, a brother and a sister. He came from an observant family and followed his father's teachings of a Jewish life.

He was a tall, striking man and presented a strong attitude of a tough guy, standing his ground, sticking to the principles of an ethical life. He was serious in his manner. His commitment to just conduct was one of respect and honor in all his dealings, connections in the community and in business. He was a constant student. He encouraged and motivated his children to acquire knowledge and education.

My mother Perl, was one of seven siblings, two brothers, she was the oldest of the five sisters. Mother was passionate in all that she undertook and had a leading position and involvement in the prosperous family business. It was an enterprise of regional distribution of foodstuff, which was established by her father, my grandfather, Shalom Boruchowicz, and grandmother, Gitel. Both sets of my grandparents died before WWII and thankfully did not have to experience the evil that befell the Jews.

Mother was a loving, no-nonsense lady. She too was observant and was educated in the Hebrew and Yiddish languages and was able to pray from the *siddur*, prayer book. She was also an excellent homemaker with focused determination. Whatever she touched was a success.

A rabbi who knew both of my parents' families, suggested that they meet and without much ado, a marriage commitment was made. Father moved to Zelechow, where he proved himself capable of hard work. He took over the management of the family business and in no time established a praiseworthy reputation that followed him all his life and in many countries.

Our home was comfortable, following the fashion of those days, as our family means could provide. Mother continued to work in the business and had a maid to help with household chores and oversee the children.

Location of the Synagogue

I was born in 1937, joining my siblings, two older sisters, Sara and Rivka and my eighteen months older brother, Sholom. As in most Jewish households, we spoke Yiddish at home, while Polish was spoken outside of the home and in business.

When WWII erupted on September 1, 1939, the Germans managed to defeat the Polish army and defenses in just a few days and entered Zelechow on September 12, 1939. Immediately they apprehended Jews on the street with ruthless abuse, looted their properties and set a number of houses on fire. The next day, on September 13, the synagogue was set on fire.

As in most of Poland, they immediately implemented anti-Jewish policies and edicts intended to demoralize, hurt, and destroy the Jewish population and culture. At the whim of the abusers, Jews were subject to harsh treatment and humiliation by both the Germans and the collaborating Poles. They stationed soldiers in town and periodically *Einzatzgrupen*, mobile killing units composed primarily of German SS and police personnel, would appear, riding in black cars or sidecar-motorcycles. Without cause, they, randomly picked up and killed Jews.

Judenrat & Community Leaders- Zelechow, 1940
(from the archives of Beit Hatfutsot, the Visual Documentation Center
- Courtesy of Zipora Shama, Israel)

They ordered that a Jewish Council, a *Judenrat*, be established in November 1939 to help them manage the community. As soon as it was set up, the Germans imposed a ransom payment, a "contribution" of 100,000 zloty. Invisible borders, lines were set beyond which Jews were not to go.

In July and August of 1940, the Germans forced all Jews from the surrounding smaller villages and towns to move to Zelechow, which overcrowded all residences, creating hardships and many shortages.

At the end of 1941, more and more refugees came to Zelechow, and the number who were pushed into a small area grew to about 13,000. Our townspeople were charitable and helpful to them, providing food, shelter and sometimes jobs. As conditions worsened and deteriorated, an epidemic of typhus broke out.

I remember occasions when we were forewarned that the black cars were coming. Mom and most other parents made the children abandon their play outside and stay in the house behind closed doors. Naturally, this would not stop the SS from entering.

As I try to summon up my own memories and what Mother told us, I recall that at first I was not afraid to play with the neighborhood children in the streets of the ghetto. I even recall that my parents did not abandon their commitment for education and at the very young age of three, my father took me to the *cheder*, a religious Hebrew school.

I recall the worried look on my mother's face, which made me apprehensive too. I did not understand what caused such concern. I must admit that it took a few years for me to understand what was happening to us. Soon these luxuries of normalcy had to be abandoned, and a rush for survival became a priority.

News of German murderous actions in other communities reached us regularly, but it was not believed. It was impossible that such atrocities could occur. Taking no chances, my parents took precautions by securing hiding places. One was a false attic in a relative's house, with provisions for about fifteen to twenty people. Two other hiding places were "*gryby*" - pits - dugouts, with provisions were established as well as for a brief stay for about the same number at the farms in Wylczyska, about five kilometers from Zelechow. These farms belonged to brothers-in-law of a client and friend of my family, Edward Turek.

Men in groups of one hundred, among them my father, were sent to the labor camp that had been established in Wilga, near Garwolyn. There they were employed digging drainage ditches in the Vistula River. This work was brutal and life meant nothing to the overseers. Jews were destined for annihilation by all means.

Zelechow's turn to be emptied of Jews, the *wyszedlenia*, expulsion, came in the fall of 1942. The ghetto was surrounded by armed SS patrols with dogs, supported by Ukrainian policemen, who spread out all over town, banging on doors, yelling "*raus - shnell*", out - fast. All were herded to the market square from which they were taken away by truck, horse and buggy or on foot to the nearest train station, Garwolyn. The gathered were loaded into cattle cars and were taken to Treblinka. The hunt continued, and those who ran or were discovered in their hiding places, about 800 people in town and nearby, were murdered.

That day, a small group of young people managed to flee from the city into the forest. About 300 Jews, who had trouble getting to the gathering place, children, the elderly, the frail, and those who were trying to hide, were murdered right then and there.

A few days before that evil day, my sisters, Rivka and Sara, were moved secretly to the farmer's hiding pit, one to each. On that day, Mom took me and my brother Sholom to the attic, carefully avoiding the chaotic crowds that were being rushed and shoved to the market place.

The *boydem*, attic, was home for us plus many more than expected, for about two weeks. Obviously there was not enough food for all and absolute quiet was essential. On one occasion, while I was sleeping under the narrow angled part of the eaves of the tin roof, possibly dreaming, I raised my head and hit the roof loudly, all were scared to death that someone had heard this bang, but luckily it was not heard by the occupiers.

One day, a German search patrol accompanied by a local Pole, the head of the community school, were searching most houses for hidden Jews. In our house, they went from room to room, thrusting rifle-bayonets into walls and floors. One of the men in the attic, lifted the trap door and saw that only the civilian was looking up. The man bravely risked discovery by the Germans by sticking out his fingers around the edge of the trap door for the civilian to see. He realized that people were hiding here. Fortunately, he was a decent man and diverted the patrol away from discovering us. He convinced the patrol to move on to other nearby homes.

Another day, our men in the attic overheard Jewish policemen walking by on the street, speaking in loud voices in Yiddish. Apparently they had learned of our hiding place, and wanted to make sure that they were heard. They described the situation in the ghetto, saying that the Germans were clearing the town and intended to burn all the houses in the ghetto in a couple of weeks. Jews in hiding should evacuate a few at a time during the night. They said that it was very dangerous to remain. Close to 13,000 Jews had resided in Zelechow at the time of the *Wysiedlenia*, expulsion. The Germans had taken away about half, and the rest had managed to run away earlier to the East or to the forests or into hiding.

Sokol Family

The two living Sokol sisters, Pela and Teresa

One night, soon after, Mother took my brother and me away from our attic hiding place. We walked guardedly toward the Sokol farm. Being a young child, it appeared like a great adventure to me, a game, but for my mother and brother, who knew the reality of our dangerous situation, it was a horror. We spent a day hiding in a barn and finally reached the Sokol farm on the second night and remained there in a pit for almost two years.

The farmhouse over the pit

The years were hard and we suffered every physical deprivation, filth, vermin, illness, hunger, cold, lack of sanitary conditions. We had to stay in darkened damp cold pits, sleeping and spending days and nights on a hard wooden plank floor, which covered the earthen ground. The entrance was very well hidden. A door camouflaged by a curtain located in a pantry hid a small opening accessed through a trap door and ladder to the *gryb*, pit, which had a tiny narrow window just above ground.

Eventually, we were over twenty people, our family, the Popowski family and an escaped Russian POW hid in this place. In a short time, stealthily, with great care and with the help from Mr. Sokol's oldest son, Jaszek, my father, two uncles and cousins managed to escape from the Wylga labor camps and joined us.

An uncle and my sisters were at the second *gryb*. There were very few visits from one pit to the other and it had to be at night. The danger was constant. If any neighbor would have seen or heard any of us, without any hesitation, they would have given us away, *maseryn*, to the Germans, who offered rewards for Jews. They were given a sack of sugar or flour, and those that hid Jews would be killed for assisting them.

Eventually, in early 1944, someone did give us away, not to the Germans but to AK, *Armia Krajowa*, Polish Folk Army. These men professed to be

270

Polish patriotic partisans working against the occupation, but in reality they were a bunch of thugs, killing especially Jews and looting for profit or pleasure. That night they surrounded the farmhouse with a small group of heavily armed men and shouted for the hidden Jews to come up immediately, calling my mother's surname. They apparently were informed and perhaps knew that our family was wealthy. They expected to get hidden jewelry and valuables.

Seeing the danger, my Aunt Sara and sister Rivka, who were coming to visit our pit that night, started to run to the nearby trees but were shot in the back. Just then my dad, who had been trying to push me out the tiny window, pulled me back when he saw Aunt Sara and Rivka fall. How does one see one's child fall dead and not scream?

After this killing, the trap door was opened, and one of Popowski boys climbed up holding a revolver and was shot instantly. I still tremble now as I recall when I climbed up barefooted from the *gryb* and stepped into a puddle of his blood.

After we were all gathered outside, their leader started negotiating with Dad to take them to town and show the hidden jewels, promising to come back the next night to take us to a safer place. Naturally Dad did not believe them. He knew that no jewels would be found, since we heard that the Jewish homes were robbed of all valuables and set on fire.

As it turned out, luck was with us, *"Got tzy danken,"* thank God. It began to get lighter. The AK also feared the German patrols. They ordered us to remain in the pit until their return at night. Not trusting them, especially seeing their cold-blooded murderous acts against my sister and the others, Dad decided that we would leave as soon as possible, but first my uncles and Dad buried the dead, as essential by Jewish law. We set off toward the northeast where Dad thought we might find some trustworthy help. He was born in Maciewic and hoped that some ex-neighbors might hide us.

The Popowskis did not come with us. Mrs. Popowska left the pit and hid in Sokol's hay barn. She was discovered the next day. She tried to convince the Germans that she was alone and that the Sokol family didn't know that she was hiding there.

Years later we learned that on July 10, 1944, a few days before the liberation, Wladislaw Sokol, a "Righteous Among the Nations," from the village of Wilczyska, was executed by the Germans for hiding three Jewish women, who were killed together with him. Sokol had concealed the Jewish families Boruchowicz, Wajnberg, and Szyfman. The Jewish community, Zelechow, was never reestablished. The few survivors live today in Israel, the United States, Brazil, Argentina, Australia and Costa Rica.

We continued to hike nightly and sleep in the rye fields during daylight. We wore threadbare clothes and had no shoes. Hunger was great. We were forced to steal from the fields and on occasion were able to get some milk, which was suspended into wells in buckets to keep it fresh in the cold water.

After four weeks of hiding in the fields, a decent farmer, who discovered that we were hiding there, warned us that the rye field would soon be harvested, and we should hide in the wheat fields, which would not be harvested for another two weeks. We took his advice, but wheat is shorter than rye so we had to remain closer to the ground during the day.

Throughout the entire time, we had no knowledge of the war's progress and expected it to go on forever. Finally, and with disbelief, we could hear the sounds of war. The explosions of artillery and shooting were getting closer. After two weeks in the wheat fields, we saw Russian tanks approaching close to us. The Russian front was moving west towards Berlin and were in Eastern Poland before the Allied invasion.

Sara, Sholom and I approached the lead tank. We had learned some Russian from the Russian POW, who was with us in the pit, and asked them to take us back to Zelechow. When they heard about our survival, they agreed to take us with them.

Our return to Zelechow was looked upon by our neighbors as if ghosts appeared. We were able to get our home back, which was returned to us without objections from the Polish squatters. They also told Father where he could find two buried Torahs, which became our treasured symbol of our Jewish town. They traveled with us wherever we went.

On July 17 of 1944, the Red Army entered Zelechów, ending the war there. We stayed in Zelechow, under Russian benevolent protection, for about a half a year. Fifty-six Jews returned and remained alive in the city. Of the six plus thousand who were not taken to the killing camps, only fifty-six individuals, including three children - my sister, brother and I, survived and returned to Zelechow as soon as it was liberated. Other survivors returned and a tiny Jewish community was established under most difficult and unnerving conditions.

And so we settled hoping to somehow rebuild our lives, but we encountered incidents of anti-Semitism and many restrictions too. Young Poles taunted and threw stones at us in the street and at our homes. Kind Poles helped in secret so that their neighbors would not find out and be angry with them. But stories were circulating that Poles were killing survivors.

Periodic public anti-Jewish acts of violence, instigated by rumors of blood libel accusations against Jews were occurring in dozens of Polish towns and many in remote villages, which were never reported. An unknown number of survivors were killed when they returned home to find no one but killers. Jews ran for their lives.

Kielce is just one tragic example. The pogrom in Kielce resulted in

272

forty-two Jews being murdered and about fifty seriously injured. This was just the tip of the iceberg that exhibited the continuing anti-Semitism and the atrocities committed against the returning Jews. The Kielce pogrom was the turning point for survivors to realize that there was no future for Jews to rebuild their lives in their previous homes. A migration out of Poland began as General Spychalski signed a decree allowing Jews to leave Poland without visas or exit permits, and the Jewish emigration, or better stated, escape from Poland increased dramatically.

My parents decided not to remain in this unwelcome town, our birthplace, and the place of visions of horrors, a town filled with torrents of tears and anguish. We packed the few belongings and traveled by horse and wagon to Warsaw. To add to our fearful existence and seeking safety, when we stopped for the night and found shelter in a barn, we were robbed of our possessions. There was little of value, but this surely was an omen that we could not and must not remain in this blood soaked land.

The next day we passed Warsaw and saw the city in complete devastation and ruins. We continued to Lodz where we found a survivors community that was offering services to the influx of survivors. There were various organizations such as HIAS, JOINT and representatives from Palestine with offices to help the growing survivor community. A *shtibl*, a small house for praying and a Jewish school was functioning. My parents immediately enrolled me in this school. This was my first secular school where I learned the alphabet. Previously, I only attended *cheder*, Hebrew religious school, at the age of two and three. That was the extent of my education in the years 1941 through 1944, except I learned to play chess with my father in the pit. He made all the game pieces by hand.

Soon the Communist government closed the borders and no exit visas were available for survivors. At the same time, there was nowhere to go since international borders were closed to survivors everywhere.

Eventually, Rabbi Herzog, from Palestine/Israel, obtained visas for about 600 to 700 orphans to secretly leave to Palestine. Not being able to fill the number of orphans that they had visas for, they opened this opportunity to children with parents. My parents, seeking a better and safer life for Sholom, Sara and me, decided to send us to safety, and they would follow later. They would escape over the mountains with my baby brother Bernard, who was born in Lodz on Yom Kippur, 1945.

First we were taken by train to an ex-military camp in Czechoslovakia, and then to Aix-le-Bain in France. We stayed in a nice enormous hotel where many kids were housed. Here we finally had food, playtime and school, mostly French and religious studies in Yiddish. This was a waiting place to eventually go to Palestine illegally. The British would not let Jews enter because of the Arab pressure.

Sara Alan Mom Salomon Bernardo Jaime

L to R: Sister Sara, Alan, Mother,
Brother Sholom, Berish,
Father, and a cousin - 1947 - Paris, France

My parents eventually made it to Paris where we were reunited and were taken out of the orphanage hotel. The six of us settled in the Hotel National near the Metro LaChapelle. The *"pletzel,"* as the public market square was called by the Jews, in the third Arrondissement, became the gathering place for survivors in Paris. They socialized, found other survivors, made new friends and searched for work or black market business.

The Jewish agencies were established here to help and offer guidance to survivors.

Dad went to these offices daily to ask for visas to America, Canada or Palestine or any better place than being stranded in limbo in Paris. He always received discouraging replies, but one day he was asked if we would go to Costa Rica. He immediately said, "Yes. Where is it?"

We learned later that Leo Weiss, a Zelechower, who published a bulletin connecting Zelechow Jews and which he distributed all over the world, facilitated the Costa Rica Zelechow Jews to sponsors us.

Approximately a few hundred, including children, born locally who had immigrated mostly in the 1920s, and a tiny number of WWII survivors settled in Costa Rica. Apparently this community organized some visas for surviving Zelechowers, especially our family, who had a very good reputation among Zelechowers everywhere, somehow communicated with the displaced persons office in Paris.

Our family sailed to Panama on the ship Jagello from Cannes in May of 1948. We could not enter Costa Rica because it was in the midst of a revolution. The Partido Nacional De Liberacion headed by Jose Figueres and Otilio Ulate were taking over from President Calderon.

We had to disembark in Panama and were housed in an ex US military camp where some local Jews came out to greet survivors and offer help. One greeter family, the Altmans, took the kids to town to a movie theatre where, for the first time, we experienced air conditioning and were introduced to eating watermelon with a spoon and drinking Coca Cola.

274

After two weeks, the revolution quieted and we flew to San Jose in a very small plane. We settled in an apartment and Dad immediately started to work to make a living. Our Zelechower reputation helped him obtain credit to buy dry goods, which he sold to people in remote areas where there were no local stores. His method of selling was by letting the buyer payout weekly until the item was paid for. In the States, they call it peddling.

The two Torahs came with us to Costa Rica and eventually one was repaired. The other could not be salvaged. We temporarily lent the repaired one to the Hebrew Academy Synagogue, in Miami Beach. One of the Torahs is now in my niece's shul, synagogue in the Beka sector of Jerusalem.

In Costa Rica, there was a traditional *shul* for regular prayers and for the first time for the kids, a public school in Spanish, the Escuela Juan Rafael Mora. We were placed by age, in grades five, four and three. Not knowing the language, we were assigned to a grade where one or more Jewish kids spoke a common language. In my class, there were three Jewish students, but they did not speak Yiddish or French, my languages. Fortunately the very nice teacher spoke a little French, and I was able to finish third grade with some Spanish skills, mostly from the "street."

During that year, Rabbi Moses Hertzog, not the same as the Israeli, came to Costa Rica on a development trip, looking for donations. He and Dad found a commonality, the Yeshiva Chachnoy Lublin, Poland. Dad had been there before the war and my brother Sholom had briefly attended a temporary post war branch in Paris. Rabbi Hertzog convinced Dad that two Jewish boys would not grow up religiously in Costa Rica, and he should send us, Sholom and me, to the Theological Hebrew Seminary, Yeshiva Chachmey Lublin, in Detroit. At the same time, we were able to attend a public high school under the auspices of the Municipal Board of Education.

Our daily routine was morning prayers, breakfast, religious studies, lunch and continued religious studies. In the late afternoon until seven in the evening, we attended public high school.

In 1955, Sholom went home for a brief visit. My parents could not afford airfare for both of us. He could not return to Detroit for a year and a half because visa rules had changed during the McCarren restriction in Congress.

When my brother and I returned to Costa Rica after graduating high school in December of 1953, we worked in the family business, by now a store, helping out during the very busy year-end season. We immediately applied for a United States residence visa at the US consul, but we had to wait five years on the Polish quota to be approved. Meanwhile we attended night school Escuela Comercial Minerva, a community college, to study accounting and finance.

The two of us also opened our own dry goods store in San Jose and a couple of years later another one in a different province, Alajuela. During weekends, we volunteered at the Costa Rican Red Cross, helping during floods and also as lifeguards at the public swimming pools Ojo de Agua near the new airport.

In Spring of 1959, we finally made it to the US and got our green cards. We settled in Miami Beach, got an apartment and jobs as bank tellers, and started night and summer school at the University of Miami, majoring in accounting. In January 1961, I switched to engineering, as a full time student with a partial scholarship and small help from home.

I graduated as an industrial engineer in January 1964 and worked for the US Naval Propellant plant in Maryland near D.C. That September, I moved to New York to attend graduate school at NYU with a full NSF scholarship and graduated in 1965. I had various jobs in management, consulting and later in executive management in the footwear and apparel industry at various locations in the US and abroad.

I married Karen in 1966 and we were blessed with wonderful children, David, Laura and Daniel and one adorable granddaughter, Anna Rose.

As I write this account of my life, my early childhood was of suffering, I saw killing and evil that children, and as a matter of fact, no one should see or experience. I don't want to forget. It is my obligation to speak and be a witness. I was there. I saw evil beyond description.

Life is not simple and all hopes and dreams sometimes have to be adjusted. And so it was with my marriage which ended in divorce in 1993.

I retired in 1999 to Maine, and then to Florida where I am enjoying an active and interesting life among wonderful friends.

Alan 2013

My very special friend is my college girlfriend Roz Lewy, who lost her husband a few years ago. We are able to renew our lives together.

When I came to Florida, I found that Florida had legislation to teach the Holocaust in schools with minimal funding. I appreciate this law and am grateful that the lesson of the Holocaust will serve as a historic fact and no denier can counter.

I associated with inSIGHT, an organization which helps fund different programs in schools to teach the lessons of the Holocaust and in general fight genocide. I also joined the Child Survivors/Hidden Children of Palm Beach County, where I have found people with common experiences and common memories. We help each other to validate our memories, while the Speakers Bureau makes a great effort to affect students so that they will know that they met a survivor, a Jew, in the hope that the students will stop discrimination and hate for all.

We, Jews, contribute and help wherever we have lived and are willing to continue, even though anti-Semitism is growing.

I speak and I am recording this history of a little child and my family so that generations will learn and fight for justice, rights and a life that is offered to all equally. I believe that we also must stand with the Holy Land of Israel. They are our voices and strength that a Holocaust will never happen again.

A picture of a page from my Uncle's Siddur. The orignal is at Yad Vashem in Jerusalem

During our years in the pits, my Uncle, Moshe Boruchowisz, wrote by hand and from memory, the entire book of prayers, *Siddur*. And one of the pages is a Memorial page with names for those that we lost.

I share with you an image of this page so that the people whose lives were cut short with cruelty will be remembered.

A copy of the Siddur is exhibited at the Jewish Museum in South Miami Beach.

A CHILD'S LIFE INTERRUPTED
A CHILDHOOD LOST

by Fran (Prawer) Zatz

The city of Warsaw, before WWII, had a Jewish population of about 400,000, approximately one third of the total population. This is where I, Frania Prawer, was born and had a secure life with my parents and little sister, Eileen, *(Chayele),* who was three years younger.

My father's parents, Shoshana and Josef Prawer raised nine children. My father, Israel, was one of four brothers and five sisters. Three of his sisters were sent to Palestine to get them away from the hoodlum element harassing them almost daily, while one of the older brothers came to the United States around 1907.

Mother's family, her mother Frieda, died leaving her father Yankev Lazer Friedman a widower, with four small children. He remarried and had another child with the new wife.

Fran Age - 5 Warsaw, Poland

Mother always dreamt of the big city life and left the small town of Kobryn for the glamour of Warsaw. She found a job as an apprentice seamstress and learned to create brassieres for small pay and keep. She worked for two years at this job and became expert.

My father was a handsome young man whose good looks, with a head-full of red hair, brought him much attention. His charming easy-going ways attracted my mother, when she attended a local dance ballroom, as was the customs of entertainment in those days. They married after a short courtship.

Mother's talent in her seamstress work and establishing some contacts gave them courage to start their own business in one of the rooms of their apartment, where they manufactured elegant lingerie sets. I don't recall any hardships. We were well provided for. I do remember that we spoke only Polish in our house and my parents did not follow the orthodoxy of their parents.

My father was always happy and carefree while my mother, Toive', was firm and ran our lives with discipline and precision, managing the house, cooking, cleaning and the business accounting. In general she set the tone of a seriousness with orderly sensibilities, overseeing all parts of our lives, freeing Father to his more carefree and jovial ways. I often found an escape from the doings of our house by sitting on the windowsill, and from this high perch, witnessing the world hurriedly going by in all directions

Father liked to dress well and loved to dance. When my serious- minded mother refused to be coaxed to dance with him, shooing him away because she had more important cares, he made me his partner and the two of us danced to many songs and styles of dancing.

When my sister was born, we moved to an apartment on the fourth floor, on Muranowska 2, a corner building overlooking the future site of the Warsaw Ghetto. Chayele enhanced my life and at the age of three, I gained a playmate and took on responsibilities to watch over her.

Father Israel, Sister Eileen, Fran, Mother Toive

It was a comfortable place where Mother ran every aspect of our lives. She managed the business and by now employed two girls using the fourth bedroom as a workshop in this enterprise.

My playmates where few, occasionally playing with children who resided in the building, since I was not allowed to play in the street unattended. I looked forward to the attention of my father, who taught me to read and took me to parks and films. I especially loved Shirley Temple movies, which captivated me. I wanted to be just like her.

I felt safe, loved and loving. My life was without any hardships. I did not know about anti-Semitism or even what it meant to be Jewish.

When Germany attacked Poland on September 1, 1939, Warsaw suffered heavy air attacks and artillery bombardments. The exploding bombs and the frightening noise of the airplanes flying overhead, strafing and shooting at anything, drove everyone to run for safety. We ran to the shelter in the cellar in our building. Every night the air raids sounded. The bombardments continued until the Polish government was beaten and surrendered. We hid in the cellar every night.

It was a terrifying time for children but having our parents with us, I did not complain and felt safe. Fortunately our building was not bombed and escaped destruction. When it quieted down, and we got to the street, we saw the city burning and the rubble all around. Amazed at the change of my neighborhood, I did not want to continue my windowsill watch anymore.

We returned to our apartment not knowing how to get back to a normal life. And normal was not to be.

German troops entered Warsaw on September 29. Within a week they ordered the establishment of a Jewish Council, *Judenrat*, who were to supervise the established ghetto, which came into being between October and mid November. The *Judenrat* had to make sure that the Jewish population would obey all edicts.

On November 23, 1939, Jews had to wear white armbands with a Star of David. Jewish schools were closed, Jewish owned property was confiscated, and Jewish men were taken away into forced labor. Countless edicts were issued against the dazed population. Life became one of suffering and fear of what will be next. Conditions deteriorated. All infrastructure stopped. There was no water, no electricity, no transportation. Restrictions of getting around were issued against Jews. My sister and I were starving, our bellies swollen. Chayele was always crying from hunger. Starvation was the norm and one could see skeletal children begging for handouts. Corpses were in the streets; no one claiming them.

To keep Father out of the grips of the roundups, my brave resourceful mother ventured out to try to trade for some bread from some Polish workers in the factories in the area.

In April 1940, construction of the ghetto walls began. From my fourth floor perch, I could see a brick wall being erected right across the street.

On October 12, 1940, the Nazis announced that all had to relocate to the ghetto. Jews from Warsaw and those deported from other places throughout Western Europe were ordered to move into the ghetto, while over 100,000 Christians were moved out of the area.

The ghetto was divided into two sections, a small ghetto at the south end and a larger one at the north end. German and Polish police guarded its entrances and a Jewish militia was formed to police the inside.

We, along with thousands of people, had to move taking only what we could carry, some bedding and clothes. Mother gave me a small leather case to carry and told me, to hold on to it with care. It held all family photos and addresses of our families in America and Palestine.

After a long exhausting walk, with German guards keeping all in line, we arrived in an abandoned building and were able to settle into an unoccupied apartment which luckily was furnished.

Out of our windows, my parents observed that on the *Umshlagplatz*, the gathering place, unsettling things were happening there. Large numbers of people were herded into the waiting cattle car trains. They sensed that something was wrong with this scene. Why were the buildings empty with all furnishings and belongings in them? My parents decided to stay there only a couple of nights and moved to another building, into empty rooms on the fifth floor. One of the rooms had a mountain of clothes laying in a pile. They left my sister and me there and went out in search of some food. Mother told me to hide in the pile of clothes if I heard anyone coming.

My little sister, too young to understand our dire condition and that food was not available, was constantly crying. I looked around in every nook and cranny trying to find something to eat but there was not a crumb anywhere to be found. I consoled the little one to be quiet saying that Mom would bring some food soon. Suddenly I heard German spoken outside of the rooms. I warned my sister that they are coming to get us, we must hide. I hid her in a cabinet under the sink shushing her, and I crawled in the mountain of clothing.

A number of soldiers stormed up the stairs and into the apartment shouting and shooting at random. Not discovering anyone, they left leaving me in terror. I ran as soon as I could to check on my sister, not knowing if they killed her. She was alive and amazingly she knew not to cry, to keep silent throughout this horrible frightening ordeal.

It was getting dark and my parents did not return. I comforted my little sister as best as I could. When I heard some voices speaking Polish coming from the attic, I followed the sounds to a camouflaged door with chairs stacked next to it. I pulled away the barricade and discovered a number of people hiding there. I wanted to get in to hide with them, but they blocked me from getting in. I began to bang and yell, shouting that they will die with me and finally they relented and let me in. Seven souls where there. I asked for some water for my sister, which they had gathered from the rainfall, and a small piece of bread. We stayed there for a couple of days when I heard my parents calling our names. Mother appeared carrying a bread. We immediately left that building and wound up in a building near Mila Street.

We settled in a cellar where many Jews were hiding. People were expressing anger and the word *Ifshtand*, uprising, was heard. I could not understand what this meant. In the days that followed, I learned what it meant and after the war when I was an adult, I learned and understood the brave boys and girls who fought and died to resist the complete murder of Jews in the Warsaw Ghetto.

Mother was determined not to sit still and decided to sneak across to the Polish side. The ghetto had factories employing Polish people. Mom got friendly with some and was able to get Polish papers. She developed some contacts and, for a while, she was able to bring in food and smuggled guns and bullets for the fighters into the ghetto.

About two days before the uprising, Mother was able to have my sister and me smuggled out of the ghetto in a Polish workers truck. When the uprising started, Father was caught and sent to Majdanek.

On the Polish side, my little sister was taken by a Polish man and another one took me by the hand and lead me away saying, "You are coming to my house and will live with my family."

His house was situation on the outskirts of Warsaw where I was met by his smiling wife. They had two children, a boy fifteen, and a girl ten. The man said to them, "This is your mother's sister's daughter, Jasia. Her parents were killed and she will live with us." I could not understand this whole development and felt strange but accepted this kindness. The woman combed my hair and comforted me. The kids, especially the boy, did not like me and felt that I was an intruder and would hit me and whispered warnings not to cry.

Toitia, aunt, Dublenko made me a place to sleep on the ground at the fireplace and assured me that all would be good. A few days later, at night, *Toitia* took me out of the house and pointed to the distant sky which was flaming red. "There is the ghetto burning. I want you to know that your parents are dead, but don't cry. I don't want you to worry. No one is going to kill you. Sunday we are going to church and you will be baptized and you will be safe forever." I did not say anything to her.

In my solitude, I cried at the fact that my parents were dead and I did not know about my sister. Eventually, I dared to ask where my sister was. The *Toitia* told me that she knew about my sister. "You can go to see her." She packed a basket of potatoes, sausage and bread, and she and her daughter took me to a fancy building where two young girls opened the door. They looked at me and said "We are like your sister." At first I could not understand what they meant, but then I realized that they too were Jewish and were passing as Polish children. They led me to a room where I found my little sister laying on a bed in a darkened room, freezing. She seemed so tiny, so forlorn. I wanted to take her with us, but *Tiotia* told me that this was not possible, we could not take her away. And we were told not to come back and not bring any food. I left in a state of distress. I thought that my sister would not survive.

In a couple of months, Mother appeared and took me away in a taxi and drove to retrieve my sister. Our reunion was a happy one although, we children did not know what to expect anymore. Mother brought us to her one room flat on the third floor of Dobra 7. She had secured Polish identity papers for all three of us and assured us that we are safe. When I asked "Where is Daddy?" She only said that we will never see him again.

Mother got a job in a German factory, working long hours. We were instructed not to walk about the room so that no one would become suspicious that we were living there too. She passed herself off as a single woman.

One day in August, Mom returned from work and told us that Polish people were fighting with sticks and rakes. They had no weapons. They were massacred by the German machine guns.

She told us to grab a few of our belongings, and we ran with hundreds of people trying to get away from this mayhem. But we were not able to escape. The Germans surrounded us and forced about five hundred people into a church, ordering "Pray." They shackled the doors and set the church on fire. As the people smelled smoke, the panic and screaming was heard. We were trapped. We thought that this was our end. Soon a door was located to a basement where an exit to the outside was discovered. All ran for their lives. The Germans shot at the running people with machine guns, bullets whizzing by. Many were killed. We succeeded to get away and came to a house on the outskirts where Mother told them that we were lost and hungry. The woman gave us some bread and water but told us that we could not stay with her. We continued on, walking through the night, and came to a town Konska Vola, a primitive settlement where we were finally able to stop and rest.

When Mom heard German spoken outside, she made us run to the back door into the nearby field where we hid behind a large haystack. While we escaped, the Germans killed all the people of the village.

We continued to run away, staying close to the road so that we could occasionally see some trucks at a distance. When we saw an open truck and recognized that these were Polish men, we came to the road. They stopped and took us along, dropping us off at a village consisting of only seven houses. When we approached one of the houses, a young peasant woman, who had two little children, asked "Pani zWarshawi? Madam are you from Warsaw?" She was intrigued and in awe that someone from that great city was now in her hut. She wanted to know all details about Warsaw and especially wanted to know when was Christmas this year since she had no calendar nor contact with the outside world.

She did not refuse us shelter and made us a bed on the floor on straw mattresses like they had and slept on. She did not turn us away and was kind to us. We stayed with her until the Russians freed the area.

Mother succeeded in getting us onto a Russian truck headed for Warsaw. As we traveled, the passing scene was of devastation. The most shocking scenes were the German soldiers corpses hanging by their feet from telephone poles. It was a surreal scene, which both frightened and gave a sense of finally not having to face the German killers.

The Russians dropped us off miles from Warsaw. It took us weeks to get home. We found Warsaw in ruins. Only skeleton walls were standing on precarious heaps of rubble. We found a Jewish organization who was helping survivors. The wall in their office was full of lists and paper notes; people searching for their families, their loved ones. We found no one looking for us and no one survived. Our entire extended family was murdered. We, the three of us, were alone in the world.

The devastation that was Poland, the killing fields, the blood-soaked earth where millions were annihilated, the danger of being killed still lurking, drove all survivors to get out. By all sorts of methods the exodus took the survivors to safe havens in the allied occupied territories of Germany and Austria. We too joined this migration and arrived to the DP Camp Bergen-Belsen, a scene out of Dante's Inferno. Typhus was raging. Over thirteen thousand people died from the disease after liberation.

Soon after our arrival, we were transferred to Eschwege where we waited for a quota and a visa from my father's brother from America.

The DP camp was a place where we regained some sense of safety. I started school where we were immersed in the study of Hebrew in order to be prepared and fit in to live in Palestine/Israel. We learned to feel safe, to have expectations that the tomorrow will come and that we had a future.

Finally in 1949, we were granted the quota. Our visa was honored and we were transported on an army ship to New York. We were met by my uncle who came to the states in 1907. He greeted us with stipulations that in America everyone had to work, and there were no handouts from anyone including him. He basically said that since his brother did not survive, that his connection with us was non-existent. He made me declare myself older so that I could work rather than go to school.

We continued to struggle and make the best of our situation and adjust. Rebuilding our lives was not an easy one, but we found our way. I worked and attended high school at night. After graduation, I found a job as a secretary-typist.

As was the case with many immigrants to the States, the newcomers formed societies and learned from each other how to exist and almost became each other's extended families.

I met my husband Hy Zatz and we got married in 1952. He was a caring, ambitious young man who provided a good stable life for me and our family.

We have three sons and five grandchildren who have enhanced our lives and rebuilt laughter and reviving a certain smile, my father's generous head of red hair, that light walk and dance that is left for me as an endowment for the future and for my generations.

We lived many happy years together, and this ended when my wonderful

Hy passed away in 1997.

It has been a difficult road for me without him. But as a survivor I learned that my life and family have value, and I must march on and live and contribute.

I cannot forget what happened in the Holocaust. I cannot forget what my eyes have seen as a young child and I will not forget that the Jewish people are heroic to have survived a brutal onslaught of murder and hate.

Fran 2012

Sharing my story leaves another picture and experience of survival, loss, suffering and rebirth, the tenacity and will to live on, overcome and not to learn to be a hater. Each life is precious.

After my own experience of observing the evil that was sent against us and the kindness that I experienced that helped me survive, I believe that people can be good. Survivors did not become bitter and thus color the attitude of their families. Their love of their lost families continued in their souls and extended doubly into their own children and generations to come.

ABOUT THE EDITORS

Zelda 2013

Zelda Marbell Fuksman, born in Poland, is a child survivor of the Holocaust. She presently is chief editor of the quarterly newsletter of the Child Survivor/Hidden Children organization of Palm Beach County, Florida.

For the past fourteen years, Zelda has devoted her seemingly limitless time, effort, and hospitality to working as editorial chairperson of the book committee. She has feverishly interviewed members of the organization, collecting and writing testimonies, and deepening our understanding of their war experiences. She has acutely observed and concentrated on the intricate memories they have of the war and has helped them articulate these memories.

In the past, when still living in Illinois, Zelda was a charter member of the Child Survivor Organization and participated in resisting the planned neo-Nazi march in Skokie, Illinois.

Now a resident of Boca Raton, Florida, she is an active speaker in schools and other venues, sharing her own war time experiences, and focusing on how we can make a better world for new generations to come. Zelda is a gift to our organization

Frieda 2013

Frieda Jaffe was born in Piotrkow-Tryb., Poland and was only two years old when Nazi Germany invaded. The city of her birth soon became the very first documented ghetto in Poland and most Jews living there were imprisoned, enslaved, and ultimately exterminated.

Frieda was just four years old when she was forced to watch her father hanged in the public square in Lututow (near Piotrkow) for refusing to cooperate with the Nazis, and later on saw her mother, baby brother and most of her immediate family taken away for extermination to the death camp Treblinka.

By 1944 Frieda was among a small group of young children still remaining alive in the ghetto. From this small remnant, the women and girls were transported to Ravensbruck Camp in Germany, and a short while later was sent to the Concentration Camp of Bergen-Belsen near Hanover Germany. A few months later, in April of 1945, when the camp was liberated by British troops, she was among the tiny group of very small and starved children who were still alive. Frieda was then seven years old.

Frieda is the Founder of The Child Survivors/Hidden Children of the Holocaust - Palm Beach Country, Florida. Her contributions are great and important. She is an active member of Temple Beth El in Boca Raton, is a speaker, writer and lecturer on her experiences in the Shoah, and has pledged herself to Jewish survival, ensuring that those who were so inhumanly slaughtered shall never be forgotten.

Judith 2013

Judith Evan Goldstein began her life in Europe, in the city of Vilna, Poland, now the capital of Lithuania. Germany invaded the city in 1941, and several months later all the Jews were placed in a ghetto. Within two years, 70,000 Jewish people were murdered in a nearby forest Ponary. After the liquidation of the ghetto in 1943, she and her mother were sent to a series of concentration camps where they faced many tunnels of death. By many miracles they survived and were liberated.

Judith reports: "I wish I was never part of the Holocaust, it was given to me and I was thrown into a sea of suffering. Still a child, I was meant to die, but I lived and survived the horrors of genocide. Many times I try to leave it all behind, but it refuses to leave me".

After the liberation, education on pre-college level and social movement helped her progress in several areas of the arts. She holds a bachelor's and master's degrees in music, attended art school and furthered her studies to become a certified music and art therapist. She worked with neurologically impaired children and taught teachers at the College of New Rochelle, N.Y, how to utilize the arts as a tool for communication and learning.

For the last eighteen years, she has exhibited her art in about twenty six museums in the USA, Israel, many galleries, universities, conferences and educational places.

As a musician, classically trained, she has composed numerous songs and lyrics, several vocalizes for piano, voice, cello, violin and flute. Also, a musical poem in four movements for piano and orchestra. Her music has been performed at museum openings, colleges, conferences and by the Chamber Philharmonic Orchestra of Westchester, New York.

Her visual art is presently in the permanent collection at Yad- Vashem, Israel; the Holocaust Museum, St. Petersburg, Florida; the Wimberly Library at the Florida Atlantic University, Boca Raton, FL; Holocaust Documentation & Education Center & Museum, Florida, and in private collections. Judith quotes, "I paint the images of my childhood and play the images I see"

She also appears in a documentary film "As Seen Through These Eyes" produced by Hilary Helstein, narrated by Maya Angelou.

Judith published two books. Her first book of art: "Images Of My Childhood From Sorrows To Joys", and her second book of art, poetry, and lyrics to her songs: "The Voice Of Color". Her art also appears on the cover of several books.

Now a retired teacher, she became a source of historical inquiry by speaking at schools, colleges, museums, and conferences, describing the genocide of the Jewish people that took place in Europe during WWII. The hope is to impress upon the future generations, that evil powers cannot rule and destroy the world we live in. These demagogues must be stopped before it is too late.

TIME LINE OF THE HOLOCAUST ERA

1933
January 30   Adolf Hitler appointed Chancellor of Germany
March 20   Dachau Concentration Camp opens
May 10   Nazis burn thousand of books

1934
August 2   President Hindenberg dies; Hitler proclaims himself Fuehrer und
                  Reichskanzler (Leader and Reich Chancellor).

1935
September 15   "Nuremberg Laws": anti-Jewish racial laws enacted

1936
July   Sachsenhausen Concentration Camp opens

1937
July 15   Buchenwald Concentration Camp opens

1938
March 13   Anschluss (incorporation of Austria): all anti-Semitic decrees
                  immediately applied in Austria
November 9   Kristallnacht - attack on Jewish people and their property - many Jews
                  murdered and 25,000 to 30,000 were arrested and placed in
                  concentration camps. 267 synagogues were destroyed and thousands of
                  homes and businesses were ransacked. Kristallnacht also served as a
                  pretext and a means for the wholesale confiscation of firearms from
                  German Jews

1939
January 30   Hitler in Reichstag speech: if war erupts it will mean the Vernichtung
                  (extermination) of European Jews
August 23   Molotov-Ribbentrop non-aggression pact signed between Soviet Union
                  and Germany - provides for partition of Poland
September 1   Beginning of World War II - Germany invades part of Poland
October 28   First Polish ghetto established in Piotrkow
November 23   Jews in German-occupied Poland - forced to wear an arm band or
                  yellow star

1940
May 7   Lodz Ghetto sealed: 165,000 people in 1.6 square miles
May 10-12   Germany invades the Netherlands, Belgium, Luxembourg, and France
May 20   Concentration camps established - Auschwitz I in May 1940;

288

| | Auschwitz II (also called Auschwitz-Birkenau) in early 1942; and Auschwitz III (also called Auschwitz-Monowitz) in October 1942, for the extermination of Jews; Gypsies, Poles, Homosexuals, and even their own disabled and mentally deficient. Russians, and others were also murdered at the camp; Zyklon B gas was used in the extermination. |
| November 15 | Warsaw Ghetto sealed - ultimately contained 500,000 people |

1941

June 22	Germany invades the Soviet Union
June 23	Einsatzgrupen begin mass murders of Jews in the Soviet Union.
July 31	Heydrich appointed by Goring to implement the "Final Solution"
Sept. 28-29	34,000 Jews massacred at Babi Yar outside Kiev, 70,000 at Ponary, a forest outside Vilno
November 24	Theresienstadt (Terezin) established as a "model camp" near Prague.
December 8	Chelmno (Kulmhof) extermination camp begins operations - 340,000 Jews, 20,000 Poles and Czechs murdered by April 1943 and additional killings in June/July 1944
December 11	United States declares war on Japan and Germany

1942

January 20	Wannsee Conference in Berlin - Heydrich outlines plan to murder Europe's Jews - "Final Solution"
March 17	Extermination begins in Belzec - by end of 1942, 600,000 Jews murdered
May 7	Extermination by gas begins in Sobibor killing center; by October 1943, 250,000 Jews murdered
July 22	Germans establish Treblinka Concentration Camp
July 28	ZOB - Zydowska Organizacja Bojowa, which means Jewish Fighting Organization was formed in the Warsaw Ghetto

1943

April 19-May 16	Warsaw Ghetto Uprising
June 19	Himmler orders the liquidation of all ghettos in Poland and the Soviet Union
October 1-2	Danes rescue 7,200 Danish Jews from impending deportation

1944

May 15	Nazis begin deporting Hungarian Jews; by June 27 - 380,000 sent to Auschwitz
June 6	D-Day: Allied invasion at Normandy
July 20	Group of German officers attempt to assassinate Hitler
July 24	Russians liberate Majdanek killing center

1945

January 17, 25	Evacuation by death marches of Auschwitz and Stutthoff
January 27	Soviet Army liberates Auschwitz
April 6-10	Death march of inmates of Buchenwald
April 30	Hitler commits suicide
May 7	Germany surrenders to the Allies, ending the war in Europe.

Financial Contributors

Adventure Club of Broken Sound
Heather R. Bennett
Rhona and Martin Bertman
Vera and Henry Bialer
Boca Woods Country Club
  Women's Club
Nancy and Richard Boyman
Bella Brookenthal
Maureen and John Carter
Center Academy
  Principal: Barbara Cooper
Dr. Pierre and Marianne Chanover
Patricia Champern
Helen and Kurt Daniel
Dr. Michael Davidson
Ida and Jerry Dressner
Mary and Joe Eckstein
Eileen and Allen Exelbierd
Dr. Daniel and Elaine Fischer
Gail and Robert Fishman
Shelley and Norman Frajman
Edith and Irwin Friedman
Nina Frisch
Zelda and Hershel Fuksman
Heni and Henri Galel
Daniel Gevirtz
June and Joseph Goldman
Marilyn Goldman

Judith and Harry Goldstein
Rosette and Gil Goldstein
Sarah and Eric M. Gordon
Ruth and Gabriel Groszman
Renee Gruskin and Jay Thomsen
Norma and Roman Haar
Jane and Edward Hait
Lore and Herman Haller
Sandy and Andy Hartmann
inSIGHT Through Education
  Roz Lewy, President
Frieda and Harold Jaffe
Lina and Gabriel Jaroslavsky
Helen Jonas
Hedviga Jungstein
Sylvia Kahana & Arie Taykan
Betty and Herbert Kammer
Beverly and John Koenigsberg
Edith Kovack
Simon and Doris Kovner
Elayne and Robert Kwait
Beatrice Levy
Selma and Benno Lindenberg
Dawn and Lewis Lindenberg
March of the Living - Southern Region - USA
  Jack Rosenbaum, Director
Mark Center of Jewish Studies
Max and Sharon Markovitz

Financial Contributors

Elaine and David Marmel
Noah Marmel
Gutki and George Miliband
Estelle Morganstein
Rhona Nelson
Next Generations
  Nancy Dershaw, President
Phyllis and Marvin Perry
Dorothy and Stanley Pierce
Pine Crest School
Dr. Henry and Marcia Rabinowitz
Tova Rabunski
Bilha and Samuel Ron
Edith and Sam Rosen
Donna Rosenthal
Henry Rosenthal
Roz and Joe Ross
Merle and Daryl Saferstein
Katherine Sattler
Larry D. Silver
Beatrice Sussman
Suzanne Sussman
Temple Beth El of Boca Raton
  Rabbi Dan Levin
Sandra and Stanley Trockman
Cantor Ann Turnoff
Dr. Bryan J. Wasserman
Peter Waxman
Victor Winston
Fran Zatz
Paula Zieselman

List of People on Back Cover Collage

(left to right)

Top Row: Henri Galel, Heni Galel, Vera Bialer, Henry Bialer, Adele Judas, Kurt Judas

Row 2: Basia McDonnell, Roman Haar, Hedviga Jungstein, Gabriel Groszman, Nina Frisch, Jay Rabunski

Row 3: Joe Henner, Frieda Jaffe, Hershel Fuksman, Zelda Fuksman, Judith Evan Goldstein, Anszel Gun

Row 4: Anya Baum, Henry Rosenthal, Beatrice Sussman, Fran Zatz, Marvin Fidler, Selma Lindenberg

Row 5: Daniel Fischer, Judy Blackman, Alan Wainberg, Eta Hecht, Kurt Daniel, Helen Daniel

Row 6: Ester Kisner, Danny Geveritz, Edith Rosen, Herbert Kammer, Jenine Sikolov, Edith Kovack

Row 7: Joe Spindel, Edith Rhodes, Joe Ross, Ida Dressner, Madeleine Goodman, Evelyn Rubin, Herman Haller